"The game of baseball best represents our country's soul, and no one has chronicled its beauty better than Roger Angell. With only class and eloquence, Roger's insights have taught us all—starting with sport and extending to humanity."

—Joe Torre, Hall of Famer and four-time World Championship manager of the New York Yankees and MLB's chief baseball officer

"Of the recent books I have read about baseball, Joe Bonomo's book chronicling the career of Roger Angell, *No Place I Would Rather Be*, is one of the best, not only for Bonomo's considerable writing skills, but also for his compelling portrayal of Angell's erudition and unique focus on the 'lesser and sweeter moments' of the sport he loves."

—Jill Brennan O'Brien, *America Magazine*

"Joe Bonomo's immensely enjoyable book examines Angell's baseball writing through the decades, shedding welcome light on the forces and events (both in the game and in Angell's life) that shaped him into the greatest baseball writer of the post–World War II era. It's an absolute must for any Angell fan and for anyone who digs great baseball writing in general."

—Dan Epstein, author of *Big Hair and Plastic Grass: A Funky Ride Through Baseball and America in the Swinging '70s*

"Joe Bonomo has curated an enjoyable journey through the career and work of Roger Angell, the godfather to generations of outsiders who set out to bring a fresh perspective to baseball coverage. If you've ever immersed yourself in Angell's prose and wondered where his incisive wit, ear for dialogue, and attention to detail came from, or wished to trace the development of recurring themes throughout his oeuvre, *No Place I Would Rather Be* is well worth your time."

—Jay Jaffe, author of *The Cooperstown Casebook* and a senior writer for FanGraphs.com

"A look behind the scenes of a remarkable career in a changing field."

—*New York Post*

"Roger Angell was in Cooperstown at the Baseball Hall of Fame to receive the J. G. Taylor Spink Award 'for meritorious contributions to baseball writing.' Joe Bonomo's book offers an infinite number of reasons why this honor was richly deserved. It is a book worth reading."

—Richard Crepeau, *New York Journal of Books*

No Place
I Would
Rather Be

No Place
I Would
Rather Be

*Roger Angell
and a Life in
Baseball Writing*

JOE BONOMO

With a new epilogue by the author

University of Nebraska Press
Lincoln

The University of Nebraska Press is part
of a land-grant institution with campuses
and programs on the past, present, and
future homelands of the Pawnee, Ponca,
Otoe-Missouria, Omaha, Dakota, Lakota,
Kaw, Cheyenne, and Arapaho Peoples, as
well as those of the relocated Ho-Chunk,
Sac and Fox, and Iowa Peoples.

First Nebraska paperback printing: 2023

Library of Congress Control Number:
2022947100

Set in ITC New Baskerville by E. Cuddy.

Frontispiece: Angell with notebook in his
New Yorker office. Photo by Elon Green.

For my dad, Phil,
and my brother, Phil

Writing is the hardest
thing in the world to do.
It's just as hard as baseball.
ROGER ANGELL

Contents

Preface   xi

Acknowledgments   xvii

Trying Out   1

Good News Forever   33

Delay on the Field   75

You Want to Laugh,
You Want More, You
Want It to Be Over   131

Epilogue   175

Notes   179

Bibliography   197

Index   203

Preface

Spring baseball heralds a fresh season and the ebb and flow of expectations. Yet it's easy for me now to view the May 10, 2013, game between the Chicago White Sox and the visiting Los Angeles Angels as nothing more than what it was: another day in a long, failed campaign. The Sox would end the season a game shy of one hundred losses, thirty games behind the first-place Detroit Tigers.

I sat with friends in chilly sunshine in the lower stands along the third base line at U.S. Cellular (now Guaranteed Rate) Field, our first game of the year. The Angels held a 5–1 lead in the bottom of the fourth when the White Sox, behind a double, two walks, a wild pitch, another double, and a single, tied it. Grab a beer. We've got a game! Things were still knotted in the top of the seventh, with none out and Hank Conger on first, when reliever Matt Lindstrom strode to the mound. He proceeded to strike out Brendan Harris but swiftly gave up singles to J. B. Shuck and to future Hall of Famer Mike Trout, the latter scoring Conger. Lindstrom endured a passed ball to the next batter, the *other* Cooperstown-bound Angel, Albert Pujols, allowing Shuck to score, and then, rattled, walked Pujols and issued a free pass to the next batter, Mark Trumbo, before mercifully inducing ground ball outs by Josh Hamilton and Howie Kendricks to end the inning. Lindstrom didn't return; Nate Jones pitched the eighth and ninth. The White Sox failed to produce more runs and lost the game, 7–5.

In the midst of the Sox pitchers' unhappy work on the mound, I noticed something in Jones's pitching delivery—you'd miss it if you weren't looking for it: an odd way of pausing slightly, mid-

windup, and holding the ball in his hand at the top of his delivery as if he were a waiter carrying a tray, hustling into the dining
room. In my seat I smiled inwardly at my modest observation,
then posed a question I've asked countless times over the years:
how would the greatest living baseball writer describe it?

Roger Angell has written about baseball for the *New Yorker* since
1962, the year he visited the fledgling New York Mets at spring
training in St. Petersburg, Florida. He was forty-one years old. Dis-
patched there by his editor, William Shawn, who was hopeful for
more sports writing in the magazine, Angell had no inkling that
the trip would inaugurate his second career—his third actually.
He'd already earned a modest reputation as an award-winning
short story writer, publishing a collection in 1960, and since 1956
he'd been a full-time fiction editor at the magazine.

But baseball, it turned out, is Angell's greatest and most reward-
ing subject. He was eager to sit in the warm stands, find his voice,
and report on what he saw and felt as a fan, filtering the action on
the field and around him in the park through a knowledgeable
yet skeptical, unabashed yet anti-sentimental love of the game
he's followed since he was a teenager. Before becoming the *New
Yorker*'s diamond authority, Angell had gotten into shape writing
about the game a couple of times for the travel magazine *Holiday*, where he'd been a writer and editor for ten years, and in a
handful of short stories and several "Talk of The Town" pieces for
the *New Yorker*. His point of view was fully formed in the stands
that first exhibition season. He put down roots in that Florida
sun, and he's bloomed perennially.

Angell's through-line in baseball astonishes. He watched Babe
Ruth and Lou Gehrig belt home runs in Yankee Stadium, and
he blogged the 2017 postseason. In his hometown he's seen his
beloved New York Giants and Brooklyn Dodgers depart; the
Polo Grounds and Ebbets Field razed and paved for apartment
complexes; old Yankee Stadium spiffed up, torn down, and then

erected again; the New York Mets arrive; and state-of-the-art Shea Stadium built, age, leveled, and replaced. He saw Joe DiMaggio stride the outfield and Barry Bonds launch epic homers. He's bathed in daylight watching Mel Ott and blinked at thousands of phones capturing a late-night October blast by Daniel Murphy, who was born nearly forty years after Ott retired. Angell recalls hearing about players boarding rickety Pullman cars that during a season stayed east of the Mississippi and has watched teams flying first-class, equipment-laden jets en route from Miami to Seattle and Los Angeles and San Diego and Montreal and Toronto.

All the while Angell has kept score religiously, from 1933—the first postseason he avidly followed, a thirteen-year-old scribbling the action on his father's yellow legal pads—through to the most recent season, along the way learning of a game's heart-stopping or trifling events through late-afternoon and early-evening newspapers; then a radio crackling in a cab or a bodega doorway; then on bright, heralding, saturating television; and finally streaming online in an avalanche of accumulating 1s and 0s. No other living baseball writer has seen and heard as much as Roger Angell has over so long a period. No other writer has written about the game as elegantly, artfully, thoughtfully, and memorably.

While writing this book, I became interested in observing Angell as he struggled with his attachments to the game. League expansion, television, all-sport stadiums, AstroTurf, free agency, escalating player salaries, work stoppages and strikes, the ominously lengthening distance between fan and player, the avalanche of statistics: all of these inevitable developments in the game affected him, and over the decades he's reacted in the magazine, sometime mildly, sometimes strongly. At times his descriptions of the challenges to his fanly allegiances—tested in the 1970s as television began exerting its strong and lasting influence and in the 1990s during the divisive labor squabbles—have been as dramatic as the games themselves. Owners, lawyers, and television producers have to varying degrees altered the sport of baseball over time, yet Angell has remained a stalwart fan, always able to plug himself into the old game's eternal rhythms and joys.

No Place I Would Rather Be is not a biography but a look at Angell's writing over the decades, including his early short stories, *New Yorker* casuals, and later autobiographical essays, and at the common threads that run through it all. (I discuss Angell's decades-long editorial position at the *New Yorker* only in passing. His parallel career as a respected and influential fiction editor, indicative of his literary interests and gifts beyond baseball writing, deserves a longer look.) Throughout I cite the dates when his baseball pieces first appeared in the magazine or online, rather than as collected in his subsequent books, to reflect a more accurate sense of the particular time of the year, season, or era that he was covering. Angell's baseball essays, especially as they matured and grew in length in the 1970s and 1980s, are *talky*—stuffed with players, and some managers, coaches, executives, and fans, holding forth. Early in his career, reserved and unsure of his credentials and amateur press box skills, he learned to listen. Hitters, pitchers, managers, and coaches—some of them anyway—love to talk about the game, its pleasures and difficulties, and its daily, often surprising, rewards, and Angell is wise enough to let these folks at it, often quoting them lengthily. Many of his pieces are so packed with enthused gabbing that they read like oral history. I'm taking a page from Angell: he writes so clearly and artfully that, as often as I can, I step aside and let his writing do the talking.

It seems unlikely that we'll ever see a baseball writer like Angell again. He wrote in an era when high-circulation magazines were bursting with lengthy articles and essays for an audience that gave itself over to long stays with the writing. Thick weeklies such as the *New Yorker* were as yet uncrowded by the high-decibel noise of the Internet, which encourages both a flood of writers and a diminution in size of what they write. Angell recognizes this. "We're all so impatient," he remarked in 2016. "People don't read much, and they spend a great deal of time looking at their phones. The average time spent on the front page on the online *New York Times* is something like forty seconds. We don't take time to read; we don't take time to have things happen."

There are distractions at ballparks as well. "People are not paying attention. They're listening to the music, or watching the lightage, or wanting to go to a restaurant, giving glances at the field or the instant replay." He adds, "Major League Baseball every night puts on highlights, where you switch to Tiger Stadium and someone's just hit a double or something spectacular has happened, and you can sit that long and it's nothing but action. But this is not what baseball is like." Angell remarked on another occasion that baseball is "stuffed with waiting." His affectionate, knowledgeable, and wryly skeptical baseball writing allows us to slow time, dive deep, and appreciate baseball and the eras in which it was played in ways that few writers attempt now. At a time when many fans, and Major League Baseball itself, are concerned about the game's languorous and antiquated pace of play in a rapidly accelerated, diverting era of entertainment options, Angell's lengthy, patient baseball essays might feel like relics. They might best be viewed as tonics.

Born and raised in Greenpoint, Brooklyn, my dad, Phil, possesses a vivid childhood memory of his older brother Anthony informing him they were heading to a Dodgers game at Ebbets Field that week; young Phil was so excited that he ran down Leonard Street and took a frog leap over a fire hydrant. His enthusiasm for the game has remained undampened, despite the Dodgers' eventual departure from town and, years later, his second-hometown Washington Senators' similar betrayal. I cherish memories of watching the hysterically entertaining late 1970s playoffs and World Series in the family rec room with my dad, his knees up, sitting on the edge of his chair like a kid. A few years later, I discovered *Late Innings* on his bookshelf, and my love of Angell's writing began.

My brother Phil is a lifelong baseball fan too. (He and my dad share not only a first name but also a birthday; my brother was born on the day Ted Williams hit a home run in his final career at bat.) The Hank Aaron poster and copies of *Baseball Digest* and *Who's Who in Baseball* in Phil's bedroom and the Strat-O-Matic games he played in the basement as I watched, a curious fan in the bleachers, are as vivid and pleasing to me as the conversations we had just last week about the game we still love. I dedicate *No Place I Would Rather Be* to them both.

Acknowledgments

Leading off, I'm grateful to Roger Angell, whose writing inspired this book and who was enthusiastic and supportive throughout the process of my researching and writing. Getting to know him has been an at-bat of a lifetime for me. Many thanks also to Peggy Moorman, who graciously and generously fact-checked the book in the draft stages and improved it considerably with her terrific editor's eye and ear.

Thanks also to Tina Brown, Ann Goldstein, Adam Gopnik, Bob Gottlieb, Janet Malcolm, Ben McGrath, Charles McGrath, Daniel Menaker, David Remnick, Mark Singer, and Amanda Urban. Thanks to Mark Singer for informing me about, and to Christopher Angell, Doris Baiza, and Allan Miller at Patterson Belknap Webb & Tyler LLP for granting me access to, a multi-session oral history of Angell's life that took place in New York City in 2010 and 2011 among Angell, Singer, and others. This intimate, wide-ranging discussion was enlightening and helpful.

Cheers to Dan Epstein, Kevin Goldstein, Jon Michaud, and Ben Yagoda for their moral support, enthusiasm, and nuts-and-bolts aid. In Cooperstown, New York, author, baseball whiz, and mayor Jeff Katz was warm and hospitable, and I was happy to share drinks with him and talk ball (and rock and roll). Thanks also to the bartenders at Cooley's Stone House Tavern, who provided convivial support, both moral and intoxicating.

Over at Baseball Freaks, thanks to General Managers Ted Cogswell (emeritus) and Bailey G. Walsh Jr. and to the fun crew there, in whose literal and/or virtual company I've enjoyed years of knowledgeable, friendly, and freakily fantastic baseball talk. Thanks to Steve Butts and Terry Cannon at the Institute for Baseball Studies for their support. Cheers and beers to Phil Bonomo (bro *and* dad), Ricky Cobb, Dan Epstein, David Goldblum, Kevin Goldstein, Dan Libman, Dave Markovitz, Amy Newman, Margaret Nissen, Keith Nyquist, Mal Thursday, Bailey Walsh, Josh Wilker, and everyone else with whom I've enjoyed many innings at the old ballpark down the years. Thanks also to ball lovers and rock and rollers Robert Jaz and Emily Seah for their thoughtfulness and generosity.

The Department of English and the College of Liberal Arts and Sciences at Northern Illinois University granted me a sabbatical to work on this book, for which I'm grateful. Thanks to Cassidy Lent and the librarians at the A. Bartlett Giamatti Research Center at the National Baseball Hall of Fame and Museum in Cooperstown, New York; to Tal Nadan, reference archivist, and the librarians at the Brooke Russell Astor Reading Room for Rare Books and Manuscripts at the New York Public Library in New York City; and to the Interlibrary Loan librarians at Founders Library at Northern Illinois University in DeKalb.

Writing this book without access to Baseball-Reference.com would have been arduous and a lot less fun. Thanks to all of the conscientious, hard-working, ball-loving folk there who devote countless hours in ensuring decades' worth of accurate game logs, box scores, and statistics. A pitcher's win-loss record may not matter much, but facts do.

Thanks to Jane Lahr and Lyn DelliQuadri at Lahr & Partners. Lyn believed in this project and kept me grounded throughout, and her editorial suggestions improved the book. Thanks to Rob Taylor, Courtney Ochsner, Sara Springsteen, Bojana Ristich, and everyone at the University of Nebraska Press who fielded the manuscript's tough hops with aplomb.

Above all, and as always, thanks and love to Amy Newman, whose love, support, and smarts inform every word in this book. I'm her number one fan.

No Place
I Would
Rather Be

Angell writing for *Brief* during World War II. Courtesy of Roger Angell.

Trying Out

On the afternoon of September 19, 1920, the New York Giants hosted the Cincinnati Reds at the Polo Grounds in Upper Manhattan. Both teams were out of playoff contention, but the game, played in pleasantly cool weather, was an exciting contest that the Giants took in eleven innings. The Giants looked to be in command early behind starter Jesse Barnes, who was cushioned with six runs through three innings. The Reds' left-handed Fritz Coumbe, who'd turn out to be the game's hard luck Renaissance Man, relieved starter Adolfo ("the Pride of Havana") Luque in the third inning, with his team down 6–2. Cincinnati drew two runs closer in the top of the fourth, then tied the game in the seventh when Coumbe, unsatisfied with merely holding the Giants to four hits, launched a homer to the right-field stands, with catcher Ivey Wingo on first. Barnes hit the showers.

The game stayed tied into extra innings. As can happen in baseball, the resolution came startlingly, and for the visitors, mercilessly quickly. In the bottom of the eleventh with none out, Coumbe walked second baseman Larry Doyle. Frank Snyder then smacked a line drive, and as left fielder Pat Duncan bobbled the ball, Doyle switched into high gear, ran hard, and slid home with the winning run. A tough result for Coumbe, who had pitched well in long relief and whose tying two-run homer made it into the eternity of the box score but in a losing cause. More than thirty-seven thousand had turned out for the inessential game, the largest crowd of the season. The thick throng of fans departed the Polo Grounds elated, many climbing the steep Brush Stairway up Coogan's Bluff to Edgecombe Avenue and reentering the long, leisurely, sunny Sunday in front of them.

Elsewhere in the city a preoccupied man and woman had their minds on other things, welcoming into their family a baby boy, their second child following a daughter, Nancy, born four years earlier. In the coming decades the boy will evolve into an ardent New York Giants fan and a regular visitor to the Polo Grounds; he'll cheer for the Yankees at the stadium across the East River too. (And in the far distant future he'll switch allegiances to the Boston Red Sox and to a futuristic local nines called "the Mets." But we're getting ahead of ourselves.)

They named him Roger, and they took him home to East Ninety-Third Street.

Born in 1889 in Cleveland, Ohio, a lifelong Indians fan, Ernest Angell grew into a robust and physically active young man, perennially challenging his body against its considerable limits. Roger Angell would write that his father was "lean and tall, with long fingers, brown eyes, and an air of energy about him." Ernest didn't know his own father, Elgin, well; he died on July 4, 1898, aboard the French liner *La Bourgogne* when it collided with a British merchant vessel off Sable Island, near Newfoundland. Adolescent grief aside, Ernest, intelligent and hard working, thrived as a student. He graduated Phi Beta Kappa from Harvard University in 1911, earning a law degree there two years later (in 1954 he'd add a law degree from Bard University as well), and then served as an infantry captain in the American Expeditionary Forces in Europe in World War I. A lawyer steeped in politics, Ernest cared passionately about social issues and disadvantaged citizens and over the course of a long career published numerous articles in law reviews. When Roger Angell was a teenager, his father served as regional administrator for New York of the Securities and Exchange Commission before joining the law firm of Spence, Windels, Walser & Hotchkins. Ernest found his true calling when he was elected national chairman of the American Civil Liberties Union, his work there often spilling into the Angell home on Ninety-Third Street in the form of books, pamphlets, and lively, sometimes heated, dinnertime conversations among family and friends.

Ernest would summer with the family in New Hampshire in the White Mountains near Chocorua, and there he met the pretty and stylish Katharine Sergeant, three years his junior, who had graduated from the elite college prep Winsor School in Boston and would later graduate from Bryn Mawr. They were married in 1913 in Brookline, Massachusetts, and for a spell lived back in Cleveland, where Ernest worked as a lawyer and where Katharine gave birth to a daughter, Nancy, in 1916. Following Ernest's hiring at a law firm, the family moved to Manhattan, where in 1924 Ernest purchased a brownstone at East Ninety-Third Street, described in a *New York Times* column as a "modern residence." Literary-minded, Katharine had already published articles and reviews in several journals when in 1925 Harold Ross hired her as a manuscript reader at a fledgling weekly magazine he was publishing called the *New Yorker*. In a profile of Katharine published in 1996, Nancy Franklin noted the role that luck played in Katharine's early career: "like thousands of other young and youngish people—when she was hired [at the *New Yorker*] she was thirty-three and was the mother of two small children—in New York in the nineteen-twenties, she was in the right place at the right time." Katharine swiftly rose to become the magazine's first fiction and poetry editor, collaborating with Ross within a richly productive working relationship, helping to shape the magazine's early tone, attitude, and audience.

In "Home and Office," an essay that ran in the December 1, 1926, issue of the social work journal *The Survey*, Katharine, assertive in her tone, careful to cover all bases, wrote about the appeal and the limitations of being a working wife. "I can hardly remember a time in my childhood, absurd a child as I must sound to admit it, when my plans for myself 'grown-up' did not include both marriage and a definite career," she begins. She acknowledges that though luck has gone her way, she'd worked hard for her professional place. A prototypical and unapologetically feminist essay, "Home and Office" charts the choppy waters navigated by a mother and working professional. Katharine debates the pros and cons and nuances of "the woman's place," helpfully offering her own daily and seasonal home and work schedules as a kind of guide for women in her position—or those dreaming of it.

"Often I am asked why I work at all and I can give no one reason," she writes. "They are countless." Among them Katharine lists her "strong personal conviction" that she's expected to work, that "[I'm] not a happy or agreeable citizen unless I am working, unless I am busy up to all my capacities, and my particular capacities do not happen to be domestic ones." (She adds: "Frankly, I do not do housework well.") She confesses to "a personal need for the opportunity to follow [her] own bent," hesitating to employ the unoriginal and "somewhat ludicrous term 'self-expression'— but if honest, I must admit to a distinct personal ambition that is thwarted and an underlying cause for unhappiness when I cannot do the work of mind, not hands, for which I am best fitted." To this catalog she adds the obvious economic benefits of working, concluding powerfully: "Most important of all, I work because I know I am a better wife and mother if I do. I personally have more to give to my children and my home, and I fondly hope that I shall continue to be to my children an individual who interests them as a person quite apart from being that important but much-taken-for-granted figure, 'Mother.'"

Key to successful working parents is a supportive and patient spouse; Katharine worked hard to balance work and home, but pressing against her happiness were Ernest's infidelities. "My mother, for her part, waited some years and then told us that it was our father's love affairs that had destroyed the marriage," Roger Angell revealed decades later. While an officer in France during the war, Ernest had picked up "different ideas about sex and marriage. He had even encouraged [Katharine] to try an affair of her own: they would be a modern couple" (living in a "modern residence"). One month before Roger Angell turned nine, his mother filed for divorce from his father. The news made it into the *Times* (dateline Reno, Nevada), which reported that the suit provided joint parental control of Nancy and Roger and an annual five thousand dollar alimony for Katharine. (Ernest would remarry in 1939.)

Thus began young Roger's dual-home adolescence, with older sister Nancy as companion until she left for boarding school: weeks spent at his father's on East Ninety-Third Street and weekends at apartments on East Eighth and, later, East Forty-Eighth Streets; and summers in Maine with his mother and E. B. White, a promising young writer whom Katharine had championed at the *New Yorker* and with whom she'd fallen in love. When Katharine married Andy (everyone who knew White personally called him Andy), she oddly neglected to tell her two children, who learned of it a couple of days after the fact when a relative spotted the item in Walter Winchell's column in the *New York Daily Mirror*. Ernest had insisted on joint custody of his children: "a big mistake for everybody, mistake for my mother, mistake for my father, mistake for the children that my father should be the main day-to-day place where we lived, but we made the best of it," Angell recalled. "My father was admirable in many ways, although he didn't know anything about being a father because he hadn't had a father of his own." As weekends and holidays were divided among homes, Angell got around, moving from the Upper East Side and the Village to alternating warm-weather days spent across the Hudson River at his father's rented cottage at Sneden's Landing in the Palisades and his stepfather's farm in Maine. He stayed focused on school and play and bonded with his school mates, all the while soaking up the sophisticated goings-on of his parents' working lives, much of it beyond his ken and tantalizingly, glamorously so.

Angell attended Lincoln School in upper Manhattan, a progressive institution that encouraged wide interests in its curious and precocious young students, and Angell enjoyed the same encouragements at home. ("No Lincoln parent was ever known to have said, 'Shut up, kid,'" he observed.) Indulging his fascination with the natural world, Angell gathered numerous animals and pets at East Ninety-Third (including, at various junctures, snakes, horned toads, salamanders, tropical fish, mice, a Boston terrier, cats, and a Javanese macaque—a gift from *New Yorker* writer Emily Hahn); enjoyed trips to city museums; and read avidly in literature and natural history books. When he was eleven, his father hired a young Columbia University student, Tex Goldschmidt, to keep company with Angell on afternoons; Tex affectionately, if unofficially, tutored Angell, quizzing him about girls and sports, all the while urging the liberal *New Republic* and Marxist *New Masses* onto him and taking him to Sergei Eisenstein films downtown. Goldschmidt generally encouraged a dynamic and healthy political and socially aware consciousness in Angell, and the brief relationship forever imprinted him. "Tex saved my life," Angell wrote frankly, "and perhaps he did more than that for Father."

There were, in the city and beyond, the enjoyable diversions of tennis matches and hockey and college football games, but the sport that consumed Angell as a young boy was baseball. Providentially he lived his childhood and adolescent years in a city where baseball prospered in a golden age. Between 1920, the year Angell was born, and 1938, his first year in college, the New York Giants and the across-the-river Yankees won or lost sixteen championships between them, five times facing off with each other. (What of the Brooklyn Dodgers? "The *lowly* Dodgers . . . were just another team in the National League to me back then," Angell acknowledged.) He pulled for both the Giants and the Yankees, and his memories of the Polo Grounds and early Yankee Stadium, and the players on the field, are vivid, stuffed with affectionate details.

"I liked it best when we came into the place from up top, rather than through the gates down at the foot of the lower-right-field stand." Angell is recalling a favorite approach, often trailing his father, to the Polo Grounds. "You reached the upper-deck turnstiles by walking down a steep, short ramp from the Speedway, the broad avenue that swept down from Coogan's Bluff and along the Harlem River, and once you got inside, the long field within the horseshoe of decked stands seemed to stretch away forever below you, toward the bleachers and the clubhouse pavilion in center." Ernest would often urge his young son to notice how, say, first baseman Bill Terry would hit for extra bases by exploiting the Grounds' enormous, odd configuration but would miss out on what would've been a home run in any other park, "and, sure enough, now and then would Terry reaffirm the parable by hammering still another triple into the pigeoned distance. Everything about the Polo Grounds was special, right down to the looped iron chains that separated each sector of box seats from its neighbor and could burn your bare arm on a summer afternoon if you weren't careful." Noting the "thin wedge of shadow for the bullpen crews" along the outfield walls, young Roger evocatively envisioned them as "cows sheltering beside a pasture shed in August." Early Metaphor.

Visiting Yankee Stadium in the Bronx was something else altogether: "If the Polo Grounds felt pastoral, Yankee Stadium was Metropole, the big city personified." Once inside the park, "up the pleasing ramps, I would stop and bend over, peering through the horizontal slot between the dark, overhanging mezzanine and the descending sweep of grandstand seats which led one's entranced eye to the sunlit green of the field and the players on it." He adds: "Then I'd look for the Babe." Of course, Ruth and others—Lou Gehrig, Bill Dickey, and Lefty Gomez among them—were gargantuan figures to Angell, and with their Giants counterparts—Mel Ott, Carl Hubbell, Dolf Luque, and the rest—acted out the sunny drama of a game that, Angell reminds us, you had to go watch in order to follow. Radio coverage was scarce in the 1930s, so sports-beat writer accounts, which Angell would gobble up in the four daily newspapers his father brought home each day, provided fans with recaps, box scores, and stories if they couldn't get to the park that day. "Sports were different in my youth—a series of events to look forward to and then to turn over in memory, rather than a huge, omnipresent industry, with its own economics and politics and crushing public relations," Angell reflected. "How it felt to be a young baseball fan in the thirties can be appreciated only if I can bring back this lighter and fresher atmosphere. Attending a game meant a lot, to adults as well as to a boy, because it was the only way you could encounter athletes and watch what they did. There was no television, no instant replay, no evening highlights. We saw the players' faces in newspaper photographs, or in the pages of *Baseball*, an engrossing monthly with an invariable red cover, to which I subscribed, and here and there in an advertisement."

"To turn over in memory." Angell, as every friend and colleague of his testifies, is blessed with a stunningly prodigious memory. As Angell kept score during games, a ritual to which he attends to this day, he cultivated evocative details and imagery. The 1933 World Series—Angell was a teenager, and this was the first postseason he followed avidly—pitted the Washington Senators against the Giants. Indicative of the growing popularity of the sport, five New York radio stations broadcast the Series that year. "I listened either to Ted Husing, on WABC, or to the old NBC warhorse, Graham McNamee, over at WEAF or WJZ," Angell remembered. "I knew how to keep score by this time, and I rushed home from school—for the four week-day games, that is—turned on the big RCA Stromberg-Carlson (with its glowing Bakelite dial), and kept track, inning by inning, on scorecards I drew on one of my father's yellow legal pads." When Ernest returned home from Wall Street, his teenage son would sit with him and run through the game, "almost pitch by pitch, telling him the baseball."

On off days, when teams were idle and the parks depressingly dark, and over the course of long winters, Angell was required to pay attention to other matters of growing up. In the fall of 1934 he matriculated at Pomfret School, a college prep boarding school in Connecticut, three hours northeast of New York City. The scholastic and intellectual demands were high, with intensive courses in Latin and Sacred Studies, the ideology of which the agnostic Angell would instinctively resist. His graduating class was small: twenty-eight students. He endured serial hazing and more than one lonely weekend while away, and at graduation earned the dubious prize of carrying the seniors' class flag, a distinction awarded to the less popular students. "There were occasional weekends which you got by keeping your marks up," he'd recall years later. "You'd go home for a weekend, by train, and that meant a lot. And vacations were absolutely wonderful and went by in a flash." When he applied himself, notably in his English classes, Angell succeeded, but he also recognized in himself a certain contrarian reserve. "I never worked very hard in school. I realized later I was a smart guy, I was a smart kid. I was a high IQ kid and I could do quite well without working." He adds, "It was a form of rebellion against my parents who had both been such serious students. My mother graduated third or fourth in her class at Bryn Mawr. It was a form of rebellion that I would not try very hard." Excess energies were diverted to literary pursuits: he coedited *The Pontefract*, a biweekly newspaper, and later cofounded the Coffee Club, a literary group that produced a magazine called *MS* (for "manuscript"), featuring stories and poems.

In 1938 Angell's mother and stepfather left Manhattan, relocating to North Brooklin, Maine, to their saltwater farm overlooking Allen's Cove and Blue Hill Bay on the village's east side. There they worked, wrote, tended the farm and gardens, and raised their son Joel, born in 1931. Katharine continued her editing work for the *New Yorker* long distance, her eighteenth-century farmhouse filling up with weekly arriving manuscripts and pencil shavings, a measure of a work ethic that Angell noticed and internalized when he'd visit in the summers. He also observed his stepfather hard at work, both in the yard and more vividly disappearing into his writing room each morning, laboring over a paragraph for a "Talk of the Town" or "Comment" piece for the *New Yorker* or for a longer "One Man's Meat" essay he'd begun contributing to *Harper's Magazine*. White never spoke with his stepson about the arduous task of writing, of sitting and marinating and worrying a phrase, an argument, an observation to perfection, all the while having it appear effortless on the page. Angell took mental notes toward a writing tutelage of which he was barely aware.

"I was entranced by Andy White. The whole *New Yorker* life represented something that was not the serious, sad life I was seeing my father living at the time, and it was literary and it was fun," he recalled later, reflecting on another occasion, "When I got older, I realized that Andy White was a wonderful model. He was there at hand, and he wrote so well. I learned things from him, the main one being to try to write simply and directly and to try to make it sound easy. Be clear, be unaffected if you can, and try to arrive at a tone that is your own tone, not somebody else's. It takes a while for you to recognize what your own tone is." White wrote on Tuesdays, closing himself in his study all day. He'd emerge looking wan and wouldn't talk. "Then he'd go back in there. He'd mail [the essay] off in the late afternoon, and then, half the time, he'd try to get it back because he thought it wasn't good enough. Of course, it was good enough, but I recognize the impulse." Angell added: "Every writer understands that."

Following his preparation at Pomfret, Angell dutifully enrolled at Harvard University in 1938. "I never had a choice," he acknowledged later. "My father had gone to Harvard and my grandfather had gone to Harvard. I'd gone to all the Harvard-Yale games. I mean, it was where I was gonna go." He majored in English, played on the squash squad, wrote and edited a bit for the *Har-*

vard Crimson newspaper, and was active in the Student Union and the fraternal DU Club. The *Red Book Yearbook* listed his intended vocation as "Publishing." He asked for some help finding summer work from those at his mother's magazine, or perhaps Katharine initiated it; either way, in 1939 *New Yorker* managing editor Ik Shuman obliged by sending feelers to the *Newark News* and *Time* and *Newsweek* magazines for potential writing or editing jobs for Angell, but nothing panned out. Angell graduated in 1942 with his AB.

Before moving to Cambridge, Angell had begun seeing Evelyn Baker, from Boston. The two dated throughout their college years and were married in October 1942; Angell was twenty-two, Evelyn a year younger. Three months earlier, on July 27, Angell had been sworn into service in the Army Air Force in a ceremony on Governor's Island. (After Pearl Harbor he'd volunteered for the navy and then the Marines, but his nearsightedness kept him civilian.) Newly married, with the war heating up, Roger and Evelyn were at the mercy of the U.S. government, as were, at once, hundreds of thousands of men and women.

Angell the draftee, it turns out, was quite fortunate. He learned early in his training that he wouldn't see combat; rather, following brisk but intensive training in a blacked-out Ritz Hotel in Atlantic City (where he and other young men trained to march along the boardwalk in the early morning, learned formations, and memorized the Articles of War), Angell boarded a train to Denver, Colorado, where at Lowry Field the air force enrolled him in armament tech school. For the next several weeks Angell endured crash courses in machine guns and power turrets and in turn was expected to teach the knowledge and operation of this equipment to rotating classes of young, poorly educated, resentful draftees, their nervous eyes on the far horizon of battles and terror. A short while later Angell became the camp's official historian. He'd made "Permanent Party" in the military parlance—that is, he wasn't going anywhere. He and Evelyn moved into an apartment in Denver, where they discovered that the life of a tech school instructor in the Rocky Mountains during wartime was a breeze; suffering one or three unavoidable inconveniences happily provided by the military, Roger and Ev, as he called her, generally spent their evenings at home with dinner and drinks and occasionally out with new friends exploring the Denver restaurants and jazz clubs.

Then, unpredictably, Angell found himself far removed from the snowy mountains. In February 1944 the air force transferred him to Hickam Field in Honolulu, Hawaii, where he joined a group of other public relations noncoms on the writing and editing staff of *Brief*, the Seventh Air Force GI magazine. "*Brief* had already started, and it wasn't very good," Angell remembers. "They knew that the Pacific was going to be a big theater and they wanted some better people, so they sent four or five of us to take over this magazine." A twenty-page weekly published on Tuesdays with a circulation of over eighteen thousand, its slick cover featuring black-and-white photos of heroic soldiers and generals or rugged beachheads and war planes zooming across skies, *Brief*'s stated purpose was to "acquaint the men with the accomplishments of the 7th AAF . . . in addition to serving as a morale and orientation publication."

Evelyn moved to Maine to live with the Whites and then on her own to Weston, near Boston, as Corporal—soon Sergeant—Roger Angell, abruptly a managing editor and wartime correspondent of sorts, contributed to *Brief*'s regular "File 13" back-pages column, reported on successful air raids on various distant Pacific islands, and wrote the occasional article. ("My column was about anything," Angell recalled, "File 13 being a waste basket." Among his military-approved stories: "It's the Sergeant's Plane—Veterans of a year in action, the groundcrews of this B-25 outfit know planes as no pilot does" and "'No Bed of Roses'—Seven Stateside veterans, newly arrived in the POA, sound off about civilians, returnees, furloughs and the tough life at home.") Angell worked at *Brief*

until the end of the war. At the odd base party that he'd bluff
his way into, he'd cock his ear toward murmuring majors and
generals and learn about key military missions and campaigns
before they were waged.

Decades later Angell would write about this strange decision of
the air force to uproot him from tech school and move him into
the relatively privileged ranks of writing and editing in the Central Pacific. "I'd just had a story published in *The New Yorker*," he
mused parenthetically, "which might have helped my chances."

Crowded with bustling street-level store fronts and towering tenement buildings peering over tops of other tenement buildings, the
cover of the March 18, 1944, issue of the *New Yorker* fairly bursts at
the seams, a colorful illustration of blaring midcentury Manhattan life. On the first page an ad from GM Diesel Power urges the
reader to "Keep America Strong—Buy War Bonds." There isn't a
table of contents, only a small square of type titled "Departments
in this Issue," tucked discreetly at the bottom of the second page,
above the magazine's address. Covered in the following ninety-
six pages, in indubitable style, are art galleries, books, the current
cinema, musical events, and sport (heavyweight boxing). There's
a "Reporter in England" column and notes on female fashions;
advertisements for Saks Fifth Avenue, Lord and Taylor, and Henri
Bendel jostle smartly with those for Bourjois perfume, United Air
Lines, and Johnnie Walker. And there are cartoons too—many
of them. (Founding editor Harold Ross initially conceived of his
magazine as a "comic paper.") In one a father enters his son's
bedroom at the precise moment the tyke uses dad's champagne
bottle to christen his toy warship; in another, an aggrieved man
on a bomb assembly line, clutching an explosive, leans toward
the Rosie the Riveter type next to him and confesses, "Miss Geb-
bert, I'm nuts about you. I stay awake all day thinking about you."

Between a review of Arthur Ripley's film noir *Voice in the Wind*
and A. J. Liebling's first installment of a three-part article on

an election in Darwen, England, you'll find "Three Ladies in the Morning," Roger Angell's first appearance in the magazine. Signed "Cpl. Roger Angell," the slight story makes for an inauspicious literary debut. In it two well-dressed women meet at a midtown hotel restaurant. One is obviously agitated and can stomach only coffee; it's revealed that she's upset with the kind of men her husband Milt is bringing home to entertain. As she finishes describing the roving hands of one man who'd claimed his wife was in a sanitarium, the cries of a woman at a nearby table interrupt the conversation. Alone and worse for wear, this distraught woman brays about her husband's abandonment of her, oddly invoking the French surgeon and suture pioneer Alexis Carrel in likening herself miserably to one of the good doctor's sponges, a lump soaking up and expanding, filling up an entire building:

> "I'm going to *stop* this," the voice said. "Got to stop being a lump. Got to start trying to be a social being, end quote. My distinguished husband, my distinguished expert says that, so must give him credit."
>
> The woman put her hands out to pull herself upright and hit her ashtray, spilling cigarette butts all over the tablecloth. She looked around wildly. "Got to apologize," she said. "Got to apologize to these other ladies and gentlemen for not being a social being. Not a lady."

Aghast, the two friends get up and leave, staring straight ahead as they pass the woman on their way out of the restaurant. "It's getting so you just can't go anywhere," one remarks to the other, unsympathetically. End of story.

One can read "Three Ladies in the Morning" as characteristic of midcentury, mid-level *New Yorker* fiction—slice-of-life, upscale, dialogue-driven, with a hint of unease and menace beneath a civil, urbane surface—and also acknowledge the story's thinness, perhaps a result of its young author's narrow frame of emotional experience. (Angell was twenty-three when the story appeared; it's based on a memory of a drunk woman he saw at the Algonquin Hotel when he was on furlough.) Are the two women embarrassed, recognizing their petty domestic travails as paling next to the real thing? Does one or both of them receive an unwanted glimpse into a dissolute, boozy future? Are they touched at all by the woman's plight, or does Angell suggest that they remain unmoved, concerned only with female propriety and the foregrounding of their own problems? No access to the women's interior lives is provided, so we remain on the outside, wondering. Whether this story's appearance inspired Angell's reassignment from Colorado tech school to *Brief*, we don't know.

After the war ended, Angel and Evelyn briefly settled in an apartment on West Forty-Seventh Street in Manhattan. In September 1947 they moved uptown to a larger apartment on Riverside Drive at 156th Street ("practically a suburb of Buffalo," Angell quipped in a letter to Gus Lobrano, an editor at the *New Yorker*), and, as the 1950s dawned, across the Hudson River into a house on Washington Springs Road in quiet, rustic Sneden's Landing in the Palisades, where Angell had so often summered as a boy. The Angells needed the room: in 1948 Evelyn gave birth to a daughter, Callie; her sister Alice arrived three years later.

In the spring of 1946 Angell accepted an editorial position at the fledgling *Magazine X*, a hopeful if doomed venture launched by Curtis Publishing of *Saturday Evening Post* and *Ladies Home Journal* renown. *X* was a glossy photo magazine modeled after the enormously successful *Life* and *Look* monthlies, edited by Ted Patrick, who'd had a profitable career on Madison Avenue in the 1930s as an ad man. Patrick's tenure at *Magazine X* was short-lived, however; in the summer of 1946 Curtis President Walter D. Fuller moved Patrick over to the Curtis-owned *Holiday*, what *Time* magazine at the time called a "flashily upholstered but unexciting" travel magazine, bringing with him much of his *Magazine X* staff. Angell moved over too, and in 1947 began a ten-year span writing for *Holiday*, car-pooling in over the George Washington Bridge, and traveling back and forth between New York and the main office in Philadelphia. He'd ultimately rise to senior editor.

"In America, the years after World War II were ones of dizzying possibility, an ideal time for a publication whose raison d'être was to offer armchair access to locales that were now accessible to the masses," observed Michael Callahan. "Transcontinental flight was beginning to boom. So were ever more luxurious hotels, tour groups, vacation packages, and travel agents. And color photography was everywhere ascendant, allowing travelers to share shots of their excursions with envious friends." A splashy entrée into a postwar world of cultural sophistication and horizon expansion, *Holiday* sold to its readers "an ideal of travel as enrichment, a literal path to intellectual and spiritual betterment. What *Vogue* did for fashion, *Holiday* did for destinations. Plus, the editorial formula was irresistible for those vagabonds providing all the words and pictures." At Curtis, Fuller made clear his intentions for *Holiday* during the magazine's early, uncertain years: "I don't want stories about how to cook supper in the backyard or how to save up 50¢ to go to Coney Island. I want articles about . . . what to do and what to see at Yellowstone Park. And in between, articles about what to wear at such places. That's what people want from a magazine called *Holiday*." He added reasonably: "Even people who can't afford to go to Bermuda want to read about it."

A decade later Clifton Fadiman wrote in *Ten Years of Holiday*, with manifesto brio, that "*Holiday* is not an organ of the intellectuals." Rather it's a magazine of "civilized entertainment. It aims at satisfying and spurring the leisure-time interests of a sizable number of moderately well-heeled Americans. It is wedded to no doctrine except that of making propaganda for the politer pleasures of our time." Fadiman claimed for *Holiday* a "new kind of American journalism" in which editor, publisher, and advertising manager "cheerfully relinquish some of their triune omnipotence, and in which the main idea is to get the writer to produce the best he has in him, on the theory that you must give him his head before you can get him to use it." Fadiman added: "The editors of *Holiday* know that fun is fun, but they are also subtly urging on us the peculiar discovery that thinking can be fun too."

The magazine was rightly celebrated for its roster of big-name writers: William Faulkner, Robert Penn Warren, Joan Didion, Carl Sandburg, Mary McCarthy, William Saroyan, Ian Fleming, Kenneth Tynan, Irwin Shaw, Paul Bowles, Ogden Nash, Arthur Miller, James Thurber, John Steinbeck, Lawrence Durrell, V. S. Pritchett, Alfred Kazin, and Alistair Cooke all wrote for *Holiday* over its lifetime. Angell wrote for the magazine also. The first opportunities for him to essay his strengths and limits as a reporter and nonfiction writer, his pieces reflected the worldly, Technicolor aspirations of the magazine: between 1947 and 1957 he wrote about diverse subjects such as New England clambakes, the African drumbeat, Boca Raton, transatlantic pilots, the Museum of Modern Art, the Westminster Dog Show, walking in Washington DC, and cooking on board the *Liberté*. "We all tried to assign ourselves pieces where we got to go somewhere," Angell recalls. "I thought of the idea of the food on the French liner. I brought this up and the other editors said, 'You bastard!' I got a free round trip, first class, where everyone on board was trying to get me to drink this wine or try this dish."

In 1948 Angell asked his stepfather for a piece on Manhattan for a New York–themed issue of *Holiday*; E. B. White obliged with "This Is New York," soon to be lauded as an all-time classic essay on the city. ("I think [White] did it for me, rather than for the money, thinking it would help me. Which it did.") Angell traveled extensively on assignments and on the lookout for article ideas, sometimes with Evelyn, often with fellow editors, enjoying first-class flights and accommodations. *Holiday* had money and wasn't shy about spending it. "For a while there, we were the shining light," Angell told Callahan.

On January 6, 1945, Angell published his first "fact" piece for
the *New Yorker*, a well-researched and solidly written "Reporter at
Large" account, first composed for *Brief*, of a harrowing bomb-
ing mission to the Japanese island of Iwo and the last flight of
"The Chambermaid," a B-24 Liberator bomber that crash-landed
after the mission. When he wasn't traveling and writing up exotic
locales for *Holiday* and in between helping raise Callie and Alice
and nursing hangovers endemic to the hard-partying magazine,
Angell concentrated on writing short stories, looking ahead and
vaguely imagining for himself a career as a serious literary writer.
(While stationed in Honolulu, Angell had received a visit from
John Cheever, who was in the Pacific on a motion picture assignment for the Army Signal Corps; Cheever had been transferred
after his first book, *The Way Some People Live*, appealed to Major
Leonard Spigelgass, an MGM executive and officer in the Signal
Corps. One can only wonder what Cheever and the young wan-
nabe Cheever talked about.)

The going was tough. The son of the magazine's cofounding
literary editor was hardly immune to rejection: many of Angell's
early stories were returned by fiction editor Gus Lobrano. On
August 9, 1945, Lobrano passed on "A Letter to the Alumni Bulle-
tin," writing carefully to Evelyn, who was receiving her husband's
mail while he was stationed in the Pacific, "We felt that it was
nicely written, but couldn't help being kind of dubious about the
theme. . . . In short, I guess we felt the values in the piece were
somewhat too black and white." Five months later, "grieved to
report," Katharine White herself passed along to Evelyn a "no"
on "Two Thousand Miles of Ocean," reminding her daughter-
in-law, "I don't vote, of course, but to be entirely honest with you
and Rog, I think I would've voted no. I feel that there are lots of
good places in it but that it doesn't work as a story." In September 1946 Angell received another rejection for "March, March
on down the Field," Lobrano sharing that he and the editors
felt, "reluctantly, that it was somewhat forced." Six months later,

concerning "Hello, Big Time," Angell opened his mail to read, this time from the comfort of his home on East Forty-Seventh, "I'm awfully sorry, but the vote was against this one. The people seem to us not entirely convincing and their relationships not definite enough." (Lobrano suggests a lunch date with Angell for later in the week, so there was that.) In June 1947 "Summer's End" was returned ("the prevailing feeling is that the situation is pretty familiar"), and on April 8, 1948, Lobrano, passing on "Field Guide," wrote, "I won't attempt to go into detailed criticism, because I understand your mother will tell you today all about our reaction to it." Angell pressed on. Instinctively, and likely evoking inspiring imagery of his mother's and stepfather's hard and determined editorial work, he recognized that the probability of rejection, and the subsequent revising in the face of failure, was tantamount to the weather to a writer: it was always there. If nothing else, Angell was receiving training in how to write tactfully honest and encouraging rejection letters, a skill he'd trade on for decades.

Through the fall of 1947, Lobrano, relaying Harold Ross's concerns, urged Angell to rework a story titled "Sooner or Later." One of Lobrano's letters to Angell nicely captures the *New Yorker*'s characteristically patient editorial attention to craft as that attention dovetails with genuine, and generous, respect for a writer's forbearance, skill, and intelligence (though how much of this kindness might've been granted to Angell for being White's son is unknown):

> [Ross] had various other suggestions and, come to think of it, I guess it would be simpler all around if I told you about them while we were both looking at the manuscript. I'll hold it here and if you're still willing to fiddle with it we can get together some day next week (which day would be best for you?) and go over it. Or you could tell us to go to hell and to send the manuscript back. I wouldn't blame you for taking that course,

but I hope you won't. Ross seems really interested in the piece and anxious to see it work out.

After addressing concerns about plot plausibility and shoring up some regional and historic inaccuracies, Angell came back with a revision retitled "Just a Matter of Time." Lobrano accepted the story in November; it ran in the January 31, 1948, *New Yorker* and twelve years later appeared in Angell's first book.

Eventually Angell's stories were routinely accepted at the magazine, though usually after some rewriting under Lobrano's influence. Angell was rewarded the first of several first-look contracts and subsequent renewals. He'd still need the occasional prod, however. "To put it quite bluntly, why in the hell haven't you written any short fiction lately?" Lobrano demanded in a letter on October 4, 1948. Likely the upside-down demands of a new baby—Callie hadn't turned one yet—and Angell's work at *Holiday* explain his diminished output; he'd also become interested in writing some of the unsigned pieces that appeared modestly in the "Talk of the Town" in the opening pages of the *New Yorker*, a form that his stepfather had mastered. William Shawn, who succeeded Ross as editor in 1952, believed that the "Talk of the Town" was the "soul of the magazine," and he enjoyed Angell's small, bemused, ironic slice-of-life pieces, though "You're doing fine," "Please do some more," and the shrugging "You obviously know how to do it" were as much gushing as the reserved Shawn would offer Angell. Over the decade Angell would publish more than a dozen of the pieces.

A life-long reader of fiction, Angell seemed truly to believe in his own stories and in himself as a fiction writer, so the work for the *New Yorker* (his sole literary target, it would appear) kept coming; between April 1946 and September 1960 he published twenty-one stories in the magazine. Before Angell could gather these stories into a book, they began receiving attention: "A Killing" was reprinted in *The Fireside Book of Baseball* and in *55 Short Stories from The New Yorker*; "Flight through the Dark" in *The Best American Short Stories, 1951*; "In an Early Winter" in *The Best American Short Stories, 1956*; and "Côte d'Azur" in *Stories from The New Yorker: 1950–1960*. Notably two of Angell's stories were adapted for television. Donald S. Sanford directed "My Own Master" for an episode of NBC's *Loretta Young Show* on December 18, 1960, and the soon-to-be-legendary Stephen Sondheim adapted "In an Early Winter" for a dramatic teleplay on *Rendezvous*, broadcast on NBC on May 20, 1959. (In 2016, Angell received an award from the New York State Writers Hall of Fame. Sondheim was a fellow honoree but couldn't attend the ceremony as he was ill. He sent a message that read, in effect, "Tell Roger Angell that my first work as a writer was to adapt a story of his into a TV show." Remarkably Sondheim's note was how Angell first learned of the adaptation, a half century after the fact.)

Little, Brown published *The Stone Arbor and Other Stories* in December 1960. Reactions were decidedly mixed, though Angell must've been buoyed by the first review he read, that of Charles Poore in the *Times*, which lauded the book as "a fine collection of *New Yorker* stories about the Button-Down-Collar Generation in crucial hours at tension and pleasure," the characters rendered with a "splendidly casual ease." Poore remarked that Angell's considerable strength was his "point of view . . . to show us the salient differences that in spite of every kind of pressure make individuals of us all." A couple of weeks later, the *Times* weighed in again, and this time reviewer Daniel Talbot virtually sneered at the book, pulling no punches in his opening: "The quality of these stories— physically and spiritually—is very *New Yorker*-ish," he sniffed, "neat prose and bland images, lighthearted attempts at delineating some of the psychic fears around town, pseudo-Proustian reminiscences and an astonishing capacity for skimming the surface of deeply felt experiences." A couple of months later, an anonymous writer in *Kirkus Reviews* complained that the "offbeat items, while convincing enough at the time, leave one only with a sense of the author's ingenuity." Robbie Macauley, in the *New Republic*, offered a more considered take, praising Angell's avoidance of cliché and evenly concluding by wondering "what might happen if [Angell] were to take some big risks, attempt some thornier subjects, use language with greater daring, and chance the errors of ambition. The results," he wrote hopefully, "might be astonishingly good."

With a handful of later exceptions, however, the stories gathered in *The Stone Arbor* would be the last serious literary fiction Angell would produce. As of this writing, the book remains out of print, a curio in online marketplaces and dusty bookstores. "When I look back on it, I was in college, and then the army, and I thought of myself as a short story writer," says Angell. "I knew I'd never be a novelist. It just wasn't in me. I was more and more involved as an editor, and that was practically a full time job." "I really didn't decide to stop," he remarked on another occasion. "I just didn't have a lot more stories to tell."

Early in his review of *The Stone Arbor*, Macauley described the kinds of situations in which Angell's characters often found themselves: "Mr. Angell's best and most frequent subject is the decent American who is, at one moment or another in life, surprised to find himself inadequate when faced with some small trial of character or emotions. Nevertheless, each one tries to muddle through in his own way and it is in this act of muddling through the discouraging self-revelation that the characters become most affecting and human." Substitute "decent American" with one of Angell's other preoccupations—namely, the baseball player—and Macauley could be describing what Angell sees when he observes a struggling slugger, a slumping pitcher, or an aggrieved manager, his muddling-through, small trials of inadequacy on the diamond as graphic as any other form of misery.

Distracted by engrossing work and his young family, Angell remained besotted with baseball and headed to his beloved Polo

Grounds and Yankee Stadium when he could, occasionally bringing his young daughters to introduce them to the game. Angell the
fan came of age in an unprecedented era. In baseball, Manhattan
reigned supreme in the midcentury: between Angell's thirteenth and
thirty-sixth birthdays, the Yankees won the World Series an astonishing thirteen times, consecutively from 1936 to '39, again from '49
to '53, and also in '41, '43, '47, and '56; they lost only two Series (in
'42 and '55) in that span. The Giants lost three Series in that era but
won it all in '33 and again in '54. (The hard-luck Brooklyn Dodgers, a team Angell generally ignored, beat those Yankees in '55.)

When given the opportunity or by his own initiative, Angell
began writing about baseball, feeling his way toward his truest
and greatest subject. He first turned to fiction, conjuring "Mrs.
Foltz" and "Mrs. Kernochan," a pair of likeable barflies and ball
fans, whom he introduced to *New Yorker* readers in a triptych of
charming stories: "A Killing" (April 20, 1946), "The Old Moxie"
(July 27, 1946), and "Opening Day" (April 22, 1950).

In the first, Linwood P. Schumacher, an enthusiastic brush
salesman, arrives one afternoon at the apartment shared, it's pre-
sumed, by the two ladies, where he's mistaken by the wildly drunk
Mrs. Kernochan for Hal Schumacher, the New York Giants' right-
handed pitcher of the 1930s. Foltz finds this all very hysterical—
she's been drinking too—and, wiping away tears of laughter,
indulges Kernochan up to a point. Flustered, Linwood doesn't
know quite what to do, torn as he is between not wishing to take
advantage of an intoxicated middle-aged baseball enthusiast and
wanting a whopping sale to crow about to the fellas back in the
office. In the end he goes for the titular kill and leaves the apartment having sold everything, including all samples, to the clueless yet none-the-wiser Kernochan, who's convinced that she'd
just met Prince Hal, the hero hurler from her youth. (Forty years
later Angell will describe famed knuckle ball pitcher Phil Niekro
in the clubhouse after a game: "Watching him take off his spikes
and his elastic sock supporters and the rest, and tuck his gear

into his square-top travel bag . . . I was reminded of an old-time travelling salesman repacking his sample case.")

We bump into Kernochan and Foltz three months later in a bar on Ninth Avenue. Kernochan's being solicited again, this time by Switzer, a panting loser who's trying in vain to convince her to go away with him on a picnic. Mr. Switzer's nothing if not persistent, but Kernochan will have none of it: she's far more interested in betting rounds of drinks with Herman the bartender over baseball trivia. Kernochan's not batting well: she's lost three rounds to Herman, who knew the name of the Giants' second baseman in the 1933 World Series (as did the story's author; that postseason was the first he followed avidly, hence its affectionate appearance here) but gained a round when Herman flubbed naming the Washington Senators' outfield in the same Series.

Exasperated by Switzer's lame entreaties, Kernochan turns and lets him have it: what he's lacking is *moxie*—what Ted Williams has, she points out helpfully. Look at Williams, she says, he's so loose up there at the plate, it's like he'd rather be in bed; it looks like he'll drop the bat at the plate; instead he wallops yet another homer. "But for God's sake, Gloria!" Switzer blurts. "I'm not a ballplayer." Poor Switzer doesn't get it and never will: with midcentury feminine subtlety, Kernochan's talking about a ballplayer's sex appeal, the confidently shrugging ease with which he plays a difficult game, the panache, the cool of it all. Switzer's no match. He's seen at the end of the story borrowing Herman's baseball stats books to brush up.

Four years on we arrive at the same bar, and time hasn't dimmed Kernochan's and Foltz's day-drinking enthusiasm. The two friends complain about endless dark winters of nothing but watching wrestling and basketball, but they're buoyed by April and their confidence that the Giants will prevail in the coming season. A man perched nearby, preoccupied by horses, overhears and joins the conversation, unwittingly setting himself up for some tart scorn and moral judging. Bar talk turns from the immorality of horse racing and gambling (and Sunday ball games) to the far more contentious topic of Giants versus Yankees—with a peaceful, agreed-upon dismissal of "them crummy Brooks." (Angell couldn't resist getting in a dig at the Dodgers.) As voices and tensions rise, Herman steps in to cool things down, and a sense of civic politeness—leavened with the forgiving balm of the start of the baseball season—prevails. After the man leaves to place a bet, Mrs. Kernochan admits to finding him "kind of cute," whereupon she's greeted with a guffaw and a friendly pinch on her ass by Foltz. "Spring is sure here, all right," Foltz remarks. Mrs. Kernochan's eyes, meanwhile, are sparkling.

Though Angell ultimately preferred to write nonfiction about baseball, "Opening Day" remains a pleasant slice of barroom hope and April optimism, less a story about baseball than about charmingly tipsy adults drinking in a bar in the afternoon as spring does its devilish work. As the title makes clear, the story pays tribute to a certain "Play Ball!" *joie de vivre*. Angell's talent for evocative narrative detail that will enliven his decades' worth of baseball writing is already vivid here with Kernochan and Foltz, and many of his baseball-related interests are present too: the ribbing among competing fans; female and kids' interests in the game; New York as the midcentury capital of baseball; and the personal possibilities between men and women against the backdrop of America's greatest game.

In 1956 "A Killing" was reprinted in Charles Einstein's popular *Fireside Book of Baseball*. (Einstein jokingly urged readers to compare the story to the tragic tale of Eddie Waitkus, the Philadelphia Phillies first baseman who'd been shot and nearly killed by a female stalker in 1949.) When Angell gathered material for *The Stone Arbor*, he included "A Killing" and "The Old Moxie" as a two-part story under the title "The Pastime," revised to reflect the gals' boozy mourning of the Giants' departure to San Francisco following the 1957 season. Curiously he neglected to include "Opening Day," perhaps deeming the story trivial or otherwise inferior or fearing that he'd merely repeated himself. When he'd sent the story to Lobrano on March 15, he'd written, "Here's another one with those two baseball nuts. . . . I don't know if it's funny, though, or funny enough." (More than a half century later, Angell admitted that he couldn't remember the story.) "Opening Day" is the last we ever hear from Kernochan and Foltz, two minor, affectionately drawn characters in the Angell baseball oeuvre who certainly had highballs to drink, daily living to kvetch about, and more ballgames to watch.

Angell twice wrote about baseball in the pages of *Holiday*. Following the Giants' and Dodgers' decampments to San Francisco and Los Angeles respectively, he wrote "Farewell, My Giants!" for the May 1958 issue. Offering a history of the team and a lament over its departure, he breezily recaps decades of highs and lows at the Polo Grounds, offering nuggets of remembered plays and players from his considerable storehouse of memory. Angell reveals that he attended the final Giants game at the park on September 29, 1957, and brought along nine-year-old Callie with him. The Giants lost to the Pirates, 9–1, and Angell describes "some history-minded fans," who dug up home plate and souvenir chunks of the outfield after the game. Leaving the park, Callie looked at her father "rather anxiously" and said, "I had a good time. That was fun. I'm sorry they lost." Angell, giving vent to a rare burst of melancholy, wrote, "I didn't feel anything—nothing at all. I guess I just couldn't believe it. But it's true, all right. The flags are down, the lights in the temple are out, and the Harlem River flows lonely to the sea." More than three decades later, the loss was still vivid. Speaking on camera to filmmaker Ken Burns for Burns's 1994 documentary *Baseball,* Angell described the Giants' departure as "absolutely heartbreaking, absolutely heartbreaking. . . . I just couldn't believe this was happening. It was as if baseball itself was ending."

This *Holiday* threnody lacks the easy humor and casually incisive turns of phrase that will come to characterize Angell's best baseball writing; to read it is to sense the work of a writer who doesn't quite yet feel the permission to take his subject as seriously as he might and who's hoarding his best metaphors for his short stories. Of greater interest is "Baseball—The Perfect Game," which ran in *Holiday* in May 1954 and which gives the impression of an essay Angell might've included in a future job application. Again he's not quite in midseason form; there are a few moments where he uncharacteristically gives in to some italicized over-emoting, and a bland sentence like "a solidly hit triple with the bases loaded is unbelievably exciting to see" might've embarrassed him a few years down the line. But in essence "Baseball—The Perfect Game" is prime Angell: casual, knowledgeable, gently persuasive without being defensive or pedantic, highly observant, anti-sentimental, funny, and literary in its attention to evocative details and telling imagery.

Angell outlines for himself and his readers what about the game might deserve his, and our, sustained, thoughtful attention, beginning by observing that the game binds us in its community-making rituals, inspiring self-identification, hometown pride, and fierce loyalties. After sharing fond memories of watching Joe DiMaggio and others play, Angell explores what will become one of the central themes in his baseball writing: the paradox of the supreme difficulty of the game and the apparent ease with which its players play. (Mrs. Kernochan would understand.) Patient with, and sympathetic to, those who find the game dull, Angell insists that it's the disconnect between boredom and elite skill, numbing routines and extravagant catastrophes that gives baseball its peculiar, renewable energy and that allows fans to halfheartedly imagine that they could be out there too.

"Unknowing people, new to the game, often complain that 'nothing happens' in a baseball game," he notes. "Innings pass, the teams change sides, yet no one scores or appears to come close to it. This, of course, is far from the truth. It is only the fantastic, almost contemptuous ease with which a big-league team completes the routine plays that make it appear, when a good pitcher is working, that it will never be scored on." Yet disaster "can descend with appalling violence and speed. A pitcher can be working beautifully after six perfect innings and then find himself, in the space of four minutes, on his way to the showers. A scratch hit, a bit of bad luck, an adverse call on a close pitch and a hit ball which just eludes the fingers of a racing outfielder, and the pitcher is done, his team defeated." There, in its richest shape, is "the drama, the perfection of baseball. Action and tragedy, defeat and triumph are suddenly enacted, against a background of apparent safety and invulnerability." He concludes with an inventory of rhetorical questions that raise the bullet points he'll cover in his long career, among them the following: "Is it any wonder then that baseball managers frequently worry themselves into the hospital with the thought that a single inconsequential April decision of theirs can mean the loss of millions of dollars in September?" and "Is it any wonder that such childishness as home-town pride and hero worship grips great segments of the population of America and that adults will pay well for the right to sit under a broiling midsummer sun on hard seats in order to scream and pray over the flight of a ball?"

Clifton Fadiman, chief editor at Simon & Schuster, felt strongly enough about "Baseball—The Perfect Game" to include it in the *Ten Years of Holiday* anthology published in 1956, though his feelings were humorously mixed. In the introduction he backhandedly observes that Angell "writes so well about baseball that he almost comes near to practically succeeding in making that organized season tic transiently, mildly semi-interesting. (To me, I mean—he will delight all decent people.)" Commissioner of Baseball Ford Frick received Angell in the commissioner's office in New York City, where Angell presented him with a bound volume of the May 1954 issue of *Holiday*. In the photograph commemorating the occasion, both men look a tad ill at ease, their countenances not reflecting their feelings toward the game they both loved and about which Angell writes so affectionately and effectively in this early heralding essay.

In 1956 Angell left *Holiday* and accepted a job as an editor of fiction at the *New Yorker*. The publication of *The Stone Arbor* and his successful, decade-long writing and senior editorship at *Holiday* qualified Angell in William Shawn's eyes, but there were surely suspicions of nepotism among colleagues. Katharine White had more or less retired from the magazine; if her word had any bearing on her son's entrée onto the twentieth floor at 25 West Forty-Third, Angell's acumen, editor's ear, writing talent, work ethic, and professional relationship with Gus Lobrano and other *New Yorker* editors would ultimately render moot the cries of favoritism. (In fact, Angell and Katharine White were simultaneously employed by the *New Yorker* for a few months before she retired. He subsequently took over the editing of several of her writers and years later moved into her corner office.) Angell's life-long familiarity with the magazine didn't guarantee a place at the table, but it bred in him a long-standing love and respect for the enterprise and a professional admiration that translated into fierce commitment and loyalty and resulted in a long, generous, and influential run as editor and contributor.

"When I came to work . . . I don't think William Shawn, the editor then, wanted any more people in that family—that cabal," Angell said. "Well, there was no cabal. Actually, Shawn wouldn't have minded, but the other people on the magazine felt, Enough already. But it was sort of a natural thing for me to come [there]. I knew the magazine, I was a contributor, and I'd grown up with *The New Yorker* as a daily presence, really, reading it and watching it being written and edited. So I had a great apprenticeship." The magazine "surrounded me on every side," he acknowledged on another occasion, "was talked about endlessly, all day long, and then some more over the weekends." He recalled that Harold Ross was mentioned by his mother and stepfather more than any single person at the White dinner table. "'Ross,' they called him, came up every day. So I paid close attention."

Angell's parents' writerly influence obviously "was important. It mattered for me in psychological terms, because my parents were divorced when I was about eight years old and I ended up with my father, which was not the best arrangement. I saw a lot of my mother, but she was away. I was young and I yearned for her, so what she did, working for *The New Yorker*, was of great significance to me. And what Andy White, my stepfather, did was attractive to me. My mother always supported my wishes to be a writer, my baby efforts." In the decades to come Angell would edit some of the great names in twentieth-century literature (John Updike, Vladimir Nabokov, and James Thurber, among others) and help discover new voices (Donald Barthelme and Ann Beattie among them), forging a distinguished career in arts and letters, consuming work that he deeply enjoyed and in which he took great pride. "It's hard to think about what he hasn't meant to the magazine," *New Yorker* editor David Remnick says, adding, "He's one of the most influential fiction editors in the history of the country." This side of Angell's professional career—a decades-long, intimate aesthetic give-and-take between editor and writer, conducted on the phone, in correspondence, and at an office desk high above Manhattan—retained a lower profile than his baseball writing.

Among *New Yorker* editorial meetings, the odd story and "casual" of his own, and film reviews (he wrote over a dozen in 1960 and '61), Angell turned to baseball. Perhaps he internalized that in the game he'd loved since he was a boy he might find something to write about that engaged him as an adult. He started with several unsigned baseball-related "Comments" in the magazine's "Talk of the Town." He'd already published two back in 1950: a May 20 piece on the lack of privacy manifested in a home plate microphone picking up a manager's comments to an umpire, and a September 30 piece on Ballplayers Day at the Polo Grounds. ("If we are going to continue to have 'days' for ballplayers," he wrote tartly, "let's have the ceremonies after the game is over, or maybe after the season is over.") A "Comment" on baseball advertisements ran in the May 11, 1957, issue, and one followed on the bittersweet departure of Casey Stengel on October 29, 1960. A year later Angell presented "Fall Classic," a tour-de-force recap of the just-concluded New York Yankees–Cincinnati Reds World Series, written in the mock-heroic style of Greek drama filtered through a modern-day baseball announcer. (More precisely via its classicist subtitle: "After an evening of Aeschylus at the City Center, followed too quickly by an afternoon of Mel Allen and the World Series.") Angell was having fun, feeling around within the parameters of the game for a voice and a tone, for what he might be able to do and say. "The more you analyze this dull, splendid game," he'd mused in "Baseball—The Perfect Game," "the more wonderful it becomes."

One afternoon in the winter of 1962, Angell was in William Shawn's office when Shawn mentioned that he'd like more sports writing in the magazine. They'd covered boxing, horse racing, hockey, college football, tennis. Thomas Meehan had been writing some "Talk of the Town" baseball pieces. Shawn wanted more, and he wanted his writers to explore what truly interested them. In a tone of voice "at once polite and venturesome, weighing and inviting," Shawn suggested to Angell that he try and write a piece about baseball; maybe he could find something interesting there. In some accounts of this conversation, in which two men gaze toward a future the grandness of which neither could've predicted, Angell is the one who broaches the idea of writing about the game. The assignment was vague and Angell admittedly apprehensive, but the editors agreed that he'd head down to Florida in March.

Wonderful, Shawn said. Take your time there. See what you find. But tell me, again, what exactly is "spring training"?

THE SPORTING SCENE

Sarasota, March 20

(named Willie ~~Roberts~~ Roberts)
This winter, a ~~Sarasota~~ mortician/dispatched to ~~local~~ Sarasota

residents and vistors a mailing of cards printed with his name
baseball
and with the schedule of ~~spring training~~ games to be played

here by the Chicago White Sox, who conduct their spring training
right
in Payne Park, ~~right~~ in the middle of town. This must be inter-

preted as a pure public service, rather than an attempt to accel-
senior citizens   unbearable
erate business by the exposure of ~~townspeople~~ to ~~unbearable~~ excite-
was ~~unbearably~~   specialist
ment; only last night, I ~~was~~ informed that a local heart/has

ordered one of his patients to attend every Sox game ~~back~~ here,
~~Spring~~ Big league ball, on
~~physicians~~ as a therapeutic measure. ~~Baseball, during the spring~~
spring
the west coast of Florida, is a/sport played by the young for the
--- a   sun-warmed, , sleepy
divertisement of the elderly/ ~~an exhibition celebrating~~

exhibition celebrating the juvenescence of the year and the senescence

of the fan. Although Florida newspapers print the "standings"

of the teams in the Grapefruit League every day, ~~winnings~~ none of
especial
the teams tries ~~any~~ hard to win; managers are looking hopefully

at their rookies and anxiously at their veteran stars, and by
no matter what the score,
the seventh or eighth inning,/most of the regulars are back in

the hotel or driving out to join their families on the beach,
youngsters up from the minors.
their places taken by ~~understudies~~   The

spectators accept this without complaint. Their loyalty to the

home club is gentle and unquestioning, and their afternoon pleasure
appears
~~is~~ scarcely affected by victory or defeat. Deeper, more emotional

attachments ~~to the home team~~ would have been badly jarred three

years ago, when the Boston Red Sox, who had trained here for many
transferred spring
years, ~~moved~~ their ~~training~~ camp to Scottsdale, Arizona, and the

265

Good News Forever

You can observe a lot by watching.
YOGI BERRA

Born of a doomed, half-baked league, cobbled together from civic pride and so-so talent, the New York Mets arrived at Major League Baseball in the spring of 1962, eager and already behind.

Following the New York Giants' and Brooklyn Dodgers' departures for California in 1957, Gotham mayor Robert Wagner was eager to bring back baseball. Surely, he reasoned, a city of sixteen million residents was large enough to support more than one team, even if that team was the lordly Yankees. Wagner contacted William Shea, a Manhattan lawyer with political ties and offices in Times Square, and asked if he'd consider chairing a committee devoted to exploring ways to return baseball to New York City. Shea agreed and, coaxing renowned baseball executive Branch Rickey out of retirement to assist him, made entreaties to the owners of the Chicago Cubs, St. Louis Cardinals, Cincinnati Reds, Philadelphia Phillies, and Pittsburgh Pirates, hopeful to lure one of them to New York. The Cubs were happy in Wrigleyville, and the Cardinals and Phillies enjoyed a monopoly over fans in their respective cities. The Reds and Pirates listened to offers but ultimately said no.

Shea and Rickey then turned their attention to the idea of a new league, the Continental, to compete with the American and National Leagues and to feature a new New York team. "We've already got five cities—New York, Toronto, Denver, Houston, and Minneapolis–St. Paul—signed up for the league," Shea crowed in 1959, "and besides Montreal there's Buffalo, Atlanta, New Orleans, Honolulu, San Juan, and Dallas-Fort Worth all anxious to sign up." He added, "It'll be a headache deciding on the three lucky cities. In my opinion, they've all earned the right to major-league ball."

Shea and Rickey hoped to have the Continental League in operation by the spring of 1961, but the league never got past the drawing board. Baseball took note of Shea's gumption, his loudly proclaimed desire to end baseball's immunity from anti-trust laws, and the interest shown in his league by various men with bags of money. In response came the announcement in July 1960 that Major League Baseball would expand by four teams, two in each league, with franchises in Los Angeles and Minne-apolis–St. Paul in the American and Houston and New York in the National. Former Yankees general manager George Weiss was hired on as president and de facto general manager (with Charlie Hurth) for the New York team, formally named the Met-ropolitan Baseball Club, nicknamed the Mets in the spring of 1961. After a bit of wooing, Weiss lured seventy-one-year-old Casey Stengel, who'd been unceremoniously fired by the Yankees in 1960, out of retirement to manage the new team. Though game-smart and thoroughly tested, the veteran Stengel must've worried about what he'd gotten himself into as the Mets were assembled, Frankenstein-like, from castoffs, old-timers, and unproven rook-ies via an expansion draft in 1961.

The motley crew arrived in St. Petersburg, Florida, for its first spring training in the late winter of 1962, and Roger Angell was on hand for the event. He was an innocent, in a sense, writing with expansive time and space at his indulgence. Before he headed south, Shawn had offered him a bit of priceless instruction: "Don't be sentimental or cynical." "That was just like [Shawn], not to plan what the story was and see how it would develop," Angell recalled later. "I went on with it because I enjoyed it so much and I seemed to find a way of writing about baseball that was easy for me, kind of like myself. You know, that's a key thing for a writer, to be yourself." "It was just natural for me not to be sentimental," he remarked on another occasion. "I'm an anti-sentimentalist. I hate goo." Ben McGrath, a staff writer at the *New Yorker* since the late 1990s and friend of Angell's, says, "By going down at age forty-one to begin this process, already established in his life, Roger didn't come at it with the same cynicism that most sports writers naturally have, sent through this machine, beginning in their twenties, writing about these athletes who don't give a shit about them. His lack of cynicism is at least as important as his lack of sentimentality."

Covering the inaugural year of the Mets was, in retrospect, a lucky gig for Angell, so rich was the team's legendary ineptitude. At the exhibition games, when he wasn't wincing at the errors and comical outfield collisions, Angell paid attention to those sitting next to him in the creaking stands—fellow, like-minded spirits. "It occurred to me fairly early on that nobody was writing about the fans. I was a fan, and I felt more like a fan than a sportswriter. I spent a lot of time in the stands. . . . And that was a great fan story, the first year of the Mets. They were these terrific losers that New York took to its heart." In his spring training game notes of the time, Angell jotted, "Kind of team this is: Players, etc.—pretty bad not like Giants, compare, v. briefly." Surely smiling, he adds: "<u>But More Fun</u>."

No human expression occurs in a vacuum, and Angell had predecessors. In the pages of the *New Yorker*, his nearest "press-box peer" was A. J. Liebling, a boxing devotee who famously detested baseball. The magazine occasionally covered the diamond. "Borough Defender," Robert Lewis Taylor's two-part profile of Brooklyn Dodgers president Larry MacPhail ran in the July 12 and 19, 1941, issues; Robert Rice profiled Branch Rickey, president, manager, and quarter owner of the Dodgers, in "Thoughts on Baseball" in the May 20, 1950, issue; John McNulty's quasi-literary-journalistic "Tryout for the Giants," in which the author visited the New York Giants camp in Melbourne, Florida, and reported on the vagaries of tryouts, contracts, and the farm club system, ran on March 22, 1952.

Yet before Angell baseball was generally treated with a light touch in the magazine, via unsigned comments in "The Talk of the Town." In the June 6, 1953, issue, E. J. Kahn Jr. wrote about a dog loose on Ebbets Field and interrupting a Dodgers and Giants game for ten minutes; in "Outside" (October 3, 1953) Peter Bunzel, Richard McCallister, and Brendan Gill collectively considered the fate of home run balls hit over the right-field fence at Ebbets Field; Thomas Meehan wrote a few "Talk of the Town" pieces, trailing the erstwhile Continental League and the New York Mets' birth (October 3, 1959) and reporting on the remodeling of the Polo Grounds for the Mets' inaugural season there (April 14, 1962). And, of course, baseball featured prominently, if seasonally, in many cartoons and in the odd poem; Rolfe Humphries's "Polo Grounds" (August 22, 1942) dramatized a midsummer inning of baseball between the Giants and Dodgers, and Donald Stewart's "Thou Mets" ("darling buds of April, we bid ye welcome") ran on March 24, 1962, heralding the Mets' arrival two weeks before Angell's first spring training piece ran.

A writer whom Angell has long respected is Red Smith, "[a] great model for me . . . a model for almost every sportswriter." Born in 1905 and raised in Green Bay, Wisconsin, Smith worked early in his career at the *Milwaukee Sentinel* and *St. Louis Journal*. From 1936 to 1945 he wrote for the *Philadelphia Record* before joining the *New York Herald Tribune* in 1945, where he'd flourish, writing three or four sports columns a week syndicated to dozens of newspapers in the United States and over two hundred worldwide. In 1976 Smith was awarded the Pulitzer Prize for Commentary, only the second sportswriter to win the award, and the J. G. Taylor Spink Award from the Baseball Hall of Fame, baseball's highest honor for journalists. "The great thing about Red Smith was that he sounded like himself," Angell remarked. "His attitude about sports was always clear. He felt himself enormously

lucky to be there in the pressbox. He was not in favor of glorify-
ing the players too much—Godding up the players, in Stanley
Woodward's phrase. But he was Red Smith in every line. You
knew what he had read and what his influences were." Elsewhere
Angell has remarked about Smith's "joyful participation" and that
Smith himself "was visible in every column. He was an erudite
guy, a college guy, and he would make knowing references. You
never felt he was writing down at any point. He was himself. The
references were complimentary because you understood them.
He always made it seem effortless and there was a lot of humor."
He added, "Everybody wanted to write like Red Smith."

As if he'd been merely eavesdropping, Smith related tales from
clubhouses and dugouts conversationally and casually, drolly
humorous and with a sharp ear for expressive dialogue. His idiosyncratic pieces on umpires (who were seldom written about),
owners, and the complex and shadowy vagaries of baseball's
backrooms made those subjects accessible and enlivening. "Red
wrote about sports without an apology, as an intelligent grown
up," Angell remembers. "And he laughed at himself and laughed
at the players a little bit, and was not manly and weepy. And there
were a lot of personal touches as well." Smith taught Angell that
a writer writing about sports could be truly himself, could be personal, and could be "smart and not apologize for loving sports."

Often blunt, Smith was unafraid of controversial subjects. His
nuanced column, "Negro Outspoken," which ran on January 25,
1962, following the announcement of Bob Feller's and Jackie
Robinson's inductions into the Baseball Hall of Fame, addressed
Robinson's career-long tendency to view the ups and downs of
his career through the lens of racism. Carefully Smith argued
that Robinson may have been missing the point all along:

> When [Robinson] was involved in controversy, and that was
> frequently, he was the first to impute bias to the other party
> or parties to the dispute.

He was a superior ballplayer who made a mighty contribution to baseball and America and human rights. This above all is the reason he belongs in the Hall of Fame and the reason he is there.

To put it in simpler words, it was primarily because of his color that he was voted in by men whom he was still accusing of bias while the ballots were being counted.

In a definitive Smithian move, the following brief, teacherly anecdote then arrives sans commentary: "Once there was a high school athlete who, called before a crowd to accept an award, blurted: 'I don't appreciate this honor, but I deserve it from the bottom of my heart.'"

Literary in his choice of details and in his evocative, snapshot narratives, Smith was dubbed the "Shakespeare of the Press Box," but he wrote as a fan as well as a journalist. His most famous and oft-quoted observation put forth an argument certainly shared by Angell: "Baseball is dull only to dull minds. Today's game is always different from yesterday's game, and tomorrow refreshingly different from today." Angell would spend his career writing variations on, and indulging in the pleasures embodied in, that fundamentally cheery, awestruck outlook.

Smith wasn't the only sportswriter who tuned his prose to a fan's sensibility. In 1955 Arnold Hano, "a bleachers guy, priding himself on inhabiting that blue-collar venue," published *A Day in the Bleachers*, a wonderful, first-person account of the 1954 World Series (the game in which Willie Mays made The Catch), cinematically bringing to life the sounds, sights, and textures of Angell's beloved Polo Grounds.

Yet one writer struck an even deeper chord. With its tabloid-flavored title, John Updike's "Hub Fans Bid Kid Adieu," which ran in the October 20, 1960, *New Yorker*, brought literary language and an eye for the telling detail to bear on Ted Williams's final game at Fenway Park on September 28, 1960, in which, famously,

Williams hit a home run in his final at bat. Updike, who wouldn't have been at the game had his hopes of meeting up with a local woman been met, sits in the stands, watches, and reflects on Williams's career and stormy relationship with his fans and the Boston reporters. Patient and curious, blending baseball history and knowledge, context, reportage, and personal response, Updike identifies Williams in three mock-heroic stages—Youth, Maturity, and Age—an approach that mythologizes Williams and elevates the sport, but Updike is careful to leaven the high-brow with a droll tone and narrative details of the playful ordinariness of a game. In short, through Updike's telling, the Splendid Splinter becomes a kind of literary character, a complex, difficult, dimensional person worthy of our attention in ways that might matter beyond the game.

Figurative language shines as brightly as sun off a field in Updike's piece: Fenway Park, painted green, seems "in curiously sharp focus, like the inside of an old-fashioned peeping-type Easter egg"; Red Sox radio and television announcer Curt Gowdy "sounds like everybody's brother-in-law"; Williams, on third, "danced down the baseline, waving his arms and stirring dust, ponderous but menacing, like an attacking goose"; Boston's second baseman "turned every grounder into a juggling act, while the shortstop did a breathtaking impersonation of an open window"; the park lights "are a wan sight in the daytime, like the burning headlights of a funeral procession"; and after Williams's home run, Williams ran "as he always ran out home runs—hurriedly, unsmiling, head down, as if our praise were a storm of rain to get out of."

Evocative and affectionate writing, without being precious or overblown: Angell was reading and listening; the essay gives the impression of Updike writing an Angell essay before Angell did. More than four decades after the lauded and oft-anthologized piece appeared, Angell reflected on its influence. "When [Updike] and I talked about the article, as we did a few times, we each admitted—I with gratitude, he with customary modesty and class—that 'Hub Fans Bid Kid Adieu' might have set the tone for my own baseball stuff, which I had not yet begun or thought of, and perhaps also encouraged *The New Yorker* to publish a few more sports pieces than it had so far." Angell recognized that "though it took me a while to become aware of it, John had already supplied my tone, while also seeming to invite me to try for a good sentence now and then, down the line, like the one he slips in when Williams fails to doff his cap after circling the bases in the wake of that homer: 'Gods do not answer letters.'" On another occasion, Angell said of Updike, admiringly, "He put himself and his grownup sensibility into the stands."

Cruising into its fourth decade, the *New Yorker* was a robust enterprise. Between 1950 and 1964, circulation grew 40 percent—from 331,574 to 464,119—as the magazine's yearly advertising pages increased by 70 percent, to 5,959. "By the midfifties," Ben Yagoda reported, "it was running more ad pages than any other general interest magazine and was second only to *Business Week* among *all* magazines." Because advertising rates rose steadily, "total ad revenue far outpaced the page gain, jumping more than *400* percent, from $5.59 million to $24.8 million, over the same fourteen years." Yagoda cites a 1958 article in the *Wall Street Journal* describing Angell's employer as a "remarkably prosperous business enterprise" with a profit margin that was "probably the highest in the field." A magazine stuffed with advertisements meant a fat magazine; *New Yorker* issues regularly sprawled to over one hundred pages, the articles and columns growing in length, depth, and complexity annually.

Fundamental to Angell's decades-long success as a baseball writer was fortune and good timing. He began his career in an era in American history when high-circulation general-interest magazines thrived and the leisure time to read them increased, and he landed, not with a little luck, at a specific magazine where he was encouraged and given plenty of room to explore, ruminate, and patiently allow his perspectives, arguments, and observations about the game to unfold; moreover, Angell was blessed with a highly literate and well-educated reading audience hospitable to, and eager for, a more literary approach to sportswriting. Erudite, well-read, a gifted writer with deep respect for the magic, music, and surprise of language, and a baseball nut: Roger Angell, settling into his sun-warmed seat in the bleachers in Florida in March 1962, notebook at the ready, was the man.

But what can a self-described "part-time, nonprofessional baseball watcher" say? Given his editor's characteristically confident blessing to roam as far afield as he wished for as long as he wished, Angell arrived at spring training with a vast canvas but no clear idea how to fill it. He reflected later, "It was clear to me that the doings of big-league baseball—the daily happenings on the field, the managerial strategies, the celebration of heroes, the medical and financial bulletins, the clubhouse gossip—were so enormously reported in the newspapers that I would have to find some other aspect of the game to study." Following Updike's lead, Angell set to writing about himself "in the stands watching what happens," adding, "I was too nervous to sit in the press box, or to talk to any of the players."

Most of all, Angell hoped to concentrate "not just on the events down on the field but on their reception and results; I wanted to pick up the feel of the game as it happened to the people around me." He was shy (for now) among sports journalists and about his modest skills as a reporter, but Angell recognized the providential position he was in: "Writing at length for a leisurely and most generous weekly magazine, I could sum things up, to be sure, and fill in a few gaps that the newspapermen were too hurried or too cramped for space to explore, but my main job, as I conceived it, was to continue to try to give the feel of things—to explain the baseball as it happened to me, at a distance and in retrospect." (One recalls nine-year-old Roger, his father's yellow

legal pads strewn before him, filled with that afternoon's scribbled scorecards, telling the story of the ballgames to his patient
and listening father after he returned from work.) For William
Shawn, Angell remarked later, "Every piece contained boundless
possibilities. He never puts limits on what one of his reporters
might discover out there, or how the subject should be attacked,
or at what length or tone the article would take in the end, or
what its writer might wish to look into next." He added: "His
patience had no boundaries, and his curiosity and passion for
facts always seemed to exceed my own."

So Angell watched, his eyes darting among the action on the
fields, the spectators in the stands, the marks on his scorecard,
and the notes in his lap, the joys of sitting in the sun watching
baseball in concert with the writer's obligation to sift his environment for sense and meaning. He went to work.

"People who write about spring training not being necessary have
never tried to throw a baseball," muttered Sandy Koufax, one
player among many in 1962 using the balm of Florida to prepare
for the long season ahead (which was soon to be longer for Koufax and the Dodgers; in 1962 the National League followed the
American's move the prior year and lengthened the season from
154 games to 162). Angell had plenty to see: he observed the Mets
practicing at Miller Huggins Field in Crescent Lake Park in St.
Petersburg and playing games at Al Lang Park, two miles away;
he also spent time a bit north in Tampa (where the Cincinnati
Reds got into fighting shape) and south of the Bay in Bradenton
(Milwaukee Braves) and Sarasota (Chicago White Sox).

Angell documented games by keeping score and taking notes,
synthesizing information gleaned from the teams' press guides
and news releases. In later years he'd flesh out this approach with
chats with fans around him in the stands; conversations with players, coaches, managers, and executives in the dugout and club
house; and information gleaned from copious reading. In Flor-

ida for the first time, he basically stayed put. He used the official fifteen-cent scorebooks offered by the teams, the tiny scorecards crowded by ads for the Bradenton Cabana Motor Hotel and its "Hideaway Cocktail Lounge," Foster's Drug Store (kindly offering the *Milwaukee Journal* and *Sentinel* for visiting Braves fans), Drive-In Package Store ("When Your Spirits Are Low Call On Joe"), Hawaiian Village ("Polynesian and American cuisine and drinks"), Hav-A-Tampa Cigar ("for good taste"), and the ubiquitous Tropicana "100% Pure Orange Juice." Angell would usually end up penning game notes—player substitutions, pinch hitters, key plays, and so on—into and all over these ads, the scorecards unable to contain everything he saw.

He used sheets of yellow 8½ x 11 paper, folded in thirds, for more comprehensive notes, filling each column top to bottom, side to side, with his characteristically excitable, herky-jerky handwriting, until both sides of the page were packed with notes and details. (In the future Angell would move on to his beloved Mead spiral stenographer notebooks; early in his career he filled up sheets of loose-leaf paper.) Later, back in his motel room or at his office at the *New Yorker*, he'd return to these notes with a discerning red pen, underlining, check-marking, circling, crossing out, correcting, adding stars and exclamation points and new observations, and emphasizing what felt ripe for further speculation, a dynamic revisiting-and-revising process he'd continue for decades.

Angell's first *New Yorker* baseball essay, "The Old Folks behind Home," ran as a "Sporting Scene" column in the April 7, 1962, issue. The title reveals Angell's chief sociological discovery in Florida and signals that Angell will be a different kind of baseball writer, one as interested in the ballpark environment and its shadings and surprises as in the action on the field between and beyond the white lines. Blending detail-rich accounts of game action and the chattery chorus of *alte kaker* pleasantries and complaints around him into virtual journalism vérité, the essay introduced the Angell persona: a quiet, observing fan alertly tuned to both key and lesser goings-on around him, unafraid to eavesdrop on conversations, occasionally (mildly, but later more strongly) editorializing, wealthy with figurative language and narrative descriptive powers, casually knowledgeable. Already the mature Angell is here: his humor, affection, sly fiction writer's eye for telling detail, and conversational but elegant style. Angellian too is his essayistic impulse, a deft and sincere movement from observing a game to sensing something larger and more complex and lasting.

"Watching the White Sox work out this morning at Payne Park reassured me that baseball is, after all, still a young man's sport and a cheerful one," he writes. "Coach Don Gutteridge broke up the early pepper games with a cry of 'Ever'body 'round!' and after the squad had circled the field once, the ritual—the same one that is practiced on every high-school, college, and professional ballfield in the country—began. Batters in the cage bunted one, hit five or six, and made room for the next man." Pitchers hit fungoes, coaches rapped out grounders, and the air was filled with "baseballs, shouts, whistles, and easy laughter. There was a raucous hoot from the players around second when a grounder hopped over [Sammy] Esposito's glove and hit him in the belly. Two young boys with fielders' gloves had joined the squad in the outfield, and I saw Floyd Robinson gravely shake hands with them both."

Marveling that anyone could come and watch the practices here at Payne, Angell observes fans from nearby hotels and cottages wandering in after their breakfasts,

> in twos and threes, and [they] slowly clambered up into the empty bleachers, where they assumed the easy, ceremonial attitude—feet up on the row in front, elbows on knees, chin in hands. There were perhaps two dozen of us in the stands, and what kept us there, what nailed us to our seats for a sweet,

boring hour or more, was not just the *whop!* of bats, the climbing white arcs of outfield flies, and the swift flight of the ball
whipped around the infield, but something more painful and
just as obvious—the knowledge that we had never made it. We
would never know the rich joke that doubled over three young
pitchers in front of the dugout; we would never be part of that
golden company on the field, which each of us, certainly for
one moment of his life, had wanted more than anything else
in the world to join.

Angell will return to this idea of the immutable distance
between players and fans again and again in his career; a brief
four years after this report, he'll observe that the "gulf between
the players and the everyday fan is almost immeasurable." He'll
eventually acknowledge that the gap grew so large as to suggest
that the wealthy, publicist-cocooned players on the other side
from us fans are, in fact, a different species of human.

Unexpected moments deeply pleased Angell, and he tried
always to remain open to them. In his notes for the March 23,
1962, Braves and Yankees game, he jotted, "have a curious sight
of [Whitey] Ford, on the mound, & [Warren] Spahn, in distance,
pitching at same instant—the two best pitchers in baseball." He
follows this observation with the word "use," circled, and a vigorous arrow pointing back to the note. He would explore the
afterimage in "The Old Folks behind Home," admitting to being
unable to concentrate on a trifling Reds and Dodgers game in
Tampa, still touched by "one of those astonishing juxtapositions
that are possible only in spring training." Describing how in the
seventh inning Ford comes in to pitch for the Yankees while
simultaneously, in the Braves' bullpen, Spahn begins loosening
up, Angell writes excitedly:

Suddenly I saw that from my seat behind first base the two
pitchers—the two best left-handers in baseball, the two best
left- or right-handers in baseball—were in a direct line with

each other, Ford exactly superimposed on Spahn. . . . It was a trick photograph, a *trompe-l'oeil*—a 158-game winner and a 309-game winner throwing baseballs in the same fragment of space. Ford, with his short, businesslike windup, was all shoulders and quickness, while, behind him, Spahn would slowly kick his right leg up high and to the left, peering over his shoulder as he leaned back, and then deliver the ball with an easy, explosive sweep. It excited me to a ridiculous extent. I couldn't get over it. I looked about me for someone to point it out to, but I couldn't find a recognizable fan-face near me.

Struck by the paradox of aloneness while surrounded by a community of like-spirits, Angell's joy blends with bitter sweetness, without a drop of treacle. He was discovering his voice.

A cultural archeologist, Angell sensed early in his baseball writing the opportunity to sift through physical remains: he's always attuned to the ages of things, of the game itself, of fans, of veteran players, and especially of stadiums, the old ones perennially threatened by architectural trends and the growing desire for better, more comfortable, and more efficient fan experiences. In "S Is for So Lovable" in the May 25, 1963, issue, Angell explores new-style Mets fans cheering for their hapless team in the last year of baseball at the Polo Grounds (the team would move to Shea Stadium in Queens, New York, the next season), fans who'd earned some frowning commentary in the media for their trash-throwing rowdiness. Angell sees the green Mets as an organic civic development, which of course they were, excitable and untamable precisely because of the their youth, as the team is "unfinished. The ultimate shape, essence, and reputation . . . are as yet invisible, and they will not be determined by an architect, a developer, a parks commissioner, a planning board, or the City Council."

The Mets, unlike the rest of us, "have their future entirely in their hands," "a youthful adventure" that's fun to watch. In his

notes Angell explored the Mets fans' messiness. "Fans <u>are</u> sometimes rowdy," he notes, because the Polo Grounds itself "jams
people in, etc. An informal, neighborly place = [everyone at
home there—] [young people alone vs. kids with fathers at sta-
dium]." Off to the side of the page Angell then mused, "PG [Polo
Grounds] as a stern-wheeler. characterize it." A lifelong amateur
sailor off the coast of Maine, Angell likes his maritime figurative
language. In 1972 he described the Chicago White Sox's Comiskey Park as a "docked paddle-wheel steamer" and extolled the
virtues of Tiger Stadium, that "grassy old boathouse." In October
1973 Shea Stadium was observed "groaning and creaking like a
great ship in the night." Two years later, in "Agincourt and After,"
Angell envisioned the legendary sixth game of the 1975 World
Series as "a well-packed but dangerously overloaded canoe." A
quarter century later "ancient" Fenway Park "sometimes felt like
F Deck aboard the *Titanic.* So did the steerage-class clubhouse,"
and at the plate Anaheim Angels batter Troy Glaus, dealing with
a challenging David Cone slider, tilted "awkwardly to starboard."
As recently as 2015 Angell saw the Mets' victory over the Dodgers
in the National League Divisional Series as "tippy as it moved
along, a rowboat overweighted at the bow." And so on. Even
the Astrodome in Houston conveyed in its interior the "aque-
ous, twilight silence of a summer lakeside cottage just before a
thunderstorm."

Tickled by this idea of the "neighborly" Polo Grounds, Angell
likens the Mets' fans' exuberance to a brand of urban life as "rich,
deplorable, and heartwarming as Rivington Street." Stirred by con-
jured images of the Lower East Side, his essayistic mind intrigued,
Angell indulges an exquisite analogy of the Polo Grounds, "in
the last few months of its disreputable life," to a warmly recalled
neighborhood, a "vast assemblage of front stoops and rusty fire
escapes. On a hot summer evening, everyone here is touching
someone else; there are no strangers, no one is private. The air
is alive with shouts, gossip, flying rubbish." Those whom he calls

the old-timers—Angell himself? He was forty-two at the time—
"know and love every corner of the crazy, crowded, proud old
neighborhood":

> the last-row walkup flats in the outermost lower grandstands,
> where one must peer through girders and pigeon nests for a
> glimpse of green; the little protruding step at the foot of each
> aisle in the upper deck that trips up the unwary beer-balancer
> on his way back to his seat; the outfield bullpens, each with
> its slanting shanty roof, beneath which the relief pitchers sit
> motionless, with their arms folded and their legs extended;
> and the good box seats just on the curve of the upper deck in
> short right and short left-front windows on the street, where
> one can watch the arching fall of a weak fly ball and know in
> advance, like one who sees a street accident in the making,
> that it will collide with that ridiculous, dangerous upper tier
> for another home run.

Few baseball writers at the time *saw* in the ways Angell saw. The
impressionistic description of a ballpark as a crowded and cor-
dially noisy neighborhood isn't simply a clever conceit: it dramatizes the park as a community meeting ground, where something
very close to neighborly and familial intimacies and connections
are recognized and forged. Though that wasn't in itself a novel
discovery, Angell's rich word painting—dimensional with narrative details, patient in its respect for where flights of fancy might
take a writer-fan, and loving its language and language's capacity
to translate visionary evocations—was something startlingly new.

The neighborhood couldn't thrive eternally. In 1964 the Polo
Grounds was razed, replaced with a literal neighborhood, or
the midcentury urban-progressive ideal of a neighborhood: the
Polo Grounds Towers complex, four thirty-story buildings hous-
ing more than 1,600 low-income apartments. In a "Talk of the
Town" piece in the April 25, 1964, issue, Angell paid tribute to
the decaying band box along the Harlem River in a moving

rendition on bereavement and befuddlement, one of the great short essays of our time on cultural loss in the face of modernity. Writing in the magazine's first-person plural, Angell mourns less the specific game memories—"Carl Hubbell's five strikeouts, Bobby Thomson's homer, Willie Mays' catch, Casey Stengel's sad torment," and the rest—than the atmosphere of the park in all of its quirkiness and, in the face of the Jet Age, its antiquity. Angell writes with a blend of grief and sighing acceptance. "What does depress us about the decease of the bony, misshapen old playground is the attendant irrevocable deprivation of habit—the amputation of so many private, repeated, and easily renewable small familiarities. The things we liked best about the Polo Grounds were sights and emotions so inconsequential that they will surely slide out of our recollection."

> A flight of pigeons flashing out of the barn-shadow of the upper stands, wheeling past the right-field foul pole, and disappearing above the inert, heat-heavy flags on the roof. The steepness of the ramp descending from the Speedway toward the upperstand gates, which pushed your toes into your shoe tips as you approached the park, tasting sweet anticipation and getting out your change to buy a program. The unmistakable, final *"Plock!"* of a line drive hitting the green wooden barrier above the stands in deep left field. The gentle, rockerlike swing of the loop of rusty chain you rested your arm upon in a box seat, and the heat of the sun-warmed iron coming through your shirtsleeve under your elbow. At a night game, the moon rising out of the scoreboard like a spongy, day-old orange balloon and then whitening over the waves of noise and the slow, shifting clouds of floodlit cigarette smoke.

We grieve for all of this "inconsequential" stuff, Angell writes, because their disappearance comprises "the death of still another neighborhood—a small landscape of distinctive and reassuring familiarity." The leveling of buildings and the subsequent modifications of the landscape "are a painful city commonplace," he acknowledges, but as our surroundings "become more undistinguished and indistinguishable, we sense, at last, that our environs are being replaced by mere events, and we are stabbed by the realization that we may not possess the score cards and record books to help us remember who we are and what we have seen and loved."

Charles Elmer Martin's illustration for the cover of the issue in which this obituary appears depicts the moon guardedly watching the earth as a satellite giddily orbits in far-fetched, yet somehow actual, modernity. The world was changing. In the unlikely event that Angell worked on this farewell to the Polo Ground with pop radio on, he'd have been assaulted by the Beatles: on April 4, 1964, they occupied the top five positions in *Billboard*'s Top 100, an astonishing feat of cultural domination that will likely never be repeated. (The All-Star lineup: "Can't Buy Me Love" at #1; "Twist and Shout," #2; "She Loves You," #3; "I Want to Hold Your Hand," #4; "Please Please Me," #5.) Within a year the Beatles would play Shea Stadium, the Mets' state-of the-art shiny new home, to shrill and deafening screams; the suburban venue was space-age new, the Polo Grounds flattened, and with it "what we have seen and loved."

In the early 1980s Angell shared a charming anecdote dating to several years before the New York Giants' final game at the Polo Grounds. Driving to a game with his young daughter Callie, adjusting the dial on the car radio, "struck by something odd, I point to the ballpark up ahead and say, 'Callie, the game we're listening to is being played right over there, right now. That's the game we're listening to, and this is the Polo Grounds, where the two teams are playing it, see? It's hard to explain, but—.' The girl nods, not much interested. Then she hears something in the broadcast and sits up suddenly and stares out at the great green barn beside her. When she turns, her eyes are wide. '*Giants* are playing in there?' she asks." Every generation of baseball fans mourns its parks and stadiums demolished for progress and the bottom line; Angell's farewell ("O lost!" he'll write of the Grounds in his following baseball essay on May 30) is indelible not only for its details and rendering of a mood and era gone, but also for its particular time in post-Kennedy, moon race newness.

The notion of baseball as an essentially rural game arose often in the notes that Angell took during his early years as a baseball writer. At a park in Bradenton, he pleasingly noticed player uniforms hanging out to dry in foul territory ("a row of shirts—black sleeves—white bodies") and the manually operated "country ballpark scoreboard." At Payne Park, the PA announcer helpfully broadcasts that a wallet had been found, the owner invited to claim it in the press box ("Imagine that in a big league park," Angell marvels, emphasizing, "A country crowd"). On the last page of his Braves/Yankees notes, he writes in red pencil, in large letters: "A country game," circling it emphatically and drawing a big arrow pointing back to it. Such details inform the rustic, friendly tone of "The Old Folks behind Home" and go a long way toward characterizing what Angell found appealing in the exhibition schedule and in the mostly elderly fans around him. The rural charm would linger in Angell's senses of the game. At the end of the 1960s he admired the expansion Montreal Expos' Jarry Park, which "much resembles a country fairground," and lamented the modernizing of the Texas Rangers' spring training park, Municipal Field, formerly "a country fairgrounds sort of place." In March 1987 in Winter Haven, Florida—where the Boston Red Sox were training—Angell observed a group of older fans removing themselves from a rain shower. "The game went on, with the sitting and standing fans quietly taking it in, and I had a sudden, oddly familiar impression (this had hit me before, in this park at this time of year) that I had found my way into a large henhouse somewhere and was surrounded by elderly farmyard fowls."

In the mid 1990s the rural appeal was still there, though the scenery was changing rapidly. Grieving the Cubs' tear-down of the "cramped but delightful" HoHoKam Park, with its "splintery redwood facade," Angell cheers up by recalling the Twins' Lee County Sports Complex in Fort Myers, "which went up only six years ago but presents an airy, rustic appearance, complete with a barn-cupola stair tower. Here the music is eight-track hits from the sixties, and you can look out beyond left field and enjoy the silent, slow moving, environmentally impeccable local entertainment. Cows." (In 2001 Angell acknowledged that "That country flavor was always an illusion, actually. Major-league baseball was always played in cities; it's an urban sport. But there was the illusion that it was a country game that moved to the city.")

By the mid-1970s the vast and cloistered business of running the game was evolving rapidly and historically. In April 1975 Angell reported from several Florida—and by then Arizona—camps, moving between, on the one hand, the clear surges of joy that March baseball gave him and, on the other, a nagging feeling that March baseball was a vestige. "My [spring training] trip was ending," he writes, "and I was beginning to feel sad about it."

In these ten days on the road, it had become clear to me that there is almost no reason for the spring baseball schedule. Most baseball people I had talked to seemed to agree with [Cardinals pitcher] Ray Sadecki that only the pitchers really needed the full six weeks in which to prepare themselves; [Orioles manager] Frank Robinson told me that the games were an interruption and that he could have used the same time to better advantage for straight instruction. Strangest of all, it seemed to me, was the fact that the baseball establishment has hardly ever tried to promote spring-training games, or to inflate them beyond their evident usefulness as a publicity device. They are still called exhibitions.

Spring baseball, Angell resolutely decided, continued for the "strangest of all possible reasons—because everyone enjoys it. It is a relic—sport pure and simple, or the closest we can come to that now. Sport for the joy of it." The essay ends restoratively: "I watched the end of the game. . . . The warm wind ruffled our hair and rattled the outfield fence, and from time to time bits of peanut shells and pieces of popcorn flew by us, airborne. Nobody said anything. Spring was over, or part of it. Dazed with sun and wind, we stared back at the distant players and the silent movements of the game."

A year later Angell found himself again struggling and uncharacteristically dejected. The gloomiest thing he'd yet written about the game, "In the Counting House," in the May 10, 1976, issue, introduced to his readers a sense of melancholy with which he'd spend the rest of his writing career wrestling, on and off, buoyed by moments of respite, leavened with his native skepticism, and shot through with optimism. "I am a baseball fan in good standing," he wrote firmly, "and my first reaction on regarding the enormous and unsavory dog's breakfast that was plunked down before me on the morning of this new season was simply to push back from the table and walk away," adding, "A lot of fans, I suspect, may be on the point of leaving the game." In his midfifties, recognizing that swift changes in the game of baseball—too many night games, for example—were affecting him negatively, he felt that the game he grew up loving was revealing, inevitably, its mercenary malice, and he was at a loss, pulled between his passion for the game and his disappointments with the sport.

No essay dramatizes these widening intervals in Angell more graphically than "In The Counting House." In the middle of ranting dismayingly about the owners' lockout that delayed that year's spring training, the sport's mounting financial injustices (both to players and fans), and the watering-down of skill levels via league expansion, Angell took a figurative deep breath and gazed around him while at a meaningless spring training game between the Cardinals and the San Diego Padres in Scottsdale, Arizona. For moments the unpleasant realities of the sport drifted away, replaced by the sensual, rhythmic sounds of the game. "I half-closed my eyes and became aware at once that the afternoon silence was not quite perfect but contained a running pattern of innocuous baseball sounds," he writes. A marvelous passage, tender and attentive, among Angell's most evocative, follows:

> I could hear the murmurous play-by-play of some radio announcer up in the press box—the words undistinguishable but their groups and phrases making a kind of sense just the same—and this was accompanied by the unending sea-sound of the crowd itself, which sometimes rose to shouts or broke apart into separate words and cries. "Hey, O.K.!" . . . *Clap, clap, clap, clap.* . . . "Hot dogs here." . . . "Hey, peanuts and hot dogs!" . . . *Clap, clap, clap.* . . . *Whoo-wheet!* (a whistle from some player in the infield). *Whoo-wheet!* . . . *Clap-clap, clap-clap, clap-clap.* . . . "The next batter, Number One, is . . . HO-SAY CARR-DENAL, right field!" (The PA announcer was giving it his best—the big, Vegas-style introduction—and the crowd tried to respond.) "O.K., *Ho*-say!" . . . "Hey-hey!" . . . "Let's *go*, Ho-say!" . . . *Clapclapclapclap.* . . . *Wheet!* There was a sudden short flat noise: *WHOCCK!*—the same sound you would hear if you let go of one end of a long one-by-eight plank, allowing it to fall back on top of a loose stack of boards. I leaned forward and watched Cardenal sprinting for first. He slowed as he took his turn and then speeded up again as he saw the ball still free in the outfield, pulling into second base with a stand-up double. Real cheering now, as the next batter stood in (". . . Number Eighteen, BILL MAD-LOCK, third base!"), but soon the game wound down again and the afternoon sounds resumed. *Clap, clap, clap.* . . . "Hey, Cokes! *Get* yer ice-cold Cokes here!" . . . *Clap, clap, clap, clap.* . . . A telephone rang and rang in the press box—*pring-pring, pring-pring, pring-pring*: a faraway, next-

door-cottage sort of noise. *Clap, clap clap.* . . . "Hey, Tim! Hey, Tim!" (a girl's voice). "Hey, Tim, over *here!*" . . . *Clap, clap.* . . . "STREEOUGH!" . . . "Aw, come *on,* Ump!" . . . *Clap, clap, clapclap- clap.* . . . "Get yer Cokes! Ice-cold Cokes here!" . . . *Whoo-wheet!* . . . *Clapclap.* . . . "Ice-cold." Then there was another noise, a regular, smothered slapping sound, with intervals in between: *Whup!* . . . *Whup!* . . . *Whup!* . . . *Whup!*—a baseball thrown back and forth by two Padre infielders warming up in short-right-field foul territory, getting ready to come into the game. The sounds flowed over me—nothing really worth remembering, but impossible entirely to forget. They were the sounds I had missed all winter, without ever knowing it.

Here is Angell at his best, his writing novelistic in its evocative details; cinematic in its modest, narrative sweep; aware of the eternal appeals of routine; attentive to the sensuous rhythms and textures of the game—above all risking mawkishness, pulling back just before the treacle.

Yet the mood can't last. Approaching as menacing storm clouds are the sport's financial concerns and the ever-widening gap between the moneyed game and its swath of old, poor, and minority fans. "In The Counting House" ends with a passage that is among the glummest of Angell's career. Perhaps recognizing the drama of the end of an essay as the proper place, he describes his experience at the Yankees' home opener, which also commemorated the reopening of Yankee Stadium, the Yankees having shared Shea Stadium with the Mets during the 1974 and '75 seasons while the House that Ruth Built was being renovated. "The new place looked fine," he observes, admiring the sweeping vista of blue seats from right field to left, the banks of escalators, and a "new, tree-line promenade outside the first-base side of the Stadium, where a street used to be." He offers mild criticism of the wall of scoreboards that "cut off our view of the elevated-station platform and the near-by apartment-house roofs, where in the old days you could always spot a few neighborhood fans watching from a great distance," adding, "The new Stadium is cut off from the city around it, and nobody can watch baseball casually there anymore." In his notes Angell opined: "that's too bad." His verdict on the new outfield wall/scoreboard scrim in the shape of the old stadium's coppery-green curtain: "A fake."

Angell sat among fifty-four thousand fans in bright sunshine as bands played; celebrities—Joe Louis, Joe DiMaggio, Mickey Mantle, and Lou Gehrig's and Babe Ruth's wives among them— arrived, smiled, and departed; and the Yankees beat the Twins, 11–4. The Bronx Bombers, Angell wrote hopefully, and correctly, "may be in the thick of things all summer long in their tough division." Yet Angell clearly wasn't enjoying himself, wrestling with the park's resplendence against the city's decay. "I don't know what to make of the new Yankee Stadium. It cost the city a hundred million dollars to rebuild and finance, and the city can't pay its bills, can't pay for new schools or hospitals, can't pay its teachers, can't keep its streets or its neighborhoods up; the South Bronx, where Yankee Stadium stands, is a disaster area."

> These are the bad realities and insolubles that we all know so well, and maybe they are the things that make us give so much attention to sports in the first place—why we need these long diversions at the ballpark. I don't think we should use sports as a hiding place, but I have always been willing to try to carry the two conflicting realities in my head at the same time—poor cities and rich sports, a lot of unnoticed kids playing in burnt-out playgrounds, and a few men playing before great crowds in a new sports palace. As the paradox deepens, however, it begins to seem as if we are trying to make the irony disappear—that we are hoping to rub out one side of the equation by vastly increasing the other.

Angell grudgingly acknowledges that he'll probably get used to the stadium (he does), "but on the first afternoon all I could think of was the quiet, slow afternoons I had just spent in Bradenton and Winter Haven and Scottsdale and Phoenix, and the games I had seen there. Those games seemed like elegies now. It was strange to be sitting in Yankee Stadium, where I had grown up watching baseball, and no longer feel at home there. I don't know what to think, because it may be that the money and the size of sport have grown too big for me after all."

Sobering stuff—"wintry," to use one of Angell's favorite words. Angell ignored much of rest of the 1976 season for the *New Yorker*. He wrote a wonderful piece on baseball scouting that ran in the August 16 issue and returned with an essay on different kinds of pitches ("On the Ball") on October 4. Finally, as if out of obligation, he turned his attention back to the season at hand for a playoffs and Yankees-Reds World Series wrap-up ("Cast a Cold Eye," on November 22). In the latter he observes (presciently or melodramatically, take your pick), "This fall, the baseball games could not distract us from the truth about baseball, which is that it may well be on the point of altering itself, if not out of existence, then out of any special or serious place in the American imagination."

Angell suffered his season of discontent in some privilege of course. The *New Yorker* financially assisted him about the country as he took in March and October games, and when on his home turf, after Yankees and Mets contests, he'd retreat, if occasionally by the dingy, graffitied subway, not into the then disastrous and fiery South Bronx but to his comfortable and roomy apartment on the Upper East Side of Manhattan. But Angell's gifts as a sympathetic commenter, as a fellow enthusiast, as a fan, enabled his humane perspectives on the game and on its roaring, hopeful, hopeless throngs.

Angell was back the following spring, reporting from camps, renewed and cautiously optimistic. The lively, riotously fun 1977 season generally revived him, but the mid-decade malaise had left a mark. He was never quite the same fan again in his essays, though over the coming years he regularly endeavored to plug himself into the eternal spring rhythms of the game.

In "Walking into the Picture" in the April 23, 1979, issue, Angell goes slightly meta while observing a journeyman pitcher (the San Francisco Giants' Gary Lavelle) warming up under the eyes of his pitching and catching coaches, Larry Shepard and Tom Haller respectively. Angell observes: "All this seemed to be happening with unusual clarity—Shepard's stance and Haller's crouch, and the sound of the ball hitting the glove, and the low slant of the afternoon sun, and the odd look of batted balls and infield throws when they are seen almost from ground level about three hundred feet away—and for a brief moment I had the feeling that I could also see myself within this scene, with my feet up on the row just below me and my elbows on my knees: I was watching myself watching baseball." Admitting that this was odd, as he'd watched virtually the same scene dozens and maybe hundreds of times, Angell nonetheless feels that on this occasion "it had seemed to be waiting for me, so to speak, and all I had to do was to walk into the picture and sit down in order to make it fresh again, and also to make it old—to bring it back just as it had always been."

Later in the essay Angell acknowledges being embarrassed by old-school baseball clichés (in this instance, a manager wanting to climb back down the ladder and become a low instructor, "to work with the kids"). But soon Angell admits that he's continually fallen for the game's clichés, that it's the transcendence of those hackneyed phrases and gestures that renews the game for him. "I'm still not entirely sure why the sight of some young pitcher warming up in spring training means so much to me, but I would almost rather watch and write about that than see Reggie Jackson or Pete Rose come up with men on base in some jam-packed, roaring stadium in October."

The old coach with his hands in his pockets watching the young man pitching is the same sports cliché—it's almost a recruiting poster for baseball—but I'm not sure that it should be resisted for that reason. Its suggestions are classical. A mystery is being elucidated before our eyes; something is being handed on. The young man may fail (probably he will), but in time he may do better. One day, he may surprise his tutors, and they will turn and begin to take note of him when he is in the game. He will become better known, possibly famous, he might even become one of the best pitchers ever. It could happen; probably it won't. Either way, it touches something in us. Because baseball changes so little, it renews itself each year without effort, but always with feeling.

He seems to be talking about more than a routine event occurring alongside a meaningless game, here as elsewhere maintaining that delicate balance between sentiment and sentimentality. The reasons that drew him to baseball camps each year, the responsibilities of his job notwithstanding, involved the hoary stereotypes of the sad, pale winter baseball fan, the lure of eternal springs, the possibility that "wait 'till next year!" (that old cliché) might mean something this year; what delights him is how the ordinary and routine keep surprising him, how the picture he keeps walking into develops subtly, with new shadings each time. That's reason enough for him to return each year.

And return he does, March after March, crisscrossing the country with his media guides, trusty notebook, tape recorder, and resolute if worn optimism, and often with his wife, Carol. Leisurely breakfasts at a palm-tree-lined motel pool, eventual dusk visits to an old park. "The sun would be slanting and the smell of grass would be there and you'd have a cup of coffee and you'd go down and sit behind the screen with somebody you knew and talk a little baseball."

As the 1980s dawned and Angell reckoned with his approaching sixtieth birthday, old doubts about his attachments to the game resurfaced in "A Learning Spring" in the April 28, 1980, issue. "Baseball is simple but never easy," he writes, pausing to reflect after attending an informal lecture given by Lary Sorensen, a Milwaukee Brewers starting pitcher, to a group of Little Leaguers visiting from Phoenix. This philosophical offering is swiftly elbowed away by a stark admission: "Each year, just before spring comes, I begin to wonder if I shouldn't give up this game."

> Surely it must be time for me to cut short my abiding, summer-consuming preoccupation with scores and standings and averages, and to put an end to all those evening and weekend hours given to the tube and morning hours given to the sports pages. Is there no cure for this second-hand passion, which makes me a partner, however unwilling, in the blather of publicity, the demeaning emptiness of hero worship, and the inconceivably wasteful outpourings of money and energy that we give to professional sports now?

Angell admits he'd gladly evade the responsibilities of "ever again having to watch the beery rage of a losing crowd in some dirty big-city stadium on a sweltering night in August, or—just as bad—suddenly noticing across the room the patronizing stare of some baseball hater, a certified adult, when he hears me mention Reggie or Yaz or Willie and watches me wave my hands or take up a stance at a make-believe plate while I tell some friends about what I have just seen or once saw, and how they should have been there, too." Angell's perhaps recalling an embarrassing instance, or several, in the hallways or offices at the *New Yorker*.

> Every year, I think about such things, often in the middle of the night, and I groan and say to myself, "Yes, all right, this is the last year for me, no more baseball after this." But then, a few days or weeks later, back in the sun in Arizona or Florida

in March, I change my mind. None of Lary Sorensen's talk to the West Side Little Leaguers at Sun City was exactly new to me, but it made me feel cheerful and instructed to hear it. I think I am almost too old for baseball, but every year I find that I need to go on learning it. Most of all, I think, baseball disarms us.

At his best Angell describes, characterizes, and evokes in the same sentence; as his essays grew substantially in length in the 1970s and 1980s, so did his sentences and paragraphs, striving syntactically to contain Angell's curious, generous, attentive sensibility and artful eye. "You can write long, but be clear," Angell remarked to sports writer Tom Verducci. "I used to have a terribly hard time starting, because when I wrote I didn't do first drafts. I wrote the whole piece on typewriters and would x out and use Scotch tape. I think I began to realize that leads weren't a big problem. You can start anywhere." Baseball is the "perfect writer's sport," he observed on another occasion. "It is perfectly linear. One thing leads to another. You can see alteration leading to a greater alteration. You can see the cause and effect. Writers like to operate in this way. He can take page after page of notes." As did his mentor Red Smith, Angell became a master of recognizing the revealing narrative moment, the wide-angle view on an ordinary scene that in a modest but elegant sweep takes in everything and situates the reader in the scene. "Every thought in my writing—every line, every moment—I'm thinking about my own suffering as a writer, but I'm also thinking basically about the reader," Angell remarked. "That is the focus of my attention, all the time: *Think of the reader, think of the reader, think of the reader.*"

In 1981 at Al Lang Park in St. Petersburg, Angell was on hand to watch the visiting Yankees play the Cardinals. During batting practice, he looked around: "the foul-ground territory around home was jam-packed with local cityside reporters, fence-hopping autograph hunters, children in baseball caps, young women with Instamatics trying to look like A.P. photogs, old codgers with baseballs to be autographed for their grandchildren, and middle-aged gents who eagerly accosted one Yankee or another with recollections of some years-past lobby encounter or with the insistent request to be remembered relayed from the player's fourth-grade teacher in Terre Haute." Slice of life, early spring.

Time and again Angell discovers, always reassuringly, that spring baseball allows us to discover the universal in the local, the timeless in the daily, however trivial that exercise may at times feel. In his languorous, extended opening paragraph in "A Heart for the Game" in the May 2, 1988, issue, Angell remarks on base-ball sights and settings "so familiar that reporters reëncountering the game at the spring-training camps in Arizona and Florida give an almost perceptible little nod as they step out onto the first field of March and find all in place once again."

Here's the tableau he's observing: batting practice, and seven or so players, "larger and younger than one has remembered (as always)," stand around the cage, waiting for turns at the plate "in easeful, half-forgotten poses that now slide back into recognition like a foot into a bedroom slipper."

> A bat rests briefly against one man's knees while he pulls the little strap on a pine-smudged batting glove tighter and presses it closed against his wrist; over here, a player hangs loose, with one spiked foot crossed in front of the other, while one palm rests on the knob of his propped-up bat, taking his weight at the hip; off to one side, a thick armed rookie seizes two hats in one hand and whirls them in a sudden circle; two more of the waiting men converse in undertones while they fussily cock and recock their batting helmets with identical gestures.

The pitching coach throws; the batter swings; he leaves the box, muttering something to himself; the next hitter stands in, looks for the pitch. Nothing new here. "And yet each time out, each spring, it feels surprising as well as comforting, utterly fresh and known by heart."

The old game in a young season. Circling the batters, the writer approaches the cage from the rear, takes up his own stance (one foot automatically finds the bottom railing of the cage, like that of a toper easing up to the bar), adjusts his own hat, and tests the tension of the knotted netting in front of him, making sure he won't catch a foul in the face. The batting coach, an old acquaintance, puts out a beefy paw in welcome, but his eyes go quickly back to the batter. A couple of the players offer recognizing smiles or head-bobs, but their attention is elsewhere; this is business.

At once a surprise: a newly arrived star player recently acquired in a trade, "a towering, famous figure, stands over there among the rookies and the regulars, looking all wrong in his strange new uniform—and then, in the same instant, looking young and dangerous in this born-again role. Ask D., the writer reminds himself in a mental note. How does it feel, etc.? Work, of a sort, has begun."

What an expansive yet intimate panorama Angell observes and creates. "D," it turns out, was Dave Parker, traded by the Cincinnati Reds to the Oakland A's in December of 1987. "The Cobra" was still a star by all rights, having slugged 26 homers and driven in nearly a hundred runs in 647 plate appearances for the Reds in 1987. Though he'd been neglected by All-Star voters for a couple of seasons and was tattooed by MLB's drug investigations in the early 1980s, he certainly still towered, at least in the physical sense. He'd go on to contribute, mostly as a designated hitter, to the dynamic Athletics' World Series runs in the late 1980s, retiring after the 1991 season. That Angell neglected to name this "famous figure" in "his strange new uniform" is of a piece with his evocative description of routine drills, of nameless players and coaches going through the motions a thousand times old, of getting in shape, getting into the swing, balancing discipline and desire, routine and hopes—silhouettes of baseball players, less personalities and superstars than types and icons. Angell writes from a wellspring of affection for baseball and its history, especially as that history tells ordinary tales, such as batting practice in March in a desert or tropics. Angell celebrates mechanisms and habits and sounds that are so old they transcend the men acting them out. The game's always bigger than the players, even the famous ones.

A decade on, in "Are We Having Fun Yet?" in the May 17, 1999, issue, writing about the exploding but dulling home run rate provided by Mark McGwire, Sammy Sosa, and the rest, as well as what he saw as overreliance on statistics by pundits, Angell again finds himself wrestling with downheartedness. "Baseball is changing at warp speed," he sighs. After summarizing the new retro ballparks in Seattle, San Francisco, Houston, Detroit, and Milwaukee, he warms a bit, offering a string of graphic and evocative memories of his favorite, long-gone parks (Polo Grounds again, Tiger Stadium, County Stadium in Milwaukee) and making a characteristic Angellian insight. "Is it youthful memory (but I wasn't all that young) that keeps hold of these inconsequential fragments, or is it the thrilling concentration of mind and appetite that the old, unhyped sport one made easy for us?" he wonders. "What baseball offers, what it does best, is to bring about moments that, because of their particularity—bottom of the eighth, two outs, three-and-one on the batter, and so on—appear to approximate the random and electric surprises of life itself, but perhaps only in these creaky, evanescing green theatres could the two, however glancingly, have seemed like one."

The business of spring training had evolved considerably by the 1990s. Angell, half-jokingly, blames himself: "People read about how great Spring Training was, probably from me! I was ruining the environment because I kept writing about it." As the small, intimate parks became more and more popular, the inevitable occurred. "They began building bigger ballparks, and one by one, these old country ballparks, the small parks with the wooden fences, disappeared and they became replicas of big city ballparks. And it became a much more citified process, and a lot of urban families began to arrive. They'd bring their kids on spring break, and the restaurants would fill up and you'd have to get reservations. And it wasn't the same. It was a little model of what was happening to all kinds of institutions around the country. Baseball was changing."

Forty years after "The Old Folks behind Home" appeared, Angell published what will likely be his last on-site spring training report, "Here Comes the Sun," a "Talk of the Town" piece that ran in the April 7, 2003, issue. Angell finds something typically generous to explore, emphasizing the environment around him in the stands as a game goes on at Scottsdale Stadium in Arizona. More leisurely at age eighty-three, Angell was nonetheless in tune enough with the vivaciousness, looseness, and distractions of youth to observe a group of women celebrating a birthday. Ever alert to detail, Angell begins with a characteristic blend of fact and evocation: "With Opening Day gone by, a visitor to the recent spring-training camps can expect to keep no more than a handful of memories of the short season, such as a low line-drive homer in Tampa by the Yankees' new import, Hideki Matsui, intensely annotated by a horde of visiting Japanese media; or a Mo Vaughn sailer at Port St. Lucie, over the right-field fence and into a sandpit, where it was excavated by an exclaiming pack of boy archeologists."

What snags his attention in Lower Box 105, Row D, is the party. Renee Conley and four friends were "dressed in jeans, tank tops, and a scattering of forward-facing baseball caps, and their occupation of this sector, close behind the backstop screen, a bit over toward the visiting-team dugout, brightened the after-noon almost as much as the sun, which had been hiding behind chilly rain clouds for the past couple of days." The game—the San Francisco Giants were hosting the Seattle Mariners—was mostly ignored by the women in favor of trying on comedy-sized cardboard "Happy Birthday" glasses and posing for many group photo shoots. Angell casually and affectionately eavesdrops on the women's conversations, evoking their personalities and honing in on individual details, all the while keeping one eye trained on a meaningless exhibition game. "'Ooo, look, the bases are loaded,' somebody said—we were in the fifth by now—but Rich Aurilia's grand slam over the left-field fence was more or less missed because the friends were so busy with the birthday cake: two Hostess cupcakes, side by side, with a candle '3' stuck in one of them and a candle '1' in the other. Renee instantly blew them out, to a screaming that became part of the wild game noise as Barry Bonds, the next man up, delivered a monster blow over the berm in right. Nobody ate the cupcakes."

In short order the women are good-naturedly hit on by a nearby cameraman, and one of them moves down front in the hopes of getting a game ball; she succeeds via an innocently flirty promise of hugs and kisses. "All that remained," Angell writes in the final paragraph, "was the next stage of the party." Because they were drinking, the women had biked to the park, and "the last party treat was a drawing of slips with various possible post-game destinations inked on them, including Zorba's Adult Shop, on Scottsdale Road, and a long-shot Las Vegas. 'We could totally do Vegas,' Angie Ray announced, but they all had to be back at work tomorrow." Nobody in Section D wanted the ballgame, the sunshine, or the clouds to go away. The previous night, Angell soberly reports, "President Bush had announced that Saddam Hussein had two more days in which to depart or face war. But this was still spring training, where nothing counts. We had this one coming."

Baseball. Sunshine. Escape from the workaday world. The buttery promises of the onrushing summer. Tipsy women: *Here's to you, Mrs. Kernochan.* If "Here Comes the Sun" is Angell's final report from spring training camps, what evocative bookends he's given us: 1962 to 2003, Mantle to Matsui, Pre-Beatles to Post-9/11, and the timeless observations that run in between, under the sun.

Following the publication in 1972 of *The Summer Game*, his first gathering of baseball writing, Angell began taking broader looks at the game, aiming to add regular, leisurely, midseason check-ins, "summer essays" that provided him an opportunity to access his spring hunches about given players and teams, take the pulse of the season (and the industry) at its midpoint or thereabouts, and, as always, reassert himself into the game's renewing myster-ies and beauty. Angell describes these essays as a "seining of the notes and scorecards and clips and moments that I kept during a couple of busy weeks at the old ball game."

In "Alfresco" in the August 5, 1985, *New Yorker*, he employs a unique and wholly evocative metaphor to describe the appeal of a baseball season in its middle. "Midseason baseball is a picnic at the beach," he writes cheerfully.

> What the experienced visitor cares about just now is not so much the water sports or who is ahead in the young people's relay races but the great family chowder cooking here just above the tideline: a warm upbubbling of innumerable tasty ingredients, some hearty and reassuring, others tantalizing and sharp-flavored—which requires many anticipatory sniffings and discussions, and perhaps an icy beer or two to deepen the long afternoon. The metaphor will not be extended by references to the ominous thunderheads gathering off to the west (Will they strike and spoil things?) or to the unpleasant behavior of the picnickers on the next dune.

In the late summer of 1986, happily watching the Boston Red Sox cruise into the postseason, Angell mused on the nature of luck, both of the good and bad variety, in "Fortuity" in the Sep-tember 1, 1986, issue. He explores the role of chance, of the vagaries of hot streaks and cold streaks that plague players and teams alike in indiscriminate, seemingly mean-spirited fashion. He concentrates on two improving teams, the San Francisco Giants and the Oakland A's, the latter a team that had suffered plenty in the decade but that seemed to be righting the ship as it had recently hired Tony La Russa, who brought a new level of acumen and confidence into the clubhouse. (La Russa would guide the A's to three World Series—in 1988, 1989, and 1990—winning in '89.) In 1986 the A's enjoyed streaks where they won games in "clusters"—a favorite word of Angell's—and endured streaks of the opposite value. From his privileged perch in the press box and via visits to clubhouses, Angell observed the A's closely (with one eye on the Red Sox ascension) and wondered, as he has on and off his whole career, about the degree to which luck guided the sport.

Near the end of the essay, he describes waking up in Brooklin, Maine, in his vacation cottage—it's late in the season—and turning to the sports pages to discover that the A's had lost yet again, this time to the Twins:

> As I studied the box score in the paper and tried to squeeze more news out of it than it could convey, I murmured to myself. "Oh, if the A's would only—." Then I stopped. Would only what? I thought about it for a moment or two, and then it came to me that what I badly seemed to want for a team I cared about was an end to bad luck, an end to bad news—no more fortuity, to use [A's general manager] Sandy Alderson's word. I wanted the exact opposite of what my friend had seen as established: I wanted good news forever.

Here Angell reaches an insight that he admits he'd never fully grasped in his decades of following and writing about the game. He mentions that Alderson had remarked that upward of 40 percent of the game was beyond his, the managers', or the players' control. "But I am a fan," Angell demands, and my lot is far worse, for everything in baseball is beyond my control; for me every part of the game is just fortuity. Because I am a fan, all I can do is care, and what I wish for, almost every day of the summer, is for things to go well—to go *perfectly*—for the teams and the players I most care about: for the Red Sox, for the A's now, for the Mets, for the Giants, for Tom Seaver and Keith Hernandez and Roy Eisenhardt and Don Baylor and Wade Boggs and Carney Lansford and Tim Shanahan and Darryl Strawberry and Roger Craig and many, many others.

Angell believes that every true fan wants this "seriously, every day of the season, but at the same time I think we don't want it at all."

We want our teams to be losers as well as winners; we must have bad luck as well as good, terrible defeats and disappointments as well as victories and thrilling surprises. We must have them, for if it were otherwise, if we could control more of the game or all of the game and make it do our bidding, we would have been granted a wish—no more losing!—that we would badly want to give back within a week. We would have lost baseball, in fact, and then we would have to look around, without much hope, for something else to care about in such a particular and arduous fashion.

Generous observations from a man who's been enjoying baseball since the 1930s and writing about it thoughtfully since the early 1960s. With its profound disappointments and trivial joys, no other sport requires the kind of duality that Angell describes here: our wish to control destiny blended with our love—or at least our begrudging acceptance—of the game's capriciousness. Angell has made a career out of exploring baseball as a narrow subject; the point of view of his fan-persona, his love and knowledge of the game, and his deliberate and searching writing about it lead him to larger subjects than the game, and his impulse to write, can contain. His best essays are both detailed observations and wide-screen rumination: the precise, evocative details cohere, as in a pointillism painting, to a vaster story. What's especially poignant about "Fortuity" is what it innocently portends. Seven weeks after this issue hit the stands, the Red Sox lost the World Series to the New York Mets in an excruciating manner: "It Got by Buckner!" being only the most infamous of the gaffes and bad breaks suffered by Red Sox Nation that fall. *No more losing!* the fans cried. Heartbreak, indeed. Yet as melancholy as that is, Angell—a Red Sox fan in his blood, who got to cheer on and write about the team's eventual 2004, '07, and '13 World Series championships—would have it no other way.

During the following summer Angell worked on "La Vida," a long essay that appeared in his book *Season Ticket.* As anyone who's deeply affectionate for the game of baseball does, Angell risks falling into maudlin weepiness at the sport's beauty, reviving mysteries, and nostalgia for childhoods past; he guards against sentimentality by an inner native temperamental, skeptical reserve. Angell employs metaphor, the generous magic trick of art, sparingly; he betrays himself as an enormous fan of baseball but stops short at mythologizing the game, letting his vivid and precise descriptions of its simple, complex pleasures do the work for him. Rarely does he sentimentalize without soon catching himself wryly, easing up with his language with an *it's-only-a-game* shake of his head. Yet any lover finds it difficult to resist the language of love. And that language is florid. Angell wrote in the early 2000s that the "one baseball sentimentality that doesn't make [him] wince" is the warm, visible camaraderie among players reuniting with those with whom they came up in the minor leagues. "Remembering your beginnings in organized ball may be a way of standing up to the vagaries of baseball fortune," he noted, "which tear people apart, not just by trades but in the fateful and merciless disposition of their talents."

"La Vida" in part explores the men who spend decades in baseball, the devoted "gamers," such as Baltimore Orioles manager Earl Weaver and (then California) Angels owner Gene Autry. Angell observes:

> Baseball is not life itself, although the resemblance keeps coming up. It's probably a good idea to keep the two sorted out, but old fans, if they're anything like me, can't help noticing how cunningly our game replicates the larger schedule, with its beguiling April optimism; the cheerful roughhouse of June; the grinding, serious, unending (surely) business of midsummer; the September settling of accounts, when hopes must be traded in for philosophies or brave smiles; and then the abrupt running-down of autumn, when we wish for—almost demand—a prolonged and glittering final adventure just before the curtain.

This metaphor is at its most graphic in "baseball's sense of slippage; our rueful, fleeting awareness that we tend to pay attention to the wrong things—to last night's rally and tomorrow's pitching match-up—while lesser and sweeter moments slide by unperceived." The mature wit of Angell's writing, the elegance of his seasonal metaphors, provoke discovery and wisdom in that last sentence: we're paying attention to the wrong stuff. This introduction of dissent, of our own silly and misguided wrongdoings, rubs up uneasily against the calendar, Angell gently suggesting that the real malfeasance is not in ignoring baseball's "lesser and sweeter moments," but in ignoring life's.

"This is kind of extraordinary," Charles McGrath, former deputy editor of the *New Yorker* and longtime friend of Angell's, says.

> Here's a guy who falls in love with baseball as a kid, and he partly falls in love with it because he's lonely. He has this crazy relationship. His mother and father are split up, and he's being raised by the father who's a good man in many ways but also

a kind of cold and unemotional one. And he's *lonely*. Baseball and movies saved his life when he was a kid. And what's interesting about it is he has this astonishing memory, so you have this love of this thing, and also this astounding facility to remember it in tranquility.

McGrath adds, "I don't want to go too far with this, but when Roger's writing about baseball, he's not just writing about baseball. He's writing about attachment; he's writing about caring; he's writing about feeling. Baseball's not a metaphor—Roger would resist that—but it's a vehicle for something else."

At the dawn of the 1980s Angell insisted, "People have said to me that I'm not writing about baseball, but I'm writing about life. That's not true. If I say personal things about baseball, it's for the love of the game. . . . Baseball is not about American life." He would add, revealingly, "Baseball is always the same but it's always changing." That reads like a working definition of life itself. Angell was sixty-six years old when he wrote "La Vida." Occasionally in the *New Yorker* he'd gently chide himself as a foolish man wasting time on a kids' game, but with age and the gift of language comes well-earned astuteness. Angell skirts mawkishness while implicating us all in the dangers of swooning to the Big Ideas when the smaller, unnoticed events are happening right behind us and without us. As Angell himself might say: *And so on.*

The balm of a Florida spring training game. Courtesy of Roger Angell.

Delay on the Field

Roger Angell didn't settle in immediately as *New Yorker*'s baseball writer-in-residence following the appearance of "The Old Folks behind Home" in 1962. Consumed by his responsibilities as fiction editor, he remained interested in exploring other kinds of sports writing, ranging far and wide as the 1960s progressed, covering the Harvard-Yale "Novemberfest" football games, amateur and professional tennis, Saratoga Springs horse racing, the Royal Ascot Meeting and Henley Royal Regatta British water festival, New York Rangers hockey, and the Olympic crew racing trials in Long Beach, California. (He even wrote about the Super Bowl in 1974.) Between the fall of 1979 and spring of 1980 he took over for the magazine's estimable film critic Pauline Kael while she was sojourning in Hollywood, penning more than two dozen film reviews of his own. He continued to contribute light verse (most notably "Greetings, Friends!"—the popular Christmas poem that he inherited from Frank Sullivan in 1978 and would compose for three decades), the odd if increasingly required obituary of cultural notables and office colleagues, and many "Talk of the Town" and "Comment" pieces unrelated to sports, including a couple of pointed responses to the war in Vietnam. "The long, almost insupportable strain of fighting an inadvertent, limited, immeasurably complicated, and morally degrading war had produced in all of us a powerful urge for certitude," he wrote in May 1967, sounding a bit like Nick Carraway.

A curio in Angell's oeuvre is a brief radio essay he recorded in 1952 for *This I Believe*, a program originally hosted by Edward R. Murrow and later revived by National Public Radio. From his suburban perch over the Hudson River, Angell explores the nature of humankind, the writing a bit stiff and unusually abstract, the tone serious-sober. Yet already intact, and characteristic, are Angell's deep belief in skepticism ("I think that a man should grasp a belief warily and carry it gingerly") and his appreciation for the surprising gift of empathy. "Once in a while, in my dealings with other men, an astonishing thing happens," he said. "Something I cannot get out of my head. Suddenly I see straight into a man and find, to my shock, only myself there. This is a rare moment, because men do not often give themselves away, only by accident or in times of great pain and happiness. In that moment, if I dare to look, I see in any man my own desires, my deeply hidden beliefs, my need for love, my inner seriousness, and my hope." Such an instance is a "lightning flash in an unlit room that suddenly illuminates all," he continues. "After it is gone, I still see, pressed on my eyes for a few instants, the shape, the bright highlights and the true vivid colors of the dark room in which I sit. In that moment, the dignity of man is an almost visible thing." Angell will employ the phrase "almost visible" countless times in his baseball writing, not to mention explore the role of empathy in modern sport. See, among other pieces, "Down for Good," his profile of pitcher Steve Blass, for the latter. This revealing essay from an obscure era in Angell's professional life was originally released in 1952 on a hefty eight-LP set by Columbia Records ("Presenting personal philosophies of thoughtful people").

Throughout the 1960s Angell continued to write satiric pieces and fictional parodies—"casuals," in the *New Yorker* parlance—that he ultimately gathered for his second book, *A Day in the Life of Roger Angell*, published in 1970. The book gives the impression of a light read, its jacket promising a "proper guidebook to chaos." The subtext is modern anxiety and urbane absurdity, the top all froth: literary parodies (of Herman Hesse, Lawrence Durrell, *Reader's Digest*, the letters section in the *New York Review of Books*, and so on); urban satires; silliness ("nonsense"); and puns and palindromes (the latter a life-long obsession of Angell's). Review-ing in the *Times*, Victor Navasky wrote, positively if backhandedly, "We couldn't help observing . . . that Mr. Angell has unwittingly, but with wit, given us a quiet parody of the magazine that made all this possible. This slim volume is elegant, pointed if often pointless, and defiantly untrendy." Most reviewers enthused over Angell's droll style: *Publishers Weekly* called the book "delight-ful"; *Booklist* praised Angell's "scintillating commentary" and his "elegant and uproarious" humor; Robert Lasson in *Book World*, though happily admitting that the book felt anachronis-tic, described it as "absolutely first rate"; *Library Journal* marveled that the book "actually makes one laugh out loud . . . as consis-tently funny as anything that has appeared in a very long time." Nimbly amusing, with nary a ponderous moment, these pieces stand in stark contrast to the conventional literary-realism that Angell produced in his stories from the 1940s and '50s; indeed the publication of *The Stone Arbor* seemed to have marked a divid-ing line of sorts in his literary pursuits.

Only two of the twenty-one selections in *A Day in the Life of Roger Angell* were baseball-related. "Fall Classic," the mock-dramatic Greek verse take on the 1961 World Series, is, on one hand, vin-tage Angell—clever, funny, knowledgeable, written out of deep affection for the game, its players (and announcers), and its history—and on the other hand, a quirky one-off, an approach never returned to by Angell in his baseball writing. He's always rolled his eyes at those who take the game too seriously, who for-get that baseball is a game, not life-or-death drama, including himself among those who get carried away at times, asking—no, demanding—more of the game and its players than it, and they, are obliged to give. By casting the World Series as a Drama, not drama, he gently pokes fun at such excessive seriousness.

The other baseball piece is a particularly funny bit titled "Over My Head," which first appeared in the June 24, 1961, *New Yorker*. Parodying George Plimpton's book *Out of My League*, in which the

Paris Review editor recounts pitching in a 1958 postseason exhibition game at Yankee Stadium to a crew of Major League All-Stars "managed" by Willie Mays and Mickey Mantle, Angell cleverly reverses the gimmick, writing from the point of view of a pro pitcher eager for the opportunity, offered by his agent, to edit the fictional *Dijon Review* for a day—participatory journalism turned on its head.

The narrator drives up to Vermont, warming up at the Bread Loaf Writer's Conference on a Remington typewriter ("I worked out for an hour, testing old muscles. My motion was good, but I wasn't hitting the space bar with the old confidence") and with a boy in the *Dijon Review* offices at whom he lobs aphorisms, quotations, and highbrow thesis statements. Greeting the editors, he's star-struck, as he "recognized most of the faces, of course; as a boy, I had pasted their likeness, clipped from Sunday book-review sections, inside my locker door." This alternate-reality conceit merits a predictable outcome: the narrator chokes while dealing with an esteemed visiting contributor, an intimidating avant-garde Romanian writer who takes the narrator to task for suggesting yoga to him. (The narrator had actually wondered about the influence on the visiting writer of *Yogi* Berra's autobiography!) Our poor man's Plimpton leaves the offices dejected, though buoyed at having tried to satisfy a childhood dream. The story ends as "sore of head and spirit," our hero leaves for the subway and sees two scraggly kids writing with chalk on the pavement, filling the sidewalk from curb to building.

> "Hey Jim-mee!" one of them yelled. "Watch me, Jim-mee! Watch me write. I'm William Styron, Jim-mee! I'm Styron writing!"
>
> "Go-wann!" the other called back, scribbling excitedly. "Lookit me. Billy. Watch *me* write! *I'm* Elizabeth Hardwick!"
>
> Touched, deeply moved by these innocent gamins, I blew my nose and began to cheer up. "The game will go on," I whispered to myself. "Even without me, it will go on. The great American pastime will never die."

"Angell was, and remains, a kind of Burkean idealist," observes *New Yorker* editor David Remnick, "wary of heedless change yet open to surprise and displays of individual genius." The game does go on. The question is, in what shape?

Among the words that Angell employs the most often in his *New Yorker* baseball essays is "startled" (and variations thereof); it is present in the first piece he wrote and appears countless times afterward, up to his 2014 speech accepting the J. G. Taylor Spink Award at the Baseball Hall of Fame in Cooperstown. (In "The Old Folks behind Home," the juxtaposition of Whitey Ford and Warren Spahn simultaneously warming up in Brandenton, Florida—discussed in "Good News Forever," above—"startled" Angell, the first of many such pleasing baseball gifts.) Angell likes to say that nothing surprises him in baseball. What he means is that he's never surprised at the number of wonders that the game offers, that "one must conclude that the only reliable precedent in baseball is surprise itself."

"For fifty some years, with the occasional digression, [Angell]'s been writing about the same subject, and yet finding ways to not repeat himself," Ben McGrath observes.

> There's an imperative to look for wonder and surprise because he's returning to the same subject and using that subject as a way to talk about life. Roger has told me that he feels it's important for great writers to have a subject because it frees them to become more inventive in their writing, to try harder to come up with new and interesting things to say. The constraint to return to the same thing over and over again brings out better writing. Roger's a baseball writer, yes, but he's writing periodical literature—it just happens to be baseball he's writing about.

McGrath adds, "Because he's been doing it for so long, he's so comfortable in that realm, and it helps him to be casual and conversational about it because he's not learning a new language or vernacular; he's steeped in it. And in the meantime he's also brought along a whole audience with him who are familiar with the same rhythms he's talking about, and he can take people places."

Tina Brown, who edited the *New Yorker* in the 1990s, hears in Angell a particularly vigorous, American voice. "He's got a freshness in his view, and that's what's wonderful and so All-American in a way. . . . His eyes are always open to new worlds. He's as enchanted by the new world as he ever was. He's still a fourteen-year-old boy watching baseball, still watching it as if it's the first time he's ever watched baseball." She adds: "'O my America, my new found land.' Isn't that what John Donne says? That's how I feel about Roger."

In 1984 Angell, commenting on the much faster players in the contemporary game—the Lou Brocks, the Rickey Hendersons—relative to the basepath plodders of his youth, wondered if this development may represent the "first breakdown of baseball's old and beautiful distances: if ninety feet from base to base is no longer enough to keep a single or a base on balls from becoming an almost automatic double, then someone may have to go back to the drawing board at last in order to restore caution to the austere sport." More than thirty years later, noting the enormous size of contemporary baseball players ("People have no idea how strong and how big these people are. They're regularly six-seven, six-eight, six-nine. They're barbaric"), Angell observed that it's still a "big surprise" to him that the dimensions of the game have held up, that there are as many bang-bang plays at first in the twenty-first century as there were in 1916. "I keep thinking that maybe they should have the bases farther apart, but that's not true," he marvels. The game always amazes. "It's not just baseball. Roger's never bored by life," observes Remnick, who took over as editor of the *New Yorker* after Brown departed in 1998. "He's alive to the new, to new things. He can get down, like the rest of us. He's had defeat and tragedies, like the rest of us. But he wants to live and he wants to be alive in the world, and he's alive to the strangeness and the wonder and the beauty and all of it. It's exemplary."

Angell has also, at times, entertained a dark realization that baseball might be changing irrevocably. A common thread in his essays from his earliest pieces onward is his sometimes grave unhappiness with the fluctuating state of the sport: attendance woes; inequalities between the two leagues; financially wobbly franchises; fractious players/owners posturing; the threat (and ultimate enactment) of work stoppages, lockouts, and strikes; the effect of the designated hitter and artificial turf on the game; the extension of the season too late into the autumn; free agency; the excessive rowdiness and anarchy of beer-fueled crowds; too many night games; suspected and documented drug offenses among players; and so on. He's been ongoingly concerned about the deleterious effect these changes might be having on the fans, himself included. In his introduction to the 1966 reissue of Bernard Malamud's novel *The Natural*, he observed, "Baseball has changed more in the last few years than in all its previous history, but I think the biggest change is . . . the disillusionment of the fans themselves—a blunting and cooling of the game's ancient loyalties. Nothing escapes the fans . . . and in recent years they have watched the owners of the game engage in a careless, greedy and wholly cynical scramble for new revenues and franchises that has strained and perhaps severed a good many of the tough, subtly wound cables that have always tied baseball to the American heart."

The corrosive effect of league expansion has been a perennial complaint of Angell's, not only for the dilution of big-league talent it portended, but also for the anonymous vastness it created. Writing in the summer of 1969, Angell sympathizes with the traditionalists who were soft for a time, "a decade ago when we all knew all sixteen big-league teams as well as we knew the faces and tones of voice of those sitting around the family dinner table at Thanksgiving." Angell acknowledges that he grew to love the changes introduced that season, including the separation of each league into East and West divisions and the subsequent new playoff system (though initially he'd refuse to call the Championship Series by its proper name, instead referring to them somewhat dismissively as "demi-pennants"), yet when something endangers the ancestral aspects of the game, when the family is threatened, Angell reacts, often passionately. "I persist in a belief that connection is one of the prime sensuous attractions of baseball," he wrote in the early 2000s. "You first notice this as a kid, on the day when a glimmering perception of the interconnectedness of today's names and batting averages and line scores and box scores—and all yesterday's, too, and others five years or five decades gone—suddenly sweeps over you in a rush, like the dawning of sex."

In the summer of 1981, in the middle of a rancorous, coming-apart-at-the-seams season, Angell observes that perusing baseball record and photography books is like "opening a family album stuffed with old letters, wedding invitations, tattered newspaper clippings, graduation programs, and curled up, darkening snapshots. Here are people from my own branches of the family—the Giants, the Red Sox, the first Mets—and, in among them, page after page, the names and looks of other departed, almost forgotten in-laws and cousins and visitors. Everyone is here." Speaking on camera to filmmaker Ken Burns for Burns's 1994 documentary *Baseball*, Angell remarked, "Baseball is like joining an enormous family, with ancestors and forebears and famous stories and histories. And it's a privilege. It means a lot. And the people who tell me that they hate baseball, or they're out of baseball, they sound bitter about it, but I think that they sense what they're missing. I think that they feel that there's something they're not in on, which is a terrible loss." He adds, "And I'm sorry for them."

No change in baseball has had as compelling and continuing an effect on Angell as television, what he's called the "biggest altering force" of the twentieth century. Angell was just shy of his nineteenth birthday and preparing for his sophomore year at Harvard when the first Major League baseball game was broadcast on television on August 26, 1939, a contest between the Cincinnati Reds and the Brooklyn Dodgers at Ebbets Field, called by announcer Red Barber on Channel One over the fledgling W2XBS (which later became WNBC). The following day, an impressed reporter for the *Times* informed readers that one "eye" (camera) was placed near the dugout, the other in a box behind the catcher, where it "commanded an extensive view of the field when outfield plays were made." The reporter enthused that technical improvements "for this sort of outdoor pick-up" had made it possible ("at times") to catch a "fleeting glimpse of the ball as it sped from the pitcher's hand toward home plate" and that "over the video-sound channels of the station, television-set owners as far away as fifty miles viewed the action and heard the roar of the crowd." (Fifty miles! Alas, if Angell was settling into his apartment on Mt. Auburn Street in Cambridge, he was well out of range of this historic broadcast.)

As a writer who's covered baseball since the early 1960s and who's been an avid fan since the Depression era, Angell has had a predictably fluid relationship to televised baseball. Watching his beloved game on the "boob tube," he's gone from being an Eisenhower-era appalled skeptic to a twenty-first-century begrudging fan. Angell has been a cultural barometer for so long that his experience with and knowledge of baseball is a gauge on which one can read his affection for the game as well as the sport's evolving, complex, multi-decades relationship with popular culture itself. In "Baseball's Strike Zone," a somewhat cranky op-ed he wrote for the *Times* in 1972 (in advance of the publication of his first baseball book, *The Summer Game*), Angell laments the results of a recent Gallup poll that indicated that football had replaced baseball as Americans' favorite sport. How, he wonders, "could baseball fade so quickly, even while seeming to keep us such good company?" Sports exist on two levels now, Angell observes, the field and the television, and discriminating fans are aware of the fundamental differences between the two. "They have discovered in the last decade that football is the finest of all televised sports (mainly because of the instant replay) and baseball very nearly the worst."

Televised baseball? It's a bore, he complains. "However nimble the camerawork or crisp the commentary, the screen offers mostly a prolonged closeup of the home-plate umpire's neck, in the foreground of a distorted two-dimensional montage of batter and battery—a tableau that is occasionally interrupted when a pitch is struck, and two or three flurried, cross-out shots hopelessly try to suggest the divergent flights of ball and base-runner and fielders across enormous spaces." Baseball's quirky dimensions and vast distances are untranslatable on television, and so too "is its lovely mystery, the slow, taut, speculative ticking of baseball time, which, conveyed upon the home screen, implacably urges a nap."

Four years later in the *New Yorker*, in "On the Ball," a smallish, meditative piece on pitching, Angell refined his defense of baseball's lovely and unique idiosyncrasies, praising the "emotions and suggestions" of his favorite game, in which the thrown-about, batted-about ball, "for all its immense energy and unpredictability," rarely escapes the players' control. "This orderliness and constraint are among the prime attractions of the sport; a handful of men, we discover, can police a great green country, forestalling unimaginable disasters." A game sloppy with errors and exhibiting loose, comical playing can at times amuse us, he observes,

> but never seems serious, and is thus never truly satisfying, for the metaphor of safety—of danger subdued by skill and courage—has been lost. Too much civilization, however, is deadly—in this game, a deadly bore. A deeper need is stifled. The ball looks impetuous and dangerous, but we perceive that in fact it lives in a slow, guarded world of order, vigilance, and

rules. Nothing can happen here. And then once again the ball is pitched—sent on its quick, planned errand. The bat flashes, there is a new, louder sound, and suddenly we see the ball streaking wild through the air and then bounding along distant and untouched in the sweet green grass. We leap up, thousands of us, and shout for its joyful flight—free, set free, free at last.

Angell's mid-1970s moodiness—likely influenced by ugly national and international affairs as well as by the unnerving changes in baseball itself—may have inspired him to the rhetorical flourishes in this passage, as close to purple as he'll get in his writing.

"Baseball is a game where the mind can both wander and be present," says Mark Singer, a *New Yorker* staff writer since 1974 and friend of Angell's. "That may contribute to the lyrical quality of baseball writing as opposed to other sports writing. There's room for language to marinate a bit longer. Why is baseball the thinking fan's game? Because of the freedom of time that comes with it. You're almost in the role of a cultural anthropologist when you're observing people quietly, and Roger was showing up at games and observing them in a very deliberate way." Singer likens Angell's patient attention at a baseball game to a nature writer's awareness out in the field. "A lot of nature writing has the same qualities to it, of noticing, and finding the language to do that. It's something you train yourself to do, but it has to come from some innate capacity to see and feel. Roger's always been an extraordinarily sensitive person, by definition." He adds, "It is a very luxurious position for a writer to be in, but it's also labor intensive. It's only you. You're there noticing this stuff and figuring out a way to make notes and literally coming back later to excavate. You've got to use everything."

Television routinely challenged Angell's in-the-field approach to watching an unfolding baseball game. In the wonderful "Four Taverns in the Town," his World Series recap that appeared in the October 26, 1963, *New Yorker*, Angell recounts his determined effort to watch the games from four different Manhattan bars, hoping to observe, anthropologically speaking, the "true Yankee fan in his October retreat—what the baseball beer commercials refer to as 'your neighborhood tavern.'" Angell visited O'Leary's at Fifty-Third Street and Eighth Avenue, the Charles Café at Vanderbilt Avenue and Forty-Third Street, the Cameo at Eighty-Seventh Street and Lexington Avenue, and the Croydon, a hotel bar at Eighty-Sixth Street and Madison Avenue. (The Los Angeles Dodgers swept the New York Yankees in the Series.)

The game's on TV in each establishment of course. When Angell isn't noting the pleasing differences among patrons—a blending of races, some people well-dressed, others casual, a mix of office workers and city employees, not many women, a handful of knowledgeable fans at each joint, Beefeater dry martini drinkers at Charles Café, beer-and-shot imbibers at O'Leary's, and so forth—he's craning his neck upward at the game, acknowledging that the "television camera, hovering over the home-plate umpire's shoulder and peering down the back of the pitcher's neck, gives a far better view of each ball and strike than any spectator can get from the stands."

Yet, as he reminds us, this World Series was lost by several Yankee miscues, "most of which were either not visible or not really understandable to television-watchers." He protests that the "lack of the third dimension on TV" makes baseball "seem less than half the game it is . . . [and] actually deprives it of its essential beauty, clarity, and excitement." (And deprives it of communal solidarity; while working on this essay, Angell scribbled on the back of a *New Yorker* manuscript envelope, "TV perfect for pitching—nothing else.—No crowd feeling, each man alone—as if watching in empty seats.") Among Angell's grievances were the otherworldly blue tint given the players on the screen and the ongoing babble of NBC announcer Mel Allen, who seemed intent on inundating viewers with inessential player and game information, sound bites Angell describes as a "dandruff of exclamation points" settling on the shoulders of viewers beneath the sets.

Angell returned to television a year later in "The Series: Two Strikes on the Image" in the October 24, 1964, *New Yorker.* Writing about the Series between the Yankees and Cardinals—couching his piece in a generally gloomy mood, 1964 being the "most shameful and destructive year the game has experienced since the Black Sox Scandal of 1919"—Angell cries, "Television is now exerting the most intense pressure on all aspects of baseball." He blames the medium for the potential destruction of the Minor Leagues and for the widening gap between have and have-not franchises. "The sports television business has never been happy with baseball, which so far includes only two big-revenue packages—the All Star Game and Series—each year." (In a note written eight years later for *The Summer Game*, he describes the Championship Series, that "inflationary autumn playoffs" round created in 1969, as "television's first contribution to the game.") That the length of any given baseball game is wonderfully unpredictable and that over the course of a long season its tension level and value varies are "almost intolerable to the young men in blazers who run sports TV":

> Their dream is fifty weekends of world championships—in football, in baseball, in surfing, in Senior Women's Marbles—that are not to be missed by the weekend watcher. Yet these sportsmen cannot be dismissed so easily, for they command an audience of millions and revenues that are almost immeasurable. It must be assumed that baseball executives will do almost anything to climb aboard this gaudy bandwagon, and that the ultimate shape of baseball in the next ten years or so—its size, its franchise locations, and even its rules—will be largely determined not by tradition or regard for the fans or regard for the delicate balances of the game, but by the demands of the little box.

A decade later Angell's mood hasn't improved much. Indeed in retrospect the mid-1970s seemed to have been Angell's season of discontent in the magazine. In "Cast a Cold Eye" in the November 22, 1976, *New Yorker*, Angell levels criticism at the garrulous broadcast crew calling postseason games for ABC, including Howard Cosell, Reggie Jackson, and Keith Jackson, normally a football announcer, "whose excited, rapid-fire delivery makes a routine double play sound like a goal-line stand. Three-man broadcasting crews, by the way, probably make sense in covering football, where a great many things happen at the same time, but baseball has no such problem, and three hyperglottal observers usually succeed only in shattering the process of waiting that is such a crucial part of the game." Again Angell sourly chides the announcers, and by extension television coverage itself, for misunderstanding "the special pace of each game, and thus [they] habitually overdramatize. Since they suggest that almost every play we see is memorable, we become distracted and then dulled, so that we are unlikely to remember the actual incidents in a game—sometimes very small ones indeed—on which the outcome truly depended."

He cites a moment in the second game of the American League Championship Series when the Yankees' Chris Chambliss, on first base, was duped by the Kansas City Royals' diminutive shortstop Freddie Patek into stopping at second on Carlos May's high-hop grounder to right; Patek had reached for the "imaginary incoming peg with such verisimilitude that Chambliss actually slid into the bag," Angell marvels, surely smiling as he describes Patek's charade, which cost the Yankees a run, as the next batter flied out. "It may even have cost them the game," Angell observes, "yet the telecast buried this pivotal moment in its customary overreporting, and it was soon forgotten. Network makes every baseball game sound just about like every other."

Difficult for Angell to stomach was the networks' habit of presenting the game as personality-driven entertainment. "While we at home may think we are simply watching a game, what we are in fact attending is Howard Cosell," he notes dryly. In his notes for "Several Stories with Sudden Endings," his season and postseason recap that appeared in the November 14, 1977, issue, Angell wrote, "On Cosell, etc.: Typical, I think, that they are now plugging Monday Night Baseball! whenever a game is close or exciting. It's the show that counts with them, not the game, not the sport. A real reporter (and Cosell always calls himself one) would say, 'Baseball!'" Angell follows this with a novel suggestion: "The way to watch ABC baseball is with the sound off after the first 2 innings or so. After all, you don't need all their kind of crap when you are at a game, so why do you need it at home?" He adds, "I like our way; turn off ABC sound and turn on Station WNCN's Composer of the Month. Watch Jim Rice swing to strains of Chopin's Etude in D Flat major!"

Fast-forward twenty years: replacing gabbing announcers with nineteenth-century classical music may have helped, but in "The Game's the Thing," in the November 27, 1995, *New Yorker*, Angell, in a funk about baseball's rancorous devolving, brought upon in part by the devastating and historic seven-and-a-half-month players' strike, gives it to television again, this time addressing the new playoffs and division expansion. Alluding to previous nail-biting October games, Angell doubts that that old style will return, citing renovations including the extra round of postseason meetings and wild card teams. "The baseball planners have increased the chances that there will be some wonderful or god-awful games somewhere in October," Angell acknowledges, "but in the process have destroyed the essential critical ingredient, which is rarity." As Angell sees it, these baseball lords have puzzled and antagonized folks who found it difficult to understand how the new postseason worked. ("Even the players had problems with this, to judge by dugout conversations I heard during the last week of the regular season," Angell remarked.) "Many friends with whom I happily used to talk baseball at the end of the summer have fallen into this category," Angell complains. "As things came down, there were thirty-one postseason games this time around (out of a mind-bending possible forty-one), which made for plenty of baseball entertainment, just as the owners and planners had hoped, but, inevitably, less that can be remembered. Baseball feels like the rest of America now: it feels like television."

Later in the piece Angell, evolving on the page, seems to change his mind about the cameras and how they might add to one's enjoyment of the game by providing "texture and filigree that you sometimes miss at the park," such as Orel Hershiser's "full-sweeping, forward and downward delivery." And: "From Seattle we were given closeups of [Carlos] Baerga's earplugs (defense against the Dome din), and also of a pleasing earlier moment, when twenty-two-year old Bob Wolcott, the Mariners' surprise starter and winner in Game One, was found sitting next to [Randy] Johnson in the dugout after giving way in the eighth to the bullpen relievers, who would sew it up for him. Both men were smiling over Wolcott's outing, and then the Unit gave him a little slap on the thigh with the back of his glove: Great game, kid." This wasn't the first time Angell admitted to enjoying baseball on television. As early as the mid-1950s, in his *Holiday* essay "Baseball—The Perfect Game," Angell enthused that despite their inadequacies, "radio and television have been responsible for creating uncounted millions of new and knowing fans (including a large proportion of women), many of whom have never been near a ball park." These fans, and the longstanding ones too, he acknowledges, are "insatiable for information about the sport."

From the 1960s onward, as the leagues grew via expansion and the number of contests increased, as traveling to watch games became more difficult or less likely, as increasing numbers of games were televised, and as Angell aged, he watched many games at home in Manhattan and in his vacation cottage in

Maine, an attentive couch spectator. He grew to appreciate, if not the bloated commentary and noisy graphics, the camera angles that televised and, later, streaming baseball provides. Of the impossibly tense and exciting 1991 World Series between the Atlanta Braves and the Minnesota Twins, Angell reported that the television coverage was "almost up to the baseball": the announcers, Tim McCarver and Jack Buck, "were into the game in all senses—prescient and useful," and the cameras found compelling imagery in the weariness of players and mangers, and of a woman "biting her lips, with her homer hankie crushed in her palm," bereft in the stands. "I don't know how many writers or fans still stop to think how much the screens and replays have added to our expertise," Angell acknowledged in the early 2000s. "Television has made scouts of us all."

About instant replay, Angell has mixed feelings. In 1991 he asked Boston Red Sox catcher Carlton Fisk if he ever watched the replay of his famous home run in Game Six of the 1975 World Series. "I turn it off or go out of the room whenever it comes along, because I want to keep it fresh in my head," Fisk replied. "I try not to talk about it or to answer questions about it either. I want to keep hold of the memory of what it felt like, as opposed to what it looks like in the screen." He added, "It's best to keep it enclosed." Angell has cited the catcher's comments on more than one occasion. In his preface to *Game Time*, Angell laments that "ESPN keeps us up to the moment, even as the rarity of the moment slips away, and instant replay supplants memory." Of course Angell doesn't want the Major League Baseball video archive to turn to dust or for a generation of kids to have been deprived of Mel Allen and *This Week In Baseball* on endless Saturday afternoons; he wants to recall favorite moments down the years via the vagaries and pleasures of memory filtered through sentimentality and skepticism.

Regardless, Angell usually tempers pleasing nods to the game with concern for the medium's entrenchment. "I watch quite a lot of televised baseball," he acknowledged in 2003, "but the trouble with televised baseball for all of us is that we've become so impatient by television in general that if nothing is happening we flick over to see what's on HBO or what's happening in that other game. If I'm watching the Yankees, I'll see what the Mets are doing. It doesn't really satisfy you in the end." He adds, "Baseball is meant to be watched all the way through. Sure, it's boring. There are boring innings and sometimes there turn out to be bad games, but you're not going to have a feeling for the good games unless you're willing to watch."

In August 1977 Angell, his wife, Carol, and their seven-year-old son, John Henry, took in an inessential Mets and Giants affair at Shea Stadium, a hot and humid, "dull, showery game" interrupted for an hour by sheets of rain. "No big plays," he later wrote in his notes. "We ate quantities of junk, and left after seven. It occurs to me that it is O.K. to teach J. H., by example, that baseball boredom is fun, too. He said he enjoyed it, at least."

Angell has certainly come around to blaring modernity—he started blogging, cheerfully, in 2008—yet memories of early television's monochromatic angles, flat dimensions, and growing troupe of crowing announcer-personalities might always intrude. Angell watched his beloved Giants at the Polo Grounds, saw Babe Ruth and Lou Gehrig hit back-to-back homers in Yankee Stadium when he was a boy, and was raised listening to baseball on the radio, that window into the cinema of the imagination, catnip to those who like to visualize a game in the "interior stadium."

Like many fans of his generation, Angell grew up in the park, where distractions were minimal and relatively quiet, where he could at times be—in fact where he expected himself to be—uninterested. This is a state of inwardness that television seems designed to guard against, dullness an other-century illness to be eradicated by a vaccine of noise and spectacle. "You should enter a ballpark the way you enter a church," pitcher Bill Lee once said. Ballparks have long been sacrosanct places for fans, though spiritual companions to Lee might've found their piety tested by the many loud, tacky diversions in the second half of the century. Beginning in the mid-1960s and cresting in the next decade, ballparks began metamorphosing from small-time affairs and funky, intimate neighborhood joints—fans squeezed tightly next to each other and right on top of the action, the parks' sizes and dimensions ruled by crowded, noisy, angled urban blocks—to monolithic stadiums, enormous and hulking, surrounded by acres of parking lots, massive footprints in the near suburbs. Natural grass was replaced by its artificial cousin from the future, and fields were often required to do double duty, hosting seasons' worth of football and other sporting events in the winters. Stadiums grew raucously louder too, the expanded (and inebriated) crowds goaded into hoarse response by giant, commanding scoreboards and deafening announcers.

From 1961 to 1982 RFK Memorial Stadium (built for the Washington Senators), Shea Stadium (New York Mets), Busch Memorial Stadium (St. Louis Cardinals), San Diego Stadium (San Diego Padres), Riverfront Stadium (Cincinnati Reds), Three Rivers Stadium (Pittsburgh Pirates), Veterans Stadium (Philadelphia Phillies), Olympic Stadium (Montreal Expos), the Kingdome (Seattle Mariners), and the Hubert H. Humphrey Metrodome (Minnesota Twins) opened for baseball and other events, each sodded, as it were, with artificial grass. The Expos', Mariners', and Twins' stadiums were domed off from the weather. "More and more these stadia remind one of motels in their perfect and dreary usefulness," Angell observed in 1970. "They are no longer parks but machines for parks." A decade later he admitted dryly, "I don't much admire the much admired Royals Stadium, a contemporary sports palace so denuded of leaf and lawn that the gentle sobriquets 'field' and 'park' are no longer heard there; it is a 'facility.'"

A new era had begun. Though RFK and Shea Stadiums were in operation in the East, the renaissance truly dawned in Texas.

Annoyed by one too many rainouts at Buffalo Stadium (the long-time home of the St. Louis Cardinals' and, more recently, the Houston Colt .45s' Minor League baseball teams) Roy Hofheinz, former Houston radio/TV station owner and since its inception in 1960 co-owner of the newly named Astros franchise, envisioned a ballpark beneath a dome, a faultless, removed-from-nature venue consistent in dry, pleasant temperature and ideal playing conditions, a virtual requirement for summer ball in frightfully hot and humid southeast Texas. The Astrodome opened in 1965, and the design firm and team publicists heralded the venue as the eighth wonder of the world. "Not since the ancient seven wonders of the world has man allowed his imagination to soar to conceive and construct another such wonder . . . until the ASTRODOME," the brochures crowed. "It too is a monument to man's daring imagination, ingenuity, intelligence. . . . It too is awesome in size, inspiring in its beauty, unique and unduplicated."

Visitors locally and nationally were suitably awestruck. "It will mark the first time that baseball, like pheasant, ever has been served under glass," marveled the *Times* columnist Arthur Daley, "offered in a monstrous indoor playpen under a domed roof and in an air-conditioned arena. It stuns the eye with such dazzling splendor that even the natives, experts at the use of superlatives, find themselves groping for words in trying to describe this Eighth Wonder that has been created by their imagination, ingenuity and oil-soaked money." As did many observers at the time, Daley relayed the sinking feeling that dawned on unhappy outfielders during practice games as they patrolled the bright green Astro-Turf: the fielders had great difficulty judging fly balls without a normal cloud-filled or overcast sky providing depth perception. "There are no clouds in the Astrodome," Daley gravely explains. "Overhead there are lacy girders instead. The blackness of night gives a certain uniformity to the glass Lucite inserts between girders and minimizes the difference. But in the daytime, the sun adds extra lights and shadows with almost kaleidoscopic effect."

(General Manager Paul Richards's cheerfully gung-ho response? "We can always place a tarpaulin over the dome and even play our day games under lights.") Despite this unforeseen problem, Daley, like many stunned by the dome's architectural and engineering audacity, felt that the Astrodome "approaches the 99 44/100 perfection of Ivory soap," that "the wildest of all sports dreams is fast approaching reality. A covered, all-weather arena is about to be opened in Texas by Texans. Superlatives still can't do justice to the Astrodome, a fantasy that defies description."

Curious and skeptical, Angell flew in from New York to visit the Astrodome a year after its debut, on Opening Day, April 18, 1966. The Astros' first season under the dome had been as popular with fans as attendance at the old Colt Stadium had been dreadful: on September 8, 1962, three months before the Harris County Commissioners Court successfully passed an issue raising nearly $10 million for construction of the Astrodome, fewer than 1,700 fans showed up at a Colt .45s–Mets game. Attendance jumped from 725,000 in 1964 to over 2 million in the dome's first year, and though the Astros finished in ninth place, there was a buzz about the team and its near future. (The Astros would remain a .500 or below team for many years.)

Sitting in an unprecedentedly cushioned seat, Angell enjoyed the baseball he watched at the dome, and, like other visitors, he too was struck by the space-age aesthetics of the venue. "During my stay, I found that when I forced myself to look at the Astrodome as a work of art, my admiration for the improbable cool bubble grew with each visit," he writes in the May 14, 1966, issue. "The exterior is especially pleasing—a broad, white-screened shell of such excellent proportions that you doubt its true dimensions until you stand at its base." The Astrodome may be the world's largest indoor arena, yet "its ramps are gentle, its portals and aisles brilliantly marked, and its various levels so stacked and tilted that immensity is reduced and made undiscouraging. There are almost no bad seats in the house, and the floors are so antiseptically clean that one hesitates before parting with a peanut shell or a cigarette butt." However, the 474-foot-long scoreboard—its immensity and spectacle soon to be *de rigueur* in ballparks—left him cold: "The giant set is impossible not to look at," he complains, "and there is no 'off' switch," adding, "The board had been the big hit of the evening."

The Astrodome's otherworldly cleanliness and the distant, airborne luxury skyboxes seemed to have rankled Angell too, as did Hofheinz's radical theories about the kinds of fans he believed wanted to watch baseball. During his stay, Angell visited Hofheinz in "His Honor's sanctum" in the dome, "a two-story business pad of such comically voluptuous decor and sybaritic furnishings that I was half convinced it had been designed by, say, John Lennon." Angell gazed about at Moorish lamps, back-lit onyx wall panels, Oriental lions, a black marble and rosewood desk, a golden telephone, a suspended baldachin. Hofheinz and Angell chatted in Hofheinz's box on an upper floor, which offered "an expansive vista of the lofty, gently breathing dome and a distant view of some Astros working out in the batting cage."

In a gold plush chair overlooking the field, drinking coffee from a gold cup, twirling his customary cigar in his hands, Hofheinz held forth about fans with an attitude toward the future that was prescient in its calculated understanding of pie-sliced attention spans and the lure of bright diversions; talking with Angell, Hofheinz seems to be staring straight into the next century. "This park keeps 'em interested enough so they don't have to keep busy with a pencil and scorecard," he boasted when Angell mentioned regretfully that few fans at the Astrodome kept score during games. "Why, in most other parks you got nothing to do but watch the game, keep score, and sit on a hard wooden seat. This place was built to keep the fans happy. They've got our good seats, fine restaurants, and our scoreboard to look at, and they don't have to make a personal sacrifice to like baseball." He argues that professional baseball clubs are competing for attention in the increasingly vast arena of sports entertainment. "You've got to create new kinds of fans," he insists. The Hofheinzian view that attending a ballgame is akin to a sacrifice rather than a luxury, as well as the owner's pious distaste for rowdiness, stymies Angell, who has one foot in the Polo Grounds era and one in contemporary culture, a native skeptic and realist recognizing the danger of nostalgia as he is sensitive to onrushing changes fated by evolving technology and trends. ("Perhaps 'traditional' should now be reserved for the rosin bag and the seventh-inning stretch," he'll sigh in the next century.)

Angell observes late in "The Cool Bubble" that baseball is an understated, multifaceted game and that its chief subtlety may be the ways it appeals to the fans in the stands. "The expensive Houston experiment does not truly affect the players or much alter the sport played down on the field, but I think it does violence to baseball—and, incidentally, threatens its own success—through a total misunderstanding of the game's old mystery." Angell disagrees with Hofheinz that a ballpark is a primary place to socialize with propriety or that many fans will continue to enjoy domed-off weather, carpeting, spotless floors, and a TV-show-like experience. "But these complaints are incidental. What matters, what appalls in Houston is the attempt being made there to alter the quality of baseball's time. Baseball's clock ticks inwardly and silently, and a man absorbed in a ball game is caught in a slow, green place of removal and concentration and in a tension that is screwed up slowly and ever more tightly with each pitcher's windup and with the almost imperceptible forward lean and little half-step with which the fielders accompany each pitch." Attempts to abolish this, to "use up" baseball with diversions, "will in fact transform the sport into another mere entertainment and thus hasten its descent to the status of a boring and stylized curiosity." The essay concludes with an Angellian kiss-off: "I do not wish them luck with this vulgar venture, and I hope that in the end they may remember that baseball has always had a capacity to create its own life-long friends—sometimes even outdoors."

It's telling how Angell develops his persona in his *New Yorker* essays, transforming raw and biased notes into an elegant, informed point of view. The observations he made while visiting Houston are particularly agitated and personal: "The park has become <u>exactly</u> like home . . . how awful! The ultimate vulgarity of it all—."

And: "Local radio (or TV) commentator's remark: 'All they need now is 50,000 artificial customers' (almost as if it will come true—)."

And: "Under it all, there is an indication that BB isn't enough—isn't interesting enough. The scoreboard must heighten our home runs—must yell for us, must outperform the home run itself. Entertainment as sport."

And: "Indoors is o.k.—<u>that's</u> not the danger, but propriety & <u>control of fans are</u>."

And: "Briefly, what it is about BB that appeals to <u>me</u>. Time passing, concentration, out-door removal, slow passage of time building (sometimes) into tension, complexity. No way to speed up the passage of time, a rural time, a <u>slow, green time</u>. Feel the air, look at faces near you, <u>watch</u>."

A decade and a half later Angell was still annoyed. Observing the Philadelphia riot police lining the field at Veterans Stadium during the concluding game of the 1980 World Series between the Philadelphia Phillies and the Kansas City Royals—"the first All-Carpet Championship of the World"—he wondered parenthetically, "What are they protecting? *AstroTurf?*"

Twenty-five years after his visit to the Astrodome, Angell was happy to find himself outdoors, this time in Baltimore, Maryland, two seasons before the opening of Oriole Park at Camden Yards, the first of several so-called retro ballparks that sprouted in the 1990s and 2000s.

A couple of years earlier, then National League president (and future commissioner of baseball) A. Bartlett Giamatti commiserated with Angell about the overwhelming blandness of the current ballparks. "More domes are coming, and I regret it," Giamatti sighed. "This game is meant to be played outdoors and on grass, but I don't see how we can expect a city to come up with a hundred-million-dollar stadium-bond issue and not want to amortize that with conventions and car-crushing contests and football and the rest, which call for all-season stadiums." Agitated, he added, "What I don't understand is the lack of imagination in ballpark design. . . . Modern ballparks are the most conventional architecture since Mussolini's social realism. Why can't we build an idiosyncratic, angular park, for a change, with all the amenities and conveniences and still make it better than anything we have now? I just don't get it. A ballpark should be a box, not a saucer—everybody knows that . . . a place of weird angles and distances and beautiful ricochets? It could be done."

It was being done. Two years after his conversation with Giamatti, touring Camden Yards and in his element, distracted from the thirty-two-day lockout in March of that year that had pushed the start of the season back a week, Angell was pleased to glance around. "This is a *fans'* park," he writes in "The Pit and the Pendulum" in the May 21, 1990, *New Yorker*. "They've done it at last."

> I had been waiting for this visit for twenty years, which is at least the length of time I have spent wondering why some team couldn't come up with a new major-league ballpark that would put an end to the weepy beatifications we writers and aficionados must still scatter down upon the rusting ancient temples of the pastime, where city grass grows deep, and where a company of fans, sometimes sitting close enough to third to tell whether Ron or Wade or Aurelio had shaved that morning, could put up a noise when needed and hear it rise and roll and reecho within those airy and wonderful chambers: Wrigley, Fenway, Comiskey, Tiger Stadium.

The visit to an uncompleted but vividly promising ballpark allows Angell to bring his imagination to bear on the attractions of parks and to muse with a hint of contained nostalgia. "Ballparks tell us more about ourselves than we think," he allows, adding, "Baseball and urban planning have always gone hand in hand, as can be deduced from the cunning placement of old downtown parks like Forbes and Ebbets Fields, Shibe Park and Fenway Park, Comiskey and Wrigley, and the rest, within their street lots and right-angled block corners. It was always a good fit: the diamond is in fact a square, and a tenement window—which is what you sometimes felt you were occupying, down front in the upper deck—invites street kibitzing and yelled advice. Baseball, at its heart, has always been a city sport."

Again Angell likens a ballpark to a neighborhood, a connection he so long ago made with the Polo Grounds, as a place where families hang out and know each other in easy familiarity, where community and a sense of belonging are stoked. He writes, "Baseball, like good design, is made up of a thousand challenges, decisions, and minute strategies, and a great contemporary ballpark, built along ancient lines but for contemporary needs and expectations, can be an amalgam of intelligence and sensual pleasure, just like a good ballgame," adding, "A little sentiment is not amiss, either, as long as it doesn't rule the enterprise." During his visit to Camden Yards' offices, Angell gazes at photos of Forbes Field, Fenway Park, Shibe Park, Wrigley Field (in Los Angeles), and Ebbets Field, describing the homey presentation as "a family album, on slides, of Camden Yards' progenitors and old aunties." Earlier in the essay he recounts standing above right field, in fair ground, the field twenty feet below him, observing a player catch a fly ball. "I could do that, I think," he writes, the reaction speaking volumes about this park's claim on his old attachments to the game. "The whole nature of what we think about athletes has changed so much," Angell remarked later. "We used to think that athletes are more or less like me, a little bit like, 'I could be that guy,' particularly in baseball."

Camden Yards opened for the 1992 season, and with its charming dimensions, throwback ambience, and urban location, it remains beloved by baseball fans. The park's influence is legendary, as it inaugurated an era of new parks: between 1994 and 2001 the Cleveland Indians, Texas Rangers, Colorado Rockies, Atlanta Braves, San Francisco Giants, Houston Astros, Detroit Tigers, and Pittsburgh Pirates franchises all followed suit and opened new parks more intimate than the 1960s and 1970s stadiums, older-leaning in style, with downtown buildings displayed prominently beyond center field. Angell was an immediate fan of Camden Yards, and his visit concludes warmly: "On the far side of the site I could see where bulldozers had already turned and smoothed the corner of the grounds directly behind home plate: a thrilling curve of the new vessel that would soon be filled and refilled, days and years on end, with fresh baseball memories." Though he'd later decry the park's small outfield and the fact that "a lot of cheap home runs get hit there," Angell remained besotted with Camden's pleasing gestures to the past.

A quarter century after his spirit-lifting visit to the Yards, Angell reported on a curious, dark, and unprecedented development there. Following the hospitalization and death in police custody of a young African American, Freddie Gray, in April 2015, Baltimore's streets turned violent and tense with rioting. Subsequently the April 29 game between the Chicago White Sox and the host Orioles was closed to the public, the first time this had happened in baseball's history. Watching the empty, tomb-like Camden Yards on television from his home in Manhattan, Angell—ninety-four at the time—was given an unanticipated reminder of the "massive and relentless add-ons and distractions of modern-day ball," including the Kiss Camera, nutty mascots, T-shirt rifles, "God Bless America," deafening music and announcers, giant souvenir shops, a restaurant in right field "with its roped-off waiting areas thoughtfully supplied with overhead screens," and so on.

Fans crave such options and diversions, Angell acknowledges, but the day's "silent anomaly" was a notice that what had been removed wasn't the crowd but the game itself, "what we came for and what we partake of now in passing fractions, often seen in a held-up smartphone." He remembers a time when the baseball and the players were "the lone attractions, barring a few outfield signboards. Nothing more, not even an organist. You watched and waited in semi-silence, ate a hot dog, drank a Moxie, watched some more, yelled when something happened, kept score, saw the shadows lengthen, then trooped home elated or disconsolate. It was a public event, modestly presented, and private in recollection. If the game was a big one, with enormous Sunday crowds and endless roaring, it was thrilling to have been there, but in some fashion you'd also been there alone, nobody else in sight."

From June to September 1985—to choose a random range—an average *New Yorker* issue ran to more than one hundred pages, remarkable for a weekly today. "Now, you know, we have less space," Angell observed in 2014. "But in those days you just wrote away. I felt that I would have as much space as I wanted." "There's a great freedom and blessing, of course, associated with not having tight deadlines and having effectively unlimited space," Ben McGrath remarks. "But there's also a burden. Once you give up on the super-confined space and restraint of the tight news peg, then your piece has to have a reason to exist. Roger availed himself of these luxuries, but then, as a result, you need to rise well above it. Of course he did."

Fortunate to have the vast number of pages available to him and indulging his native inquisitiveness, Angell often used his baseball essays to explore particular subjects at great length and in great detail, perhaps in response to the expansive leisurely pace of a season where games can feel as endless as summer itself—extra-inning essays, as it were. In the August 16, 1976, issue Angell wrote a lengthy profile of baseball scout Ray Scarborough, followed on October 4 by "On the Ball," a piece about pitchers' mentalities and quirks and the different kinds of pitches they throw. The April 9, 1979, issue featured the prescient "Sharing the Beat," a heavily researched and thoughtful piece about the dawning controversy of female sportswriters in the locker room. (It is interesting that this was the sole essay of Angell's about which his editor, William Shawn, expressed doubt: "This was a new thing—woman newspaper reporters were coming in and reporting on sports," Angell said. "They were running into a lot of prejudice and a lot of trouble. . . . I went to Shawn and he said, 'Really? I hope it's going to be funny.' And then he read the piece and came back to me and apologized. He said, 'I'm sorry about what I said. That's so terrible.'") In 1981 three essays were devoted to particulars: "One Hard Way to Make a Living," in April, about the mysterious vagaries of hitting; "The Web of the Game," in July, on the Yale-St. John's game in New Haven, where students and future stars Ron Darling and Frank Viola faced off and where Angell sat with and gently profiled ninety-one-year-old Smoky Joe Wood, a former Yale coach and right-handed pitcher for the Boston Red Sox; and in August, the wonderfully cinematic "In the Country" about former Minor League pitcher Ron Goble and his supportive girlfriend, the poetry-loving and enthusiastic letter writer Linda Kittell.

Other notable essays in this vein include "Three for the Tigers" (published in September 1973), about a trio of old-timer Tigers fans with whom Angell hung out in Detroit; "The Companions of the Game" (September 1975), about departing New York/San Francisco Giants president Horace Stoneham; "Being Green" (August 1983), a lengthy profile of Oakland A's president Roy Eisenhardt; "In the Fire" (March 1984), about catchers whom Angell watched and spoke to during spring training and regular season; "Taking Infield" (May 1985), about infielders; "Quis"

(September 1985), a profile of Kansas City Royals relief pitcher Dan Quisenberry, whom Angell greatly admired; "Up at the Hall" (August 1987), about a visit to the National Baseball Hall of Fame and Museum in Cooperstown, New York; "No, But I Saw the Game" (July 1989), about baseball movies (*Bull Durham, The Pride of the Yankees, Bang the Drum Slowly, The Natural,* and *Eight Men Out* among them); "Homeric Tales" (May 1991), recounting players' stories of home runs, both of the clouting and given-up variety; "Dinosaur" (August 1992), about the restorative charms of Minor League baseball and a trip upstate to watch the Oneonta Yankees; "Wings of Fire" (May 1998), about the alarming rise in the number of baseball pitchers facing orthopedic surgery; and "The Bard in the Booth" (August 1999), a profile of lauded radio and television color analyst and former player Tim McCarver.

Though Angell never profiled Earl Weaver at length, the diminutive, fiery Baltimore Orioles manager was a favorite of his; a brilliant game strategist, Weaver would often hold forth in the clubhouse, after a win or a loss, stark naked and chewing on a chicken wing while swigging a beer. Angell also admires the calm, long-tenured New York Yankee skipper Joe Torre for his implacability in the face of owner George Steinbrenner's wrath and for his modesty, compassion for his players, baseball smarts, and "lifer" wisdoms. Angell wonderfully evokes Torre's easy, friendly presence in "Front Running" in the August 17, 1998, *New Yorker.* The Yanks are riding high; that October they'll capture their second World Series in three years and then win two more in a row. Paying a pregame visit to the clubhouse, Angell observes Torre, bench coach Don Zimmer ("pink and freshly shaved"), and a few visitors engage in a "river of baseball" talk, the conversation moving casually among last night's game (David Cone's ten strikeout domination), ancient affairs (the '78 Yanks–Red Sox battles), amusing quirks of old players (Jeffrey Leonard's "broken-wing" homerun trot), and favorite names ("Fir-po *Mar*-berry!"). All the while, Torre is "climbing into his uniform," smiling gently at the old memories as he provides one of his own: "Our conversation ends, in any case, when Torre finishes tying his shoes and stands up. 'Well, yesterday was my anniversary,' he announces. 'Twenty-three years since I hit into four double plays in one game.'"

This warmly sketched scene embedded in a midsummer piece displays Angell's confident ease in discovering those precise details that evoke the presence and character of players and managers. When Torre arrived in the Bronx in 1996, following mixed results managing the St. Louis Cardinals, Atlanta Braves, and New York Mets, Angell quickly honed in on his admirable and handy stoicism. "No one—well, no one since Casey Stengel—had moved into the manager's office at the Stadium with more aplomb and fewer glances upstairs," he observed. Recalling Torre's playing days, Angell remarked that an eighteen-year career "produced in him a calm tension that appeared impervious to ego or job anxiety"; elsewhere he noticed Torre's "instinctive fairness," born of his "firsthand knowledge of the inexorable built-in swoops and lurches of baseball fortune." Torre's physical features tickled Angell also, and as so often happens when Angell's struck by someone's distinctive mien, his language rises to the occasion: witness Torre's "saggy, dark-eyed gaze," "rumpled face," the "late-game streakings of his lucky red candy, around the mouth," and his "Don-like (Calabria, not Oxford) sidewise tilt and cocked ear for the ceaseless dugout gerbillings and counsellings" of Zimmer. On another occasion he observed that Torre, "with his long face, dark eyes, and ruminative pauses, exudes the wisdom of an elderly hunting dog—a celebrated bluetick, with memories of fabled night runs and ancient treeings to call up at will." And this delight, among Angell's most remarkable descriptions: Torre's "prairie mortician's gait" as he headed for the mound to remove a pitcher. No one but Angell envisions a manager walking in such a way, the image evoking unhappy labor of all stripes, suggestive of both a lone man's walk and that walk's glum universality. Men at work.

Two of Angell's lengthy profiles drew great acclaim. In "Down the Drain" in the June 23, 1975, *New Yorker*, Angell writes about hard-luck Pittsburgh Pirates hurler Steve Blass, who suffered from the bizarrely sudden inability to control his pitches. Angell was both fascinated with and disturbed by the affliction that settled upon Blass, whom he'd seen pitch in the 1971 World Series and about whom he'd written with admiration. (Blass, "the marvel of the third game," had pitched "with an almost surgical finesse.") Blass's problems—generally referred to among players and observers as "the yips"—began during the following season, when he lost his control and began bouncing pitches in front of home plate or sailing them over batters' heads. He suffered for the next couple of years in both the Major and the Minor Leagues in an attempt to straighten himself out.

Blass had been in and out of professional baseball for a while when Angell visited him for a week in April 1975. He found a genial, uncomplicated man, not prone to introspection or, for that matter, much chatting. "Blass was not a great talker," Angell recalled later.

He was, in the sense that he spoke for himself and revealed constantly who he was—a lighthearted person who disliked complexity, or distrusted complexity in himself. He had a deep distrust of his own complexity. He was always moving away from it, and this terrible dilemma that he found himself in—this inability to pitch—eventually took him to a place where every fan, his teammates, his coaches, and his friends would say, *What's going on? What's happening here?* And he really didn't want to hear their conjectures. He kept saying, *Well, it's probably nothing very complicated.* That's the way he is. And that's why the story is, in a way, sad. Because it is a complicated story. I don't know the answer.

Angell watched Blass pitch and visited a Pirates game with him, but he brings the aggrieved pitcher to life most fully while describing him on his home turf, coaching a Little League game or sitting with his family. (At home Blass seemed wistful: "I noticed that it seems difficult for Blass to talk about his baseball career as a thing of the past; now and then he slipped into the present tense—as if it were still going on.") What interests Angell the most in Blass's story is the abrupt failure at an elite level and the uniqueness of his problem. "The frustrating, bewildering part of it all was that while working alone with a catcher Blass continued to throw as well as he ever had; his fastball was alive, and his slider and curve shaved the corners of the plate," Angell writes. "But the moment a batter stood in against him he became a different pitcher, especially when throwing a fastball—a pitcher apparently afraid of seriously injuring somebody." As a result, Angell notes soberly, "he was of very little use to the Pirates even in batting practice."

This unexpected demotion in craft and poise on a profoundly large stage strikes a note of compassion inside Angell. He's long been cognizant of the unrealistic, even childish, demands that fans place on professional players, a hostility that often stems from envy, especially since the labor skirmishes of the 1960s and 1970s detonated the exploding rate of pay that ballplayers received for playing a so-called kids' game. As demands on players increase, so does the pressure those players—particularly the highly paid, publicized, and successful ones—feel to live up to expectations, many of which they recognize as having placed on sports heroes of their own when they were young. "Professional sports have a powerful hold on us because they display and glorify remarkable physical capacities, and because the artificial demands of games played for very high rewards produce vivid responses," Angell observes. "But sometimes, of course, what is happening on the field seems to speak to something deeper within us; we stop cheering and look on in uneasy silence, for the man out there is no longer just another great athlete, an idealized hero, but only a man—only ourself. We are no longer at a game. . . .

Sport is no longer a release from the harsh everyday American business world but its continuation and apotheosis."

Near the end of "Down the Drain" Angell ticks off possible reasons or explanations for Blass's bedeviling, career-ending syndrome—including fears of being injured or of injuring a batter, a slump that resulted in a loss of confidence, and excessive grief over the death of teammate Roberto Clemente—and speaks with teammates and coaches, many of whom remain as baffled as Angell. At this point in the piece "the reader has gone through a lot," Angell commented later. "He's learned a lot, and he hasn't come to the answer. He hasn't come to a solution. And then you bring in his friends, who don't have the solution, either. So let them talk. We're now going to talk together about this central mystery, which doesn't get answered in the piece. They're down to guesses."

Angell ends the profile in Blass's home, in the family room, playing an imaginary game of baseball with Blass, a large-hearted gesture on the part of Angell, who suggested the activity, and a crucial and moving narrative pivot that renders the sympathetic Blass on a human-scale, as a member of an extended family. Angell writes, "It had occurred to me that in spite of his enforced and now permanent exile from the game, he still possessed a rare body of precise and hard-won pitching information. He still knew most of the hitters in his league, and, probably as well as any other pitcher around, he knew what to pitch to them in a given situation." Angell admits to always wanting to listen to a pitcher "say exactly what he would throw next and why, and now I invited Blass to throw against the Cincinnati Reds, the toughest lineup of hitters anywhere. I would call the balls and strikes and hits. I promised he would have no control problems."

Sitting comfortably on the couch next to Angell at ten in the morning, smoking a cigar thoughtfully, Blass proceeds to "pitch" to Pete Rose, Joe Morgan, Dan Driessen, Johnny Bench, and Tony Perez—a formidable lineup!—imagining what he'd throw to each batter given the hitter's tendencies and the game situations. "First of all, I'm going to try to keep [Rose] off base if I can, because they have so many tough hitters coming up"; "Joe Morgan is strictly a fastball hitter, so I want to throw him a bad fastball to start him off"; "Perez is not a good high, hard fastball hitter. I'll begin him with that pitch, because I don't want to get into any more trouble with the slider and have him dunk one in. A letter-high fastball, with good mustard on it." And so on. In the end Perez swung and missed for the third out, stranding Morgan at second and Bench at first. "Pretty good inning," Angell said to Blass, provoking easy laughter from the pitcher.

This proposal to Blass that he imagine standing on the mound again, in control—in all aspects of that word—"was the best idea I ever had as a reporter," Angell acknowledged in 2014. "I mean, this is a guy who can't pitch anymore, and we've spent the whole piece watching him lose his stuff. And he cannot do it; he cannot pitch. He's out of the major leagues. And I bring him back. And he's going to pitch, and he's going to have perfect control. And for a half hour we sit and pitch this imaginary game. I thought, *Good for you, Roger.*" He added, *"*It also lightens the whole thing for the reader. How do you pitch to the Reds? Well, it is the best way to end it, it seems to me. It lightens up a gloomy piece. And he still seems very young, which is a big thing to remember about ballplayers. They're young. They have to do all the serious parts of their lives while they're still in their 20s. That's why it's so hard for them to give it up later, because they don't have anything else coming along as interesting as this." Blass was grateful for the idea. "We knew we wouldn't see each other again," Angell said.

Another player with whom Angell was long intrigued is legendary Cardinals pitcher and Hall of Famer Bob Gibson; "Distance" appeared in the September 22, 1980, issue. On the mound Gibson was tough to hit; off the field, he was hard to know. "Distance" accomplishes a profoundly difficult task in bringing to life a man infamous for his stony and often misunderstood silences, the title of the piece evoking not only the feet and inches between the mound and home plate, but also the divide between Gibson and those whom he kept at arm's length, many of whom found him enigmatic and difficult. "He was the best pitcher in baseball and also the scariest and most unapproachable," Angell observed. Angell had esteemed Gibson for many years, writing the following of him in the 1967 World Series between the Cardinals and Boston Red Sox: "Gibson, hardly taking a deep breath between pitches, was simply overpowering, throwing fast balls past the hitters with his sweeping right-handed delivery, which he finishes with a sudden lunge toward first base"; he later writes that the Red Sox were stymied by Gibson when they learned that "he was not merely a thrower but a pitcher."

"Distance" originates in a moment in the Cardinals' locker room after the first game of the 1968 World Series, in which Gibson struck out a record seventeen Detroit Tigers en route to a five-hit shutout. Crowded by reporters armed with notebooks and microphones, Angell among them, Gibson was asked if he'd been surprised by his achievements on the field that day. He replied, "I'm never surprised by anything I do." Angell recounted this moment in the *New Yorker* that fall; twelve years later, recalling the moment in "Distance," he writes that "the shock of this went out across the ten-deep bank of writer faces like a seismic wave, and the returning, murmurous counterwaves of reaction were made up of uneasy laughter and whispers of '*What* did he say?' and some ripples of disbelieving silence and (it seemed to me) a considerable, almost visible wave of dislike, or perhaps hatred."

Writing from the perspective of a dozen culturally noisy years later, Angell observes, "This occasion, it should be remembered, was before the time when players' enormous salaries and their accompanying television-bred notoriety had given birth to a kind of athlete who could choose to become famous for his sullenness and foul temper, just as another might be identified by his gentle smile and unvarying sweetness of disposition. In 1968, ballplayers, particularly black ballplayers in near-Southern cities like St. Louis, did not talk outrageously to the press. Bob Gibson, however, was not projecting an image but telling us a fact about himself." In this moment, Gibson "was beyond us, it seemed, but the truth of the matter is that no one at Busch Stadium should have been much surprised by his achievement that afternoon."

The confident, almost unreal murmur from Gibson remained with Angell, defining Gibson not only as a professional athlete, but also as a man. For several days in July 1980 Angell visited Gibson and his family at Gibson's home in Omaha, Nebraska, and shadowed him at his post-retirement place of business, Gibby's restaurant and bar, which Gibson owned. Angell grew friendly with Gibson's wife, Wendy, and watched Gibson relax at home by the pool and with his daughters, though guardedly—"as always, there was a silence about him: an air not of something held back but of a space within him that is not quite filled." The thread in Angell's conversations with Gibson often wound around the knotty relationship between the star and the press; Angell was interested in what made Gibson tick, and he needed to ask probing questions, first of Gibson's ex-teammates and managers, then of Gibson himself about his game and his temperament.

Though he eventually trusted Angell and opened up to him, Gibson remained reserved, partially closed off. In his notes to the piece Angell listed the qualities about Gibson that intrigued him as a subject: "He seems intelligent, withdrawn, unhappy (or unsatisfied), edgy, intuitive, businesslike, unsentimental, energetic, but not quick-moving, alert. Willing to open up if he trusts you. (He didn't know me, but after we talked for awhile I got the feeling, possibly wrongly, that he would tell me almost anything.)" "There is a standoff here," Angell observes in "Distance."

The price of Bob Gibson's owning St. Louis seems to be his agreeing—in his mind, at least—to let the press own him. I have considerable sympathy for any writer who had to ask Bob Gibson some sharp, news-producing questions two or three times a week over the span of a decade or more, but wanting Gibson with a sunny, less obdurate temperament would be to want him a less difficult, less dangerous man on the mound—not quite a Bob Gibson, not quite a great pitcher. The man is indivisible, and it is the wonder of him.

In seeing Gibson as emblematic of the price of fame, to both the athlete basking in praise and the fan lofting it, Angell takes up an issue he's long considered. "It is my own suspicion that both sportswriters and fans are increasingly resentful of the fame and adulation and immense wealth that are now bestowed so swiftly upon so many young professional athletes, and are envious of their privileged and apparently carefree style of living," he writes. He feels that this stems from the semi-conscious recognition among fans and media that they in essence made these young men and want to possess them, demand peerless performances from them, and be allowed to glimpse their private lives on demand. Angell notes, pointedly and admiringly, that Gibson "has always kept his distance and his strangeness, and there is something upright and old-fashioned about such stubborn propriety. He is there if anyone really wants to close that space—the whole man, and not a piece of him or an image of him—but many of us may prefer not to do so, because at a distance (from sixty feet six inches away, perhaps) he stands whole and undiminished, and beyond our envy: the athlete incarnate, the player."

This cohering insight originated in a note that Angell dashed off while working on "Distance" and then later refined:

SAY THAT: I too understand the problem that the press had with him. The fact is, he isn't private at all, the way everyone said, but so open that one must always deal with the whole man, and not with some affable, approachable public face. He doesn't hide, and if one wants to write something easy and light about him, one feels faced with his unblinking, serious, steady regard. He says, in effect, Take me whole and take me seriously. There is no side or easy charm to him and no effort at self-explanation or self-dramatization. He deals from strength, and one feels a little minor, a bit trifling, in the presence of such wholeness. I think this is what batters must have felt, looking out at him. He could bring all himself to bear on every pitch—full concentration, the whole beam of light at full intensity, because that's the way he deals with everything and everybody. Here I am. Here's the pitch . . . go ahead: hit it if you can.

Just after the observation of Gibson's "steady regard," Angell penciled between the lines the phrases "that look" and "plant this," with an arrow, an underline, and a star denoting their importance to the piece. He then added, "NOT BAD."

Gibson's countenance—that look, steady and serious, distancing—fascinated and at times troubled Angell as a writer; how to make sense of it? Near the end of the piece Angell tells Gibson that he was at times aware of a sadness in him. Gibson responded uncomprehendingly. "No, I'm not sad. I just think I've been spoiled. When you've been an athlete, there's no place for you to go. You're much harder to please. But where I am right now is where the average person has been all along. I'm like millions of others now, and I'm finding out what that's like. I don't think the ordinary person ever gets to do anything they enjoy nearly as much as I enjoyed playing ball. I haven't found my niche now that that's over—or maybe I have found it and I don't know it." Gibson added, "Maybe I'll still find something I like as much as I liked pitching, but I don't know if I will. I sure hope so."

In his notes, his handwriting excitedly, tellingly untidy, Angell jotted, "Say that he was sounding like the man who said that nothing he ever did surprised him but that I wasn't startled anymore, or put off by this. His directness is part of him, and you come to accept." Above this note Angell scribbled, "FIND A CLOSING

QUOTE." A red arrow points to an observation on the right of the page—"Nothing he ever did would surprise me"—around which Angell drew a box. He had his finish. He closed "Distance" with that sentence.

Pitchers have long fascinated Angell, what with their singular, lonely, seemingly impossible tasks. In "The Arms Talks," a lengthy spring training piece in the May 4, 1987, *New Yorker*, Angell explored the many kinds of pitches—old war horses such as the heater and the curveball, as well as the slider, the then dawning split-finger fastball, and the soon-to-dominate cut fastball—and the many ways to throw them, talking with young and old (and retired) hurlers, coaches, and managers in the Arizona and Florida camps about changes on the mound over time. As Angell's essays in the 1970s and 1980s grew in length and breadth, helped into maturity in part by elastic deadlines and the ample-and-growing space he enjoyed at the magazine, he complemented his exceptional journalistic reporting with a kind of poor man's thirst for knowledge. In short, he endeavors to learn more about the game he loves, out of his native curiosity, to generate material, and also to protect himself from the game's "overattachments and repeated buffetings," a balm especially appreciated, one assumes, after the intense Red Sox and Mets World Series the previous autumn. Angell admits that as the years have passed, attempting to learn the game has become for him "almost the best part of baseball," and though as fans we'll never *quite* learn, there are "rewards in trying" in that one might "learn something you thought you already knew." On another occasion he explained simply, "I learned more about baseball as I went along and had more that I wanted to pass on."

The education in pitching has been lifelong. Angell threw as a boy, ultimately learning to toss a "pleasing roundhouse curve that sometimes sailed over a corner of the plate (or a cap or newspaper)" to the wonder of his school buddies. Cheered, he worked up a screwball and could eventually toss "something that infinitesimally broke the wrong way, although always too high to invite a swing." In his early teens Angell started self-consciously strolling through the Lincoln School hallways with the palm of his pitching hand turned outward like that of his idol Carl Hubbell's, "but nobody noticed." He wore out his arm at age thirteen while working on his screwball. He continued pitching at Pomfret School in Connecticut but didn't make the varsity cut. "By that time, the batters I faced were smarter and did frightful things to my trusty roundhouse. I fanned a batter here and there, but took up smoking and irony in self-defense. A short career."

Nearing his eightieth birthday, Angell embarked upon his most ambitious project to date, a full-length book about David Cone, whom Angell followed in games, clubhouses, and training rooms, and met with Cone's extended family and friends in New York, at home, and on the long road throughout the 2000 exhibition and regular seasons. *A Pitcher's Story: Innings with David Cone* was published in 2001. Angell was besotted with Cone and had followed him avidly when he pitched for the Mets in the late 1980s and early 1990s. He wrote about him at length in "Conic Projection" in the May 20, 1996, *New Yorker*, in which he briefly discussed Cone's childhood and adolescence in Kansas City and the surgery to repair an aneurysm on the front of Cone's right shoulder (his throwing arm).

"Everybody was interested in that strange medical business, which very few other pitchers had experienced," Angell said. "And [Cone] then said, 'How would you like to write a book about me?' I said, 'I don't do that. I've never written a front-to-back book.' He said, 'Well, maybe you'll change your mind.'" Cone was persistent, and after Warner Books got wind of the idea and made a sizeable offer to Angel, he decided to go for it. "I was scared the whole way." (He added, "Of course, the story changed.") Cone fully trusted Angell, and as Cone's physical breakdowns came to dominate and alter the book's narrative in unexpected ways, and as some (among them the New York Yankees' august stadium announcer Bob Sheppard) mildly suggested to Angell that he reconsider the book, Cone urged Angell to continue. It's your book, he'd plainly remind Angell.

The guy on the mound, Angell noticed, is the only player on the field with an offensive plan. "Everything else in the game is defensive and reactive. The batter has to react to what the pitcher does, and the fielders react to what the batter does." In Cone's case "the great part about him is that he's so emotional out there, and also you could see what he was doing. He has this great variety of visible pitches. . . . The minute he throws it, you can see the fastball, a couple of kinds of sliders, the curveball, the splitter, the two-seamer, and so forth. All that stuff was highly visible, so you could see what he was thinking," adding, "And he could talk about it afterwards, which is a pretty good combination for a writer."

Struck by Cone's demeanor, poise, and unique, up-and-down career (divided among stints with the Kansas City Royals, New York Mets, Toronto Blue Jays, and New York Yankees), Angell was pleased to be "watching and talking with someone at his stage of a great career as he sets about winning again—winning when it's work, with hard days and nights to get through, and times when the fastball is snoozing and the slider has gone off to the dentist or to the races." Above all, Cone's contradictions interested Angell: worth exploring were the pitcher's maturation from a hard-partying young stud with the Mets, snagged in several lurid sex scandals, to a knowledgeable, confident, and articulate Players Association representative during the debilitating 1994–95 strike, and his dogged back and forth between woeful, sore-arm performances and sterling starts (including a perfect game and another in which he struck out nineteen batters). "Nothing about him is simple," Angell marvels. "He is emotional but also extremely intelligent: a power pitcher with an idea."

Cone's 2000 season veered wildly off its expected, hoped-for course, and so, by necessity, did Angell's book. Cone was making $12 million to pitch, the third-highest salary in base-ball that year, but was thirty-seven as the season began and at the start of spring training was already receiving regular treat-ment, including acupuncture, for his sore shoulder. Pitching in pain, and erratically, throughout the year, his fastball several tics lower than in previous seasons and his devastating slider inconsistent, Cone was placed by Yankees manager Joe Torre in the bullpen by the All-Star break, was forced to skip several starts, and in September at Kaufman Stadium in Kansas City, while fielding a grounder, fell on his shoulder, wrenching it out of the socket. His season devolved unhappily from that grisly injury; he'd end up starting 29 games and throwing 155 innings but ended the year with an awful 6.91 ERA and a 1.768 WHIP (Walks-Plus-Hits per Inning Pitched, an analytic mea-surement of the number of base runners a pitcher allows per inning; generally a WHIP above 1.5 is considered poor). He won only 4 games against 14 losses.

Angell faced a rethink. He'd hoped in his book to study an elite and intellectually savvy pitcher's skills and techniques and the degree to which a pitcher may or may not "own" his own arm, but he was faced with the reality of that pitcher's break-down. Hovering over Cone and his career was the hint of final-ity, of the end of the road approaching; in 1987, writing about the cocaine abuse issues and stays in rehab of Cone's teammate Dwight Gooden, Angell wrote, "The pain and sadness we feel about this are off to one side of baseball, I think—or should be—but there is a sense of loss that reminds us of the kind of wishful hero worship that every real fan had within him or her, even in middle age; we think we have outgrown it, but in truth we can hardly wait for the next shy and shining, extraordinarily talented young man to come along and make the game thrilling for us once again."

For years Cone had been that shining young man. Now the glow was dulling. Over the course of *A Pitcher's Story*, in which Angell reprinted passages from "Conic Projection" and other writings on Cone he'd produced for the *New Yorker*, Angell pivoted from the 2000 season and earlier Cone glories (with the loud and lively Mets, his 1992 postseason efforts with the Toronto Blue Jays, his 1994 Cy Young Award as a Kansas City Royal, his efficient and at times inspiring work as a Players Association representative during rancorous times for the sport, the perfect game in 1999 as a Yankee at Yankee Stadium on Yogi Berra Day) to cinematic, evocative portraits of Cone with his many eager fans, to whom he was tirelessly available; his fiancée and later wife, Lynn; his parents, Ed and Joan; his siblings, longtime friends, and hangers-on; and finally to larger questions about athletic durability and the unrealistic expectations that fans (Angell included) place on their sports heroes. Cone became a kind of tragic figure, broken but honorable, fiercely committed to a game as his skills inevitably eroded. Cone's final appearance with the Yankees came in Game Four of the 2000 World Series against the Mets, a lone stint out of the bullpen. The Yankees won the Series. Cone left the team shortly thereafter. He returned in 2001 to pitch a surprisingly strong season for the Red Sox; Angell covered the campaign for the paperback edition of *A Pitcher's Story*. After a year away Cone signed a contract with the Mets, but a heralded, for-the-ages comeback season wasn't to be. He retired after a final appearance on the mound on May 28, 2003, sore of hip and realistically clear about his future.

"Sports renew us because they're about youth and the thrilling things the species is capable of at its early best," Angell writes late in the book. "But I believe that its other face has to do with a harder, more complicated side of our experience. Nellie King, a former pitcher and broadcaster with the Pirates, once said to me, 'Being good up here is tough—people have no idea. It gets much worse when you have to repeat it: "We know you're great.

Now go and do that again for me.'" If these words didn't come to my mind during [the 2000 World Series], it was because they'd been there all summer long." A handful of Angell's friends and acquaintances who weren't baseball fans had scoffed at Cone's poor season, wondering aloud why he couldn't succeed any more, seemingly "relieved and released," as Angell saw it, by the fact that Cone now no longer seemed out of reach, was no longer immortal. "I didn't feel that way. While I missed the air of brisk hostility that once set Cone apart, I felt closer to him and began to sense, in glimmers, that I was getting a better sense of pitching than I'd had. The difficulty and complexity of the work showed itself in absorbing and excruciating detail now that he was struggling, while the boring mystery of success still shone in my mind, even as I saw it slip away." Angell may as well have been writing about Steve Blass. A bit later he confesses, "The more I saw Cone in confusion and pain, the better I liked him."

In a lesser writer's hands, this shuffling of expectations might've come across as rationalizing, as if the writer had become determined to care about his now wayward and unpredictable subject matter. In actuality Angell was alertly paying attention, a well-earned writer's habit, letting the narrative come to him rather than imposing one. The surprises and vagaries of playing baseball, its stubborn way of imposing its own design and skein of bad luck or indifference to the serious manner in which elite players play, expecting to succeed, revealed itself as the book's true subject all along. "We were friends, and I kept thinking that he would say, 'I can't do this anymore,' and I would say 'Okay,' and that would be the end. But he hung on, which was an enormous tribute to him; he was so deeply embarrassed and shocked by what he was going through. And I kept saying, 'Losing is more interesting than winning,' and he said, 'Well, if you say so.'" Indeed Angell's determination to write and finish the book that he believed some friends, colleagues, and beat writer acquaintances probably felt was finished given Cone's lousy season was inspired in part by

Cone's own determination in the face of the unwelcome turn of events: "My book was nothing compared to his reputation and his record, of course, but he'd seen it though, too, at whatever cost."

Blass, Gibson, and Cone each dealt in his own way with the cumulative effects on his body and soul of time, physical and mental routine, expectations, and the violent motion of the pitching delivery, and to a man Angell discovered an inner and outer toughness and common sense, though in differing degrees and to vastly different outcomes. Similar among the men, too, was a sober understanding of when was the right time to leave the game. One measure of the differences among Blass, Gibson, and Cone is the staggering salaries Cone earned during his career, a total nearing $66 million by the end, unheard of riches to Blass, Gibson, and most players who played or began their careers in the pre–free agent era.

In one passage Cone's wife, Lynn, shows Angell around the Cones' renovated mansion-in-progress in Greenwich, Connecticut, walking "confidently through a succession of plasterboarded, plywood-floor spaces—a family room, a couple of bars, a billiard room, a smoking room, a library, a wine cellar, four or five bedrooms and baths, two children's rooms with a shared overhead loft, a sizable upstairs guest area, and a main living room with an indoor stonework pool and spa at its center, opening onto the sky and nearby woods." The Cones designed many of these architectural show pieces themselves, making "cozier and more sensible use of what had been a sprawl of lofty, cathedral-style spaces. Outside, there were flagstone paths and walkways, and terraces with handsome limestone walls." Suitably impressed, Angell observes that the house and grounds look like a "setting for a wedding or a movie shoot."

Compared to the relatively modest homes into which Blass and Gibson had invited Angell, Cone's residence is palatial. At an earlier point in the book Angell speaks with Cone alongside Cone's pool, as he had with Gibson alongside Gibson's pool

some twenty years earlier. Cone's gleamed resplendent in a large
property within a gated community. Same game, different era.
A star nearly out of reach.

Since midcentury owner and player clashes and the threat of
work stoppages and strikes loomed over baseball. Ever hopeful
to keep his eyes on the field, Angell was nonetheless distracted,
as most baseball fans were, by the many off-field commotions.
Commissioner Bowie Kuhn had staved off several last-minute
stoppages in the 1960s, but eight interruptions besmirched the
game between 1972 and 1995; the seven-and-a-half-month strike
in 1994 into 1995 resulted in the first cancellation of the World
Series in ninety years. Fans were reminded, again and again, that
the game they'd loved since childhood was indeed a multibillion
dollar business helmed by men and women whose job it was to
keep the money flowing, to placate investors and stockholders,
and to profit as fully as possible.

   In the mid-1970s Angell wondered on future claims on the
game, poised as an observing fan casting a look back at old-time
owners, such as the Cubs' William Wrigley Jr. and the New York/
San Francisco Giants' Horace Stoneham, and forward at the rapidly changing, multi-interest, machine-like phalanx of owners:
"A typical modern ball team is operated coldly and at a distance,
just like any other conglomerate subentity with interesting tax-
depletion build-ins and excellent PR overtones. Their owners and
operators are men whose money derives from, and whose deepest
loyalties adhere to, insurance companies, broadcasting chains, oil
wells, whiskey manufacture, real-estate sales, trucking and ship-
ping lines, quick-lunch chains and the like." Baseball is infamously
exempt from antitrust laws—an irony, argues David Greenberg,
in that the owners and players "prove day after day that they
consider baseball above all a business. But the exemption stems
from the government's naive insistence that baseball is only a
game. Alone among professional sports, baseball enjoys immu-

nity from antitrust prosecution because neither Congress nor the Supreme Court has been willing to overturn an ancient decision that baseball is merely an amusement, not a commercial enterprise." Certain owners, flexing their collective muscle, went about the curious and unique business of waging a twentieth-century version of nineteenth-century capitalism—the players in the role of light entertainment, the owners in charge of the fun fair.

As player-versus-management skirmishes arose, Angell often found himself on the side of the players, their grievances and arguments striking a deep, sympathetic chord. Aligning with the players and with Players Association union chief Marvin Miller, whom Angell had long admired, did not always place him in kind country. To many observers, the young, cocky multimillionaires playing a kid's game in the spring and summer—and, if they were fortunate, in the fall—had no right to complain, were absurdly lucky, and should gratefully take whatever the owners offered them. The owners rarely opened their franchises' books for clear accounting and transparency, as Angell, to his credit, regularly reported and complained about in the *New Yorker* and grumbled publicly about the players' escalating salaries—set in motion by the epochal Curt Flood case and exploding into the free agent era—at the same time lamenting out-of-control business costs while local television and cable deals were minting piles and piles of money for their clubs.

The players often felt the scorn of fans and non-fans who read about salaries that were so widely, science fictionally disparate from their own, the scorn amplified to toxic levels when those same players struggled under immense pressures, as of course they inevitably did, and when those struggles looked suspiciously like entitled apathy. "There's a big misconception that all the strikes were for higher salaries," Angell observes.

There was never a strike about higher salaries; it was about free agency. Fans think the players don't care. But the thing about professional athletes which I've noticed over and over and over again is how deeply, deeply they care. They really want to do well. They don't want to look bad out there. If a guy is running out his contract at the end of the year with nothing ahead, he might not run out the ball, or there are players like Robinson Cano who always looks as if he wasn't trying. It looked that way. It was his manner, but he was always trying, and a great player. They do try. You see them weeping unexpectedly when things don't go their way.

The divide between the owners and players—the two groups were never comfortably or warmly close—widened steadily during the second half of the century. Attempts on the players' part to right what they saw as the grievous wrongs on the owners' part in maintaining the status quo came to loudly dominate the game's off-field narrative. Angell took the few work stoppages in the 1970s in stride, though with caution; none of them resulted in the cancellation of regular season games, yet the forebodings were vivid. The 1981 strike hit Angell deeply, as it cancelled over seven hundred games and forced a split season. In the July 6, 1981, *New Yorker*, Angell addressed the nearly month-old strike in a "Comment" piece, presented, in throwback style, as a letter from a "friend of ours here in the city." The interruption of baseball and its rhythms and comforting, familiar annual contours clearly affected Angell. He recounts a cab drive up Sixth Avenue with his wife, Carol, after seeing some friends in the Village—it's a summer evening, a week or so into the strike—and how he was hit with a "terrific jolt of unhappiness and mourning" when he recognized that there was no baseball news on the cab's radio. "Without knowing it, I had been waiting for those other particular sounds, for that other part of the summer night, but it was missing, of course," he writes, "no line scores, no winning and losing pitchers, no homers and highlights, no records approached or streaks cut short, no 'Meanwhile, over in the National League,' no double-zip early innings from Anaheim or Chavez Ravine, no Valenzuela and no Rose, no Goose and no Tom, no Yaz, no Mazz, no nothing."

As an "attentive and patient fan," Angell knew that he'd wait out the unprecedented strike until it was settled, finding other diversions to fill the "empty evenings and morningtimes I had once spent (I did not say 'wasted'; I would never say 'wasted') before the tube and with the sports pages," adding, "It might even be better for me to do without baseball for a while, although I could not imagine why." But this "brave nonsense" was obliterated in that moment in the quiet cab, and "suddenly the loss of that murmurous little ribbon of baseball-by-radio, the ordinary news of the game, seemed to explain a lot of things about the much larger loss we fans are all experiencing because of the strike," among them the choruses of late-night baseball scores, the sound of a ballgame on television in a near room, and the "baseball conversation in the elevator that goes away when two men get off together at the eleventh floor, taking the game with them."

Contemplating the abstract, "riverlike flow of baseball," Angell pulls wide and makes contact with eternal qualities of the game, moved and risking the kind of sentimental "goo" that he abhors in so much baseball commentary. He observes, with the air of a solemnly poetic natural scientist, "The slow, inexorable progression of baseball events—balls and strikes, outs and innings, batters stepping up and batters being retired, pitchers and sides changing on the field, innings turning into games and games into series, and all these merging and continuing, in turn, in the box scores and the averages and the slowly fluctuous standings—are what make the game quietly and uniquely satisfying." Baseball streams before fans, unceasingly, throughout the summer—"it is one of the reasons that summer exists"—and wherever we happen to be "on its green banks we can sense with only a glance across its shiny expanse that the long, unhurrying swirl and down-flowing have their own purpose and direction, that the river is headed, in its own sweet time, toward a downsummer broadening and debouchment and to its end in the estuary of October."

Perhaps recalling endless afternoons along the Hudson as a boy at Sneden's Landing, vacationing with his parents and sister, Angell ends the "Comment" with the appearance of "river people"—those who grow up or spend time alongside or near a river—who can "count on the noises and movement of nearby water, even without knowing it, and feel uneasy and unaccountably diminished if they must move away for a while and stay among plains inhabitants." The situation is almost that bad for baseball fans during this delay in the game, Angell laments, "but it is worse than that, really, because this time it is the river that has gone away—just stopped—and all of us who live along these banks feel a fretful sense of loss and a profound disquiet over the sudden cessation of our reliable old stream." Angell gathers himself enough to report that the central sticking point of the strike involves compensation for owners who lost a player to free agency, "but what compensation can ever be made to us, the fans, who are the true owners and neighbors and keepers of the game, for this dry, soundless summer and for the loss of our joy?"

Four months later, in "Asterisks," his grumpy summation of the fractious and glued-together '81 season and postseason, Angell cries out again from the fan's perspective. "Fans looking back on the strike—this fan among them—can hardly remember now what it was all about," he protests. "They were left with the numbing knowledge that they were never consulted about it and that, as usual, they have no place to go with their grievance. They sense that the old fixed shape of the game has shifted somehow, away from its past pleasures and assured summer sounds and rituals, and that the only response available to them now is to give way to their anger—to care less about what they once cared about so much, and perhaps to stay away from games altogether." He adds gravely, "They have been silenced." The discovery Angell makes in these obligatory and unhappy siftings through the strike and its aftereffects is large-minded and unsurprisingly familial in theme: "What is going on here, I believe, is the same old psychodrama about American fathers and sons, work and play, money and sex and sports." On other occasions Angell has likened the owners to distant, imperious father figures, envious of the players' youth, beauty, talent, easy access to casual sex on the road, and, most of all, their immense promise yet to be fulfilled.

Casting owners as bitter dads living their lost youth vicariously through ball-playing sons might be seen as a carelessly generalized or sentimental rhetorical gesture, yet little of what Angell writes is not thoroughly and thoughtfully considered, and this view of the owners is of a piece with Angell's long-standing sense of, and identification with, baseball as a figurative extended family, at times warmly intimate, at other times rancorously feuding. In 1996 he wrote that baseball provides for players and fans alike as many "interconnections and possibilities and opportunities for interesting disaster as a Cheever Thanksgiving dinner," on another occasion recalling that when he was young and there were only sixteen MLB teams, the same clubs "turned up again at Yankee Stadium with something like the frequency of a persistent aunt at home." (Elsewhere he writes that as he grew into his teenage years, he began to think of those teams as "personalities—sixteen different but familiar faces ranged around a large dinner table, as it were.") At Yankee Stadium the voice of esteemed public-address announcer Bob Sheppard "fell over the big crowd like a father's voice at the dinner table, conveying news, continuity, and patience, and a light-baritone blanket of calm." Upon Yankee great Mariano Rivera's retirement in 2013, Angell noted that imagery of the pitcher's storied delivery has been "as familiar to us as our dad's light cough from the next room, or the dimples on the back of our once-three-year-old daughter's hands, but, like these, must now only be recalled."

After the Yankees' talented and popular catcher Thurman Munson died when the plane he was piloting went down in August

1979, Angell mourned him in "Wilver's Way," his season and postseason recap, in the November 16 *New Yorker*. Angell was a month away from his sixtieth birthday when Munson died, and the tragedy triggered an unusually personal response in him. The death "kept coming back as a shock and a loss. I was startled, because I was certain that my admiration for the many hundreds of gifted or brilliant players I have watched was based almost entirely on how they played the game; I had always tried to concentrate more on what they did on the field than on what they said or who they seemed to be away from the diamond," adding, "It was all right, or almost all right, to be a middle-aged fan as long as I had this sorted out." But Munson's death resonated at a deeper, more profound level. "Now I am beginning to suspect that athletes may play a larger part in our lives than we are willing to admit. Without our quite being aware of it, they may have begun to seem like members of our family, or like trusted friends."

Angell confesses that he may know more about two or three dozen ballplayers than he does about some of his own friends, the intimate circle of which is closing, inevitably. "I can only conclude that these adopted, seasonal relatives have filled a real need for me, and perhaps for other fans as well. The lives of most baseball players may be trifling, but there is always fresh news of them; something is happening to them every day, which is more than we can say with certainty about ourselves." Sounding a theme long present in his baseball writing, he adds, "Belonging anywhere now is terribly difficult, I think, and the old childhood dream of *really* belonging will not go away. . . . We want to know all about ballplayers, because then somehow they will know about *us*, and then we will belong, too." "Sometimes I wish I had private portraits, of friends or loves gone by, that stayed as clear as these," he admits on another occasion. Given his own temperament and psychologies, his parents' divorce and the hush surrounding it, his complicated family past, his affection for the game and its players, many of whom he's become friendly with, Angell likely would find it impossible to ignore the domestic themes and the scrim of family identification through which he's long viewed the game.

In the mid-1990s the relationship between the symbolic sons and fathers reached a grievous breaking point. The owners had long felt that a hard salary cap was crucial to the game's healthy future and that unless teams agreed to share local broadcast moneys, the so-called small-market teams (Pittsburgh, Kansas City, Baltimore, and Montreal among them) would wither on the vine; the players fiercely opposed a ceiling erected over their hard-won salaries and limits on their freedoms to negotiate. Why should they be penalized for the owners' willingness to pony up dough to attract elite star players to their teams? Owners' representative Richard Ravitch revealed the ownership proposal on June 14, 1994; $1 billion in salary and benefits for the players was guaranteed, but among other changes, salary arbitration—the opportunity, after a numbers of years in the game, for a player to have his worth to his team calculated by an objective third-party, a particular nuisance to the owners and a hard-earned prize that the players cherished—would have been abolished.

On July 18 executive director of the MLB Players Association Donald Fehr rejected the owners' offer. Four months later, on New Year's Eve, Major League Baseball's collective bargaining agreement expired with no new agreement signed, and the consequences were inevitable: the players voted to strike. Baseball's eighth work stoppage was by far the longest interruption in the game's history, forcing the cancellation of 948 games in total. The walkout lasted 232 days, wiped out the remainder of the 1994 season, and erased the possibility of a postseason and World Series, the first time that the Series had been cancelled since 1904. (That Series would have pitted the American League's Boston Americans—now the Red Sox—against the New York Giants.)

After the 1981 strike Angell admitted to some reluctance in taking up position along the old riverbank again. ("Like a lot of other fans, I was slow to come back to the games.") A dozen years later that unwillingness morphed into something graver. He wrote a small piece titled "Bad Call" in the days before the 1994 strike began, and the *New Yorker* featured it as the sole "Comment" in the August 15 issue. "Without realizing it, the clueless owners surely envision the players as their psychic sons: kids who play a game for a living, who have been handed far too much money for their own good (who could have done a thing like that?), and who get all the girls. All because they got lucky at this easy-looking but weirdly elusive sport—they could actually hit the ball now and then, which is something that their dads and the rest of us could never pull off."

Two months later, deep in the cold dark of the lost postseason, the game's present in disarray and its future in flux, Angell posits the unthinkable: "The owners (and the players, too) may not welcome any suggestions from me about where the money should come from to rebalance their playing field and put their finances in order—although I can think of six or eight ways to set about this—but what they do need is to find a way to invite me, and millions like me, to come back to their waiting parks first thing next spring. . . . I'll probably want to go, but right now—and here's another baseball first—I'm not too sure about that."

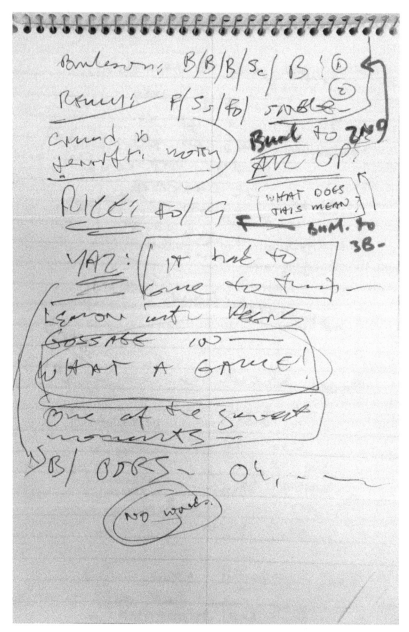

Angell's notes for the New York Yankees–Boston Red Sox playoff game, October 2, 1978. National Baseball Hall of Fame and Museum.

You Want to Laugh, You Want More, You Want It to Be Over

People ask me what I do in winter when there's no baseball.
I'll tell you what I do. I stare out the window and wait for spring.

ROGERS HORNSBY

On March 31, 1995, Judge Sonia Sotomayor of the U.S. District Court for the Southern District of New York issued a preliminary injunction against baseball team owners, effectively prohibiting them from using the replacement players they'd threatened to employ in order to spur a new season. Players returned to work on Sunday, April 2, and play resumed on April 25. The season lasted 144 games and was the first to feature the Divisional Series in the playoffs, in which a wild card team battled the winner of one of the three new divisions. (In 2012 a second wild card team was added to the postseason.) The Atlanta Braves beat the Cleveland Indians in the World Series, four games to two.

Of course Angell returned when play resumed. "I came home from Arizona and unpacked, and in a twinkling, it seemed, found myself hurrying down the gum-blackened, malodorous steps of the IRT 161st Street El station on my way to another season." The strike couldn't stiff-arm him for long, despite the somber sighing and wintry concerns he voiced at the time in the pages of the magazine. "Nothing had changed: the cops and Sabrett wagons, the TV trucks and pigeons and handball players, and, of course, Yankee Stadium itself, patiently waiting there for us—the same junky old high-wall sanitarium, and, inside, swarms of pale-faced fellow-inmates, released to the yard after our long stretch in solitary, gravely shaking hands and squinting in the thin spring sunshine." For many fans, the egregious and protracted strike, the images on television and in newspapers of untouchable millionaires glaring at each other across tables in sealed-off boardrooms, permanently marred the so-called national pastime. Scores of fans stayed away when play resumed and for a long time afterward.

A year or so after the resolution of the strike Angell sat onstage at a baseball reading and discussion in San Francisco. He faced out at the crowd, one member of which admitted bitterly that he'd given up on the game, so disgusted was he by the strike and by the owner-player dramas. "For once, the right answer came to me, there on the spot, instead of later," Angell recalls. "I said I'd heard that the San Francisco Symphony was also out on strike just then. How was that going?

"'Yes, they are,' [the fan] responded. 'It doesn't look good. They've been out for a couple of months now.'

"'And you?' I said. 'You've given up on Mozart and Chopin and Schubert forever?'

"My wiseguy answer drew a mixed response—there were laughs and a few boos, and then applause—but suddenly I felt great about baseball again and terrifically lucky to be a part of it. For me, the music was still playing."

Autumn baseball paradoxically renews. At midsummer, for all of its deep, sunlit pleasures, baseball is "slovenly and excessive," Angell observes, "with its onrolling daily cascade of line scores and box scores, shifting statistics, highlights and lowlights, dingers and shutouts, streaks and slumps, DL listings, rumors, trades, yesterdays blown saves, tomorrow's starting pitchers, and (here it comes again on the replay!) the never-seen-before catch at the wall." Contrary to other sports, baseball demands a "summing up and restoration of order at the end of the season." On another occasion Angell remarks that baseball "is such a powerful, and complicated, and beautiful sport that every year in the post season it renews itself, and people begin to watch games from beginning to end, because they care, or they get hooked. And then, over a period of three weeks to a month people go, 'Wow, wow,' people who don't really pay much attention to baseball saying that all over again." In the fall of 1975, startled by the epic greatness of the Boston Red Sox–Cincinnati Reds battle, Angell acknowledged simply: "Much is expected of the World Series."

Angell cherished the 1933 fall matchup between his New York Giants and the Washington Senators, the first Series he avidly followed. He listened to the action at his home on Ninety-Third Street, a thirteen-year-old glued to the RCA Stromberg-Carlson radio, keeping score pitch-by-pitch, his "interior stadium" alight. Listening, he imagined the throng of more than twenty-eight thousand spectators in Griffith Stadium in the District of Columbia, then a sleepy Southern town; he pictured the geometry of Mel Ott's homerun in Game Five and Fred Schulte at the wall— and then *over* the wall—attempting to snag it; he cheered as the Senators' hopes were snuffed when Dolf Luque struck out Joe Kuhel on three pitches to end the Series, the first to go the Giants' way in a decade.

Alas, Angell's first swing at a postseason recap for the *New Yorker* resulted in a dribbler to the mound. The 1962 San Francisco Giants–New York Yankees matchup took nearly two weeks to play out, affected by rain delays on both coasts and, consequently, by a deadline back at the office. Games Five and Six, in New York and San Francisco respectively, were postponed by showers, so Angell had little choice but to file a truncated summary, concluding his October 20 piece by admitting to an "odd conviction that this championship can have no satisfactory conclusion." A victory by the Yankees "will merely encourage smugness among their adherents, whose mouths are already perpetually stuffed with feathers, and will reinforce the San Francisco fans' conviction of their own fundamental insufficiency." The defending champion Yankees did indeed eventually win the Series (though no one, least of all Angell, could have sensed that the great Yankees would soon face a string of meager years) with a famous—*in*famous in the Bay Area—Game Seven, in which the Giants, down by one run in the bottom of the ninth, brought their slugger Willie McCovey to the plate with two out and with Willie Mays at second and Matty Alou at third, ninety feet from home; McCovey smacked a hard liner off of Yankee pitcher Bill Terry right at second baseman Bobby Richardson, who moved a step and a half to his left and snagged the streaking ball with his glove—the game, and Series, over. Had nature cooperated and allowed Angell a full reportorial shot at these games, he would've marveled at this moment, in his seat in the stands at chilly Candlestick Park. (A decade later in *The Summer Game*, he tacked on a summarizing note to the Series.)

What Angell couldn't find room for was an observation he'd made at Yankee Stadium after Game Three, which the Giants lost by a run (coming agonizingly close on catcher Ed Bailey's two-run blast in the top of the ninth inning). On his yellow, folded-in-thirds page of game notes, he'd scrawled: "After the game: Carl Hubbell on subway platform, signs auto[graph] with left hand. Rides car with hand over face." Underneath Angell wrote, questioningly, "HOW USE" and an arrow pointing back to the note. Ultimately he couldn't find a place in the piece for this startling image of his boyhood hero, whose pitching hand the teenage Angell had so often mimicked by turning his own hand outward as he walked his school's corridors and who here, thirty years later, long retired but on the Giants' payroll for life, fresh with familiar defeat in his old, East Coast city, hides his face with that famous Hall of Fame paw.

Postseason heroics magnify under the gaze of millions. Often unlikely and surprising feats enter the history and iconography of the game, and the World Series has provided numerous theatrical moments: Babe Ruth's "Called Shot" in Game Three of the 1932 World Series; Willie Mays's epic catch in center field in the first game of the '54 Series; Don Larsen's perfect game in '56; Bill Mazeroski's deciding home run in Game Seven of the '60 Series; Reggie Jackson's three home runs in Game Six of the '77 Series; umpire Don Dekinger's blown call at first base in Game Six of the '85 Series; Kirk Gibson's cinematic game-winning pinch-hit homer in the first game of the '88 Series; Jack Morris's ten-inning shutout victory in Game Seven of the '91 Series; the Arizona Diamondbacks' stirring, come-from-behind Game Seven upset of the Yankees in the 9/11-shadowed 2001 Series; David Freese's two-strike, two-out, bottom-of-the ninth game-tying triple in Game Six of the '11 Series. And so on.

Nearly overcome by gloom in "Cast a Cold Eye" in November 1976, Angell roused himself to recap one of the more iconic postseason baseball moments of the 1970s. Chris Chambliss's bottom-of-the-ninth, game-winning home run in Game Five of the 1976 Championship Series between the New York Yankees and Kansas City Royals is remembered mostly for its aftermath: the vivid assault of the field by overjoyed (and overserved) Yankees fans and Chambliss's tense, insane attempt to circle the bases and touch home plate. In describing the homer and subsequent bedlam in cinematic terms, Angell turns chaos and frenzy into a crisp, vivid story; his writing is evocative and deceptively organized, simultaneously reveling in the present-tense madness of it all and taking it in with a wide-angle lens, offering further evidence that no one describes a plate appearance quite like Angell. "Frame 1: Chris Chambliss has just swung at Mark Littell's very first pitch of the ninth inning, a fastball," he writes. "He has swung from the heels, and the ball is now suspended somewhere out in the darkness above the right-center-field fence. Chambliss stands motionless at the plate, with his feet together and the bat still in his right hand and his head tipped back as he watches the ball—watching not in admiration (as Reggie Jackson has been known to do) but in true astonishment and anxiety."

In Frame 2 Al Cowens and Hal McRae, the Kansas City center fielder and right fielder, stand at the outfield wall, "waiting and looking straight up in the air, like a pair of bird-watchers anxious to confirm a rare species." In the third and fourth frames McRae leaps for the ball yet comes down empty-handed; Chambliss leaps joyfully in the fifth frame and begins to round the bases,

> running slowly at first and then (Frame 6, Frame 7) with increasing attention and urgency, as he sees surging, converging waves of out-scattering, frantically leaping spectators pouring onto the field from the left-field and right-field grandstands. These people sprint through descending streamers of toilet paper and torn-up newspaper and other debris, and through the reverberating, doubly and triply reechoed explosions of shouting. They all meet near second base—Chambliss, the thickening and tumbling crowds, the waves of noise, and the waves of people (multiple frames here, faster and faster, all blurring together)—and now it is plain that he is almost running for his life.

Chambliss is knocked down but rises, "holding on to his batting helmet and running now like a fullback, twisting and dodging through the appalling scene: attempts a mad dash to home, a new game—one for which we have no name yet, and no rules." Chambliss finally arrives at the dugout, "with his uniform shirt half torn away and the look on his face now is not one of joy or fear or relief but just the closed, expressionless, neutral subway look that we all see and all wear when abroad in the enormous and inexplicable city. Later, Chambliss comes back onto the ripped-up, debris-strewn field with two cops, and after a few minutes' search they find home plate and he steps on it." Angell didn't seem too pleased with the uncouth fans (he'd wag his finger at them for a few more years before shrugging his shoulders and accepting the clamor), but he was delighted that the game could still surprise him—us—with moments like Chambliss's homer and subsequent pent-up Bronx mania, which catapulted the Yankees into the World Series for the first time since 1964.

"Given a choice of watching a World Series or reading Roger Angell's account in *The New Yorker* months later, I'll wait for the Angell," David Remnick, then a young reporter for the *Washington Post*, wrote in the mid-1980s. A decade and a half later, now the editor of the *New Yorker*, Remnick accompanied Angell to Game Five of the 2000 World Series, "the greatest night of my life that didn't involve my family," he says. The two were high up in the left-field deck, where, as the game unfolded, Angell described watching Babe Ruth play and being at Ebbets Field for Game Four of the 1941 World Series, when Dodgers catcher Mickey Owen allowed a passed ball in the ninth inning, sending Tommy Henrich to first—Henrich later scored in the Yankees victory—and "being a baseball fan before you could know anything about the game other than read about it in the paper the next day, or attend the game. This was a magical thing for me." After the Series-clinching Yankees victory ("which pleased me"), Remnick accompanied Angell to the clubhouse, where by that point in his career "only a few players knew him, but it was very clear that the people who knew him best were people like Don Zimmer and Joe Torre, the elders of the game. So, that was thrilling."

A handful of well-played, nail-biting Series stirred Angell as a fan and a writer. For every unexciting or events-lacking Series sweep, there were the 1967, '68, '69, '71, '77, '91, and 2001 affairs, each epic and memorable in different ways, each affecting Angell deeply. During the eleven-year span between 1975 and 1986 several autumn skirmishes tested Angell both as a devotee and as a professional, inspiring him to some of his greatest and most personal writing about the game as he balanced intense, deeply pleasurable yet at times agonizing homerism with the objective and detached responsibilities of good writing and reporting.

Raised a Giants fan, Angell over time felt his "passionate boyhood attachments" weakened by the team's departure for San Francisco in 1958 and by the "pale neutrality of middle age." He grew to love the Boston Red Sox and New York Mets. (He's kept up with the Giants in San Francisco and harbors a lifelong, neighborly affection for and rooting interest in the Yankees, especially admiring the Joe Torre–Derek Jeter–Mariano Rivera era, though he has consistently and publicly disliked owner George Steinbrenner.) Angell covered the Mets in their inaugural season—in *his* inaugural season as a baseball writer—and the arc from their laughable growing pains to their eventual maturation into the 1973 pennant-winning and 1969 and 1986 world champion teams warmed his native, din-loving New York soul and strengthened attachments to the team.

The Red Sox were his mother's favorite team. His fondness for them deepened in flavor and complexity throughout the decades of regular family trips up to the Whites' farm in hilly Maine and the surrounding small villages stuffed with long-suffering Red Sox lifers, the ballgames on the radio, and baseball conversation, everywhere. In a letter from Brooklin, Maine, composed during the tense 1967 World Series between the Red Sox and the Cardinals, Katherine White wrote to her son that "the transistor [radio] goes everywhere and Andy tells me that the men who are building wooden frames and pouring cement for the dam across our brook have had transistors going through all the games." At Williams Store, where every man in town stopped at 6:30 in the morning to grab his *Bangor Daily News* (it's "the great yak yak place"), there was so much lively talk about the games, in addition to the standard town stuff, that people couldn't tear themselves away. "Now it is all Yaz and the Sox," she wrote, adding, "the lobster men are more interested in the games than in the price of lobster."

The sixth game of the 1975 World Series between the Cincinnati Reds and the Red Sox is widely considered among the greatest in

Series history. Played in Boston after three days of rain, the contest is infamous for Carlton Fisk's eleventh inning game-winning home run that permanently enshrined the catcher in the Icon Hall of Fame. As he sat in the stands surveying Fenway before that game, Angell was reminded of the privilege of attending ballgames at the park. "Maybe my last look at this beautiful landscape," he wrote in his notes, pridefully observing the field as if it were a national park—this in sharp contrast to his mood when the Series shifted to Cincinnati and to "the cheerless, circular, Monsantoed close of Riverfront Stadium," where the glass-walled, air-conditioned press box is "utterly cut off from the sounds of baseball action and baseball cheering." After a few innings there Angell began to feel as if he were "suffering from the effects of a mild stroke, and so gave up my privileged niche and moved outdoors to a less favored spot in an auxiliary press section in the stands, where I was surrounded by the short-haired but vociferous multitudes of the Cincinnati." A fan surrounded by fans.

A side-session: the 1975 Series allowed Angell a close-up look at Luis Tiant, one of his favorite players to write about. Angell admired the portly Cuban hurler's presence on the mound, which he found equal parts regal, confounding, and hilarious. In "In Search of a Season" in the July 1, 1972, *New Yorker*, writing in a consciously staccato, note-taking style, Angell memorably described the pitcher's lengthy deliberations on the mound during an inessential game against the White Sox at Comiskey Park: "Stands on hill like sunstruck archeologist at Knossos. Regards ruins. Studies sun. Studies landscape. Looks at artifact in hand. Wonders: Keep this potsherd or throw it away? Does Smithsonian want it? Hmm. Prepares to throw it away. Pauses. Sudd. discovers writing on object. Hmm. Possible Linear B inscript.? Sighs. Decides. Throws. Wipes face. Repeats whole thing. Innings 8: hours creep by. Spectators clap, yawn, droop, expire. In stands, 57 disloc. jaws set new modern AL record, single game. Somebody wins game in end, can't remember who." Three years later, at Fenway for Game One of the World Series, Tiant's as appealing and humorous as ever. "The venerable stopper . . . did not have much of a fastball on this particular afternoon, so we were treated to the splendid full range of Tiantic mime," Angell observed. "His repertoire begins with an exaggerated mid-windup pivot, during which he turns his back on the batter and seems to examine the infield directly behind the mound for signs of crabgrass. With men on bases, his stretch consists of a succession of minute downward waggles and pauses of the glove, and a menacing sidewise, slit-eyed, Valentino-like gaze over his shoulder at the base runner. The full flower of his art, however, comes during the actual delivery, which is executed with a perfect variety show of accompanying gestures and impersonations." Several case-study examples of Tiant's idiosyncratic deliveries follow, among them "Call the Osteopath," "Falling off the Fence," and "The Slipper-Kick."

By the time Game Six rolled around, Fenway Park was rigid with tension. "Game Six, Game Six . . . what can we say of it without seeming to diminish it by recapitulation or dull it with detail?" Angell wondered in his *New Yorker* recap. The legendary game was a seesaw affair, tied at three runs apiece in the ninth. In the bottom of that frame the Red Sox loaded the bases against Will McEnaney with a walk to Brian Doyle, a single by Carl Yastrzemski, and an intentional walk to Carlton Fisk, but Doyle, darting homeward on Fred Lynn's pop-up to left-field foul territory, was nabbed at the plate by George Foster's strong throw. Two innings later Joe Morgan hit a deep drive to right that Dwight Evans, twisting in pursuit, caught against the fence; Evans then doubled Ken Griffey off of first base. In his game notes Angell wrote, "WHAT AN INNING! *WHAT A* GAME*!* SOX ARE HARD TO BELIEVE." Later, in demonstrative red ink, he wrote in the margin about Evans's acrobatics: "KEY TO THE WHOLE GAME."

The affair went to the twelfth. After a Reds rally was snuffed in the top of the inning, Fisk batted against Pat Darcy, taking his second pitch deep and high to left field, where it caromed off of the foul pole. Of this famous and heroic home run, made vivid for generations to come by the televised image of Fisk willing the ball with flailing arms to stay fair, Angell wrote in his game notes simply: "HR OFF TOP OF FOUL POLE—glances off." Only when he was writing a week or so later did he consider the moment in context: "I was watching the ball, of course, so I missed what everyone on television saw." Angell watched Fisk circle the bases, surrounded by several hundred fans, and jump on home plate "with both feet, [while] John Kiley, the Fenway Park organist, played Handel's "Hallelujah Chorus," *fortissimo*, and then followed with other appropriately exuberant classical selections."

Earlier, in the anxious pause before the Red Sox came to bat in the bottom of the eighth inning, Angell had jotted a half-notion in his Steno pad: "Sudden thoughts of my friends in Maine, silent in front of their sets." After Bernie Carbo tied the game that inning on a two-out, three-run monster shot to the center-field bleachers, electrifying Fenway Park, Angell hurriedly scribbled, "What's happening in Brooklin <u>NOW</u>!" Working on his *New Yorker* piece later, filtering the thrill of that game through his years of Red Sox fandom, Angell composed one of his most moving passages on baseball and its deep and undying connections among fans, alive with a fiction writer's eye for rich, anecdotal detail and for large, familiar themes of belonging and cherishing, experienced from one's school days through to adulthood.

> For the second time that evening I suddenly remembered all my old absent and distant Sox-afflicted friends (and all the other Red Sox fans, all over New England), and I thought of them—in Brookline, Mass., and Brooklin, Maine; in Beverly Farms and Mashpee and Presque Isle and North Conway and Damariscotta; in Pomfret, Connecticut, and Pomfret, Vermont;

in Wayland and Providence and Revere and Nashua and in both the Concords and all five Manchesters; and in Raymond, New Hampshire (where Carlton Fisk lives), and Bellows Falls, Vermont (where Carlton Fisk was born), and I saw all of the dancing and shouting and kissing and leaping about like the fans at Fenway—jumping up and down in their bedrooms and kitchens and living rooms, and in bars and trailers and even in some boats here and there, I suppose and on back-country roads (a lone driver getting the news over the radio and blowing his horn over and over, and finally pulling up and getting out and leaping up and down on the cold macadam, yelling into the night), and all of them for once at least, utterly joyful and believing in that joy—alight with it.

A paragraph later, acknowledging that Reds fans were obviously more joyful, as their team beat the Red Sox in the seventh game, Angell allows his regional sentiments to widen and deepen, exploring the game's humane and generous aspects, a theme common to much of his baseball writing: "What I do know is that this belonging and caring is what our games are all about; this is what we come for. It is foolish and childish, on the face of it, to affiliate ourselves with anything so insignificant and patently contrived and commercially exploitative as a professional sports team, and the amused superiority and icy scorn that the non-fan directs at the sports nut (I know this look—I know it by heart) is understandable and almost unanswerable. Almost." What such a reckoning ignores, Angell continues, is "the business of caring—caring deeply and passionately, really caring—which is a capacity or an emotion that has almost gone out of our lives."

And so it seems possible that we have come to a time when it no longer matters so much what the caring is about, how frail or foolish is the object of that concern, as long as the feeling itself can be saved. Naïveté—the infantile and ignoble joy that sends a grown man or woman to dancing and shouting with joy in the middle of the night over the haphazardous flight of a distant ball—seems a small price to pay for such a gift.

"Agincourt and After" ran in the November 17 *New Yorker*, the title a nod to the historic Hundred Years' War battle waged victoriously by the English over the French on October 25, 1415; Angell described Game Six as Boston's Agincourt, a stout and historic, if draining, victory. Three years later the Red Sox and their weary fans would find their mettle tested yet again. On the last day of the 1978 season the Red Sox and New York Yankees, each with 99 wins, found themselves tied for first place in the American League East Division. In mid-July the Yankees had been 14 games out of first place, but the Red Sox suffered a frightful collapse in September, and the dangerous Yankees charged Fenway Park on October 2 for a one-off playoff game to determine the East Division winner. The game is infamously remembered, painfully by Red Sox fans, for Bucky Dent's seventh-inning three-run home run into the screen above the Green Monster that gave the Yankees a slim one-run lead. Just prior to Dent's homer, Angell had written in his game notes, "It's still extremely quiet here. <u>The Silent Game</u>." After the blast he wrote: "And now it <u>is</u> quiet here. I can't believe it."

The Red Sox would draw within a run in the bottom of the eighth against closer Goose Gossage. Angell was watching the game from his customary place in the press box, but his heart was in the stands. Stirred by the game's excitement, he abruptly moved from the press box to the "dark, ancient grandstand" along the first base line "among hundreds of clustered, afflicted rooters who had gathered behind the sloping stands for a closer look at the end of it." "I'm in crowd with weak knees," he scribbled in his notes. After Rick Burleson walked, Jerry Remy struck a drive to right field, where Lou Piniella, though blinded by the intense, late afternoon sun, snagged the ball on a hop, holding Burrelson at second. Jim Rice flied out to right, and Burleson moved to third. "Crowd is terrifically noisy," Angell wrote in his pad, standing shoulder-to-shoulder with hoarse Boston rooters. Carl Yastrzemski strode to the plate with the tying run at third. "A whole season, thousands of innings, had gone into this tableau," Angell wrote later. "My hands were trembling. The faces around me looked haggard. Gossage, the enormous pitcher, reared and threw a fastball: ball one. He flailed and fired again, and Yastrzemski swung and popped the ball into very short left-field foul ground, where Graig Nettles, backing up, made the easy out. It was over."

Angell's game notes, scrawled in his ruled steno pad under high-pitch tension and alongside jostling fans, are barely legible. Deciphered, they reveal his deep and abject disappointment as a longtime Red Sox fan and Yastrzemski admirer. "YAZ: it had to come to this— . . . Gossage in—WHAT A GAME! One of the great moments—."

He then writes: "POPS—Oh,—NO words."

Angell eventually found the words. A week or so later, high above West Forty-Third or in the reflective stillness of his apartment, he took a wide-angle lens on the setback. "In the biggest ballgame of his life, [Yastrzemski] had homered and singled and had driven in two runs, but almost no one would remember that," he wrote in "City Lights: Heartthrobs, Prodigies, Winners, Lost Children" in the November 20 *New Yorker*. "He is thirty-nine years old, and he has never played on a world-championship team; it is the one remaining goal of his career. He emerged after a while, dry-eyed, and sat by his locker and answered our questions quietly. He looked old. He looked fifty." Angell quoted Emily Vermeule, a professor of classics at Harvard, who days after the game had written in the *Boston Globe* with Senecian stoicism, "The hero must go under at last, after prodigious deeds, to be remembered and immortal and to have poets sing his tale." Angell understood this. "I will sing the tale of Yaz always," he wrote, "but I still don't quite see why it couldn't have been arranged for him to single to right center, or to double off the wall. I'd have sung *that*, too. I think God was shelling a peanut."

Throughout the summer of 1969 the team that Angell had observed as it bumbled its way through its inaugural season provided fans with the thrills of winning and not a little cognitive dissonance. "Disbelief persists, then, and one can see now that disbelief itself was one of the Mets' most powerful assets all through the season," Angell wrote in "Days and Nights with the Unbored" in the November 1, 1969, *New Yorker*. "Again and again this summer, fans or friends, sitting next to me in the stands at Shea Stadium would fill out their scorecards just before game time, and then turn and shake their heads and say, 'There is no way—just *no* way—the Mets can take this team tonight.' I would compare the two lineups and agree." Late that evening or the next morning, marveling at yet another improbable victory by the onrushing Mets, Angell would "find it hard to recall just how they *had* won it, for there was still no way, *no* way, it could have happened." These Mets, "the famous and comical losers," were a squad "that had built a fortune and a following out of defeat and perversity, a team that had lost seven hundred and thirty-seven games in seven years and had finished a total of two hundred and eighty-eight and a half games away from first place. No way, and yet it happened and went on happening." The terrific Series that pitted the Mets against the heavily favored Baltimore Orioles, which the Mets won in five, was for Angell "an assemblage of brilliant parables illustrating every varied aspect of the beautiful game."

Struggling to describe just how the confetti-laden Amazin's had pulled off a magical season and a more magical October, Angell fell back on the vagaries of the game itself. In addition to stout pitching, timely hitting, sharp defense, cunning managing by Gil Hodges, fizzy youth, and old fashioned luck, it was likely that these "intuitive, self-aware athletes sensed, however vaguely, that they might be among the few to achieve splendor in a profession that is so often disappointing, tedious, and degrading," he wrote. "Their immense good fortune was to find themselves together at the same moment of sudden maturity, combined skills, and high spirits. Perhaps they won only because they didn't want this ended." He added, "Perhaps they won because they were unbored."

A decade and a half later Angell found himself in a delectable bind. Loud and momentous postseason events, marked by tense, bruising games and hysterical, hard-to-believe changes of fortune, brought his two favorite teams face-to-face in the World Series. Angell was watching with a racing heart and a mild concern for bias. "As readers of these reports may know by now," he wrote in "Not So, Boston" in the December 8, 1986, issue of the *New Yorker*, "I am a baseball fan as well as a baseball writer (most scribes, however grizzled and game-worn, are fans at heart, although they love to deny it), and although I am capable of an infatuated interest in almost any accomplished or klutzy nine that I happen to watch over a span of four or five games, the true objects of my affection down the years have been the Mets and the Red Sox." He added, "I have written almost as many words about these two clubs as I have put down about the twenty-four other major-league teams combined." It did not occur to Angell he might be forced one autumn to "discover and then declare an ultimate loyalty." Figuring that the odds against any two particular teams meeting in a Series were great, he'd felt "safe in moonily wishing for this dream date: when it came closer, during this year's pennant races and then again late in the playoffs, I became hopeful and irritable, exalted and apprehensive, for I didn't know—had no idea at all—which outcome would delight me if they did play, and which would break my heart." He sighed, "In dreams begin responsibilities, damn it."

The 1986 Series is remembered chiefly for the larger-than-life sixth game at deafeningly noisy Shea Stadium and for first baseman Bill Buckner's tenth-inning error in that game that delivered the heartbreaking climax of Boston's multi-act fate. A win away from their first World Series in seven decades, the Sox held a 3–2 lead going into the bottom of the eighth, needing only six more outs to vouchsafe New England. But a Lee Mazzilli single, a sacrifice bunt by Lenny Dykstra moving up Mazzilli, a bunt by Wally Backman, and an intentional walk to Keith Hernandez loaded the bases for Gary Carter, who hit a deep fly to left to score Mazzilli with the tying run, sending Shea Stadium and most of Manhattan and Queens into tumult. Neither team scored in the ninth inning, setting the stage for the tenth, in the top of which the Red Sox scored twice, on a Dave Henderson home run (Angell in his notes: "Shea goes dead—a great lid on the bowl") and a single by Marty Barrett knocking in Wade Boggs from second. Heading into the bottom of the inning—it was past midnight, by now—the Red Sox, three outs from victory, sent in Calvin Schiraldi for his third straight inning of relief; he quickly induced noise-cancelling fly ball outs by Backman and Hernandez.

What occurred next, Angell wrote, "happened slowly but all at once, it seemed later." Facing elimination, Carter and pinch hitter Kevin Mitchell each singled, and Ray Knight, enduring a two-strike, Series-ending count, also singled, scoring Carter. With Shea thundering, Red Sox manager John McNamara brought in Bob Stanley to face Mookie Wilson, who'd also during his at-bat face a two-strike count; on his seventh offering Stanley uncorked a wild pitch, and Mitchell scurried home with the tying run. Wilson then hit a meek ground ball to Buckner at first. Hobbling from season-long ankle and shin injuries, Buckner couldn't get his glove down effectively, and the ball scooted through his legs into right field. Knight roared around third with the winning run. Shea devolved into bedlam; Boggs crumpled into tears on the visitors' bench; millions watching at home sat in disbelief. In his game notes Angell wrote, "Horribly sad for Buckner.—Jesus.

What a way to go—." adding, in concert with countless grieving Sox fans: "Why was he still in there?"

Angell had been watching, marveling, and agonizing from his seat high above home plate, but between halves of the tenth inning he moved down to the main press box, "ready for a dash to the clubhouses." There he spied a handful of Mets fans, "sadly coming along the main aisles down below me, headed for home." The scoreboard operator had mistakenly flashed a "Congratulations!" to the Red Sox for their Series victory. The Sox clubhouse had been champagne-proofed in sheets of plastic, prepared for festivities as television cameras and Bob Costas waited to fete the victorious, long-due Red Sox. Writer Nicholas Dawidoff, a twenty-three year-old reporter in 1986, recalls being near Angell and sportswriter Peter Gammons in the press box that night. "Throngs of sportswriters were climbing aboard the elevator to see the Red Sox as they came inside to celebrate the long-awaited triumph," he wrote. "Mr. Angell and Mr. Gammons, however, didn't move, so neither did I." When the ball rolled between Buckner's legs, Dawidoff had the feeling that "we were the only three left up there to see. It's as if they knew."

It wasn't to be. Two days later the Sox lost Game Seven, 8–5, and the Mets—more than once a strike away from losing the Series—were world champions.

Three hastily written observations in Angell's '86 Series notes reveal the games' wear and tear on his fidelity:

(1) Between the halves of the tenth inning of Game Six, he wrote, "I think that I'm a METS FAN." He commemorated this unvoiced epiphany with two big, cheery stars. Yet moments later he scribbled, "AH, NEW ENGLAND!!!—At Last??"

(2) After the game he wrote—he *confessed*: "I've never run on the field—but I ran on the field." This he circled.

(3) Moments before Game Seven, he was still undecided. "Here we go! And who am I for?" He supplied the answer underneath, in minuscule handwriting: "The <u>Mets</u>, I realize." He circled this too.

Angell often referred to the Mets as "we" and "us" in his game notes, his allegiance to the team that effectively replaced his beloved Giants made clear by the swiftness of pen. "There was a surprise for me, there at the end," he wrote several weeks later. "I am a Mets fan. I had no idea how this private Series would come out, but when the Mets almost lost the next-to-last game of the Series I suddenly realized that my pain and foreboding were even deeper than what I had felt when the Red Sox came to the very brink out in Anaheim [in the American League Championship Series against the California Angels]. I suppose most of my old Red Sox friends will attack me for perfidy, and perhaps accuse me of front-running and other failures of character, but there is no help for it." He added, "I don't think much has been lost, to tell the truth. I will root and suffer for the Sox and the Mets next summer and the summers after that, and if they ever come up against each other again in the World Series—well, who knows? Ask me again in a hundred and sixty-seven years."

Of course the Red Sox eventually claimed a World Series title in 2004, winning again in '07 and '13. Reflecting after the third triumph, Angell acknowledged that the so-called Curse of the Bambino and the "New England paranoias" that comprised his writing and "night thoughts for so many years" have vanished. Yet he added, "Winning almost all the time has a lot to be said for it, but not quite winning, barely missing again and again, keeps you whining and breathing, and might even be more fun in the end."

In his notes to "Distance," his profile of Cardinals pitcher Bob Gibson, Angell jotted down a revealing directive: "*Use a lot of myself." Angell indeed figures prominently in "Distance." He visits Gibson at his home and place of business, and rather than hover on the edges of the piece, he centralizes his point of view and personal attitude about Gibson. Yet this impulse to insert himself into his work is rare. In his baseball writing readers occasionally catch a glimpse of Angell's family members, a reference to a summer cottage in Maine, or a colleague or three but few details that shed light on his private life. Around the time he began his career in baseball writing, his marriage to Evelyn ended. In 1964 he wed Carol Rogge, who'd worked at the *New Yorker,* and in 1970 they welcomed a son, John Henry. Carol had attended Bucknell University and Teachers College at Columbia University's Graduate School of Education, worked for some time as a copy editor at *American Heritage,* and then joined the faculty at the all-girls Brearley School on the Upper East Side of Manhattan, where she worked in the Department of Reading and Testing and was chair from 1997 to 2006. Roger and Carol remained together until her death in 2012.

In 1973 Ernest Angell died. Angell's relationship with his father had always been complex, his parents' largely unspoken feelings about their divorce dovetailing with Ernest's wounded dignity and his game, if complicated, commitment to raising his sister and him. "'Parenting' in its contemporary sense was not a concept most fathers would have understood back then," Angell reflects, "but if it was pride that first made him fight to keep his children, he then plunged right ahead with fatherhood, striding up its trail at full charge." Ernest's remarriage in 1939 to Elizabeth Brosius Higgins lasted until her death in 1970. They raised twins, Abigail and Christopher, with whom Angell is still close.

Ernest was fiercely athletic and spirited, and he passed on his robust energies and *joie de vivre* to his son. ("Unlike his colleagues, [Angell] is intensely competitive," remembered longtime *New Yorker* writer Brendan Gill. "Any challenge, mental or physical, exhilarates him. . . . Angell's mastery of certain unexpected feats—for example, his ability to leap straight up onto a table from a standing start—fills the rest of us with awe.") "The plain truth about him," Angell remarked about his father at a memorial in New York a month after his death, "was that he remained a young man all his life."

Closing in on his thirtieth birthday, Angell wrote "Tennis," a short story that appeared in the July 8, 1950, *New Yorker* and that he included in *The Stone Arbor*. The narrator recounts his history of playing against his father, a tireless competitor and a very good player, even into his forties. The narrator "never played well against him" the many times they battled, once churlishly reacting to a girlfriend who'd admired out loud his father's athleticism. (Angell wrote to his editor Gus Lobrano: "I think that [the narrator] would hate to admit to the girl that his father was remarkable," before adding, "Maybe I'm wrong about this.") He admits that he felt shame as a boy as he watched for the first time as his father lost a game and then greater shame when, later, he privately hoped that his father would lose to a younger player. The father and son got along well, but beneath the surface was a competitive streak and a battle for vigor and potency. Near the end of the story the father suffers a heart attack. He's forced to give up the game. Later, as the narrator plays a casual match with friends, his enfeebled father watches nearby from a chair. He remains alive at the story's close. "I'd never wanted to beat him—not really," the son reflects at the end. "I think I had only wanted him to notice me, but he'd been too busy living up to something he'd promised himself a long time before. All that time, all those years, I had only been trying to grow up and he had been trying to keep young, and we'd both done it on the tennis court. And now our struggle was over."

Unsurprisingly all of this was thinly veiled. Angell acknowledged years later that the story "drew heavily on the struggles [he] was still experiencing in beating Father at singles." Angell shared the story in its manuscript stages with Ernest, "who saw the connection, of course" and who told his son how proud he was of him. Life would imitate art: "Four or five years after this, almost inevitably, after my father and I had been playing Sunday doubles together at his friend Stuart Chase's court in Redding, he complained in the car of a heaviness and some twinges in his chest: a full-blown coronary, it turned out." Angell called a doctor. As his father waited calmly, "lying out on an old Victorian sofa in his tennis whites," Angell ventured to him, "This is weird, isn't it?"

"'I've been thinking that, too,' he said, with a little gleam of pleasure.

"'Just remember the script,' I said. 'If you die now, I'll never forgive you.'

"'O.K.,' he said, 'I won't die.' And he didn't—not for a long time." At Ernest's memorial, Angell spoke of his father's spirit, of his

> Joy. Dash. Verve. Panache . . . detergent nouns [that] keep their energy and meaning when we think of this man. There was about him a youthfulness and fervor that somehow seem to belong to the century in which he was born. I think we can call it naiveté, if we understand it as a life-giving and essential and conserved naiveté that may be the ultimate attribute of a truly civilized and contemporary man. All of us must learn innocence from our fathers now, if we are to survive, and we can be grateful for these vivid and cheerful lessons. The ball is still in play.

Ernest lived long enough to see that his son dedicated his first baseball book to him.

Katharine White passed away in 1977; eight years later her devoted husband, E. B. White, followed. Katharine had been in declining health in the later years of the marriage—skin disease, a spinal-fusion operation, a procedure to clear a carotid artery, and painful bone deterioration from steroid treatments—and in old age her lifelong propensity toward worry had come in large part to define her. Angell's memories of his mother and step-father are heartening and respectful, shot through with deep admiration for their lifelong work and romantic partnership but complicated by the couple's elder-years illnesses (in Andy's case mild hypochondria and, near the end of his life, a serious fall at the farm in Maine). "To me, the Whites' later concern with their health was a substitute joint effort, more loving than angry, and constituted a fresh form of intimacy as the two grew older," Angell wrote in 2005. "Andy missed the joy and youth that he had known in my mother and the passion that she had brought to her work as an editor, an obsessive gardener, and a non-stop letter-writer; once he told me how he mourned the day when she decided that she'd have to give up her evening Martini or Old-Fashioned." He adds, "I've come to believe that his anxieties were a neurotic remnant of childhood" and that "what is certain is the way that writing about death became a strength for him, and brought a lasting power in his best work."

Two years after his mother's death Angell wrote about the surprisingly deep pleasure he experienced from Willie Mays's election to the Baseball Hall of Fame. "I suspect that his enshrinement allowed me to remember Mays as he had been in his wonderful youth," he writes,

> the brilliant boy gliding across the long meadows of the Polo Grounds, or running the bases in a cloud of speed and dust and excitement—and to forget the old, uncertain, querulous Willie Mays who came to the Mets in his final few seasons and who had so clearly stayed too long in the game. The shift in my feelings was like the change that sometimes comes when we remember a close relative or a friend who has died in old age or after a long illness; suddenly one morning, our sad last view of that person fades away and we are left instead with an earlier and more vivid picture—the one that stays with us. It is a miracle of sorts.

A quarter century later, in "Here Below," an essay he wrote about his mother, Angell names William Maxwell as the source for this wisdom. Maxwell—a novelist and short story writer who served as a fiction editor at the *New Yorker* from 1936 to 1975— had remarked to Angell that "one of the great mercies we are provided with is that within a few months after someone close to us has died the vision of him in sickness or great age is replaced with a much younger memory of that same parent or husband or friend, now seen at his youthful best." Angell acknowledges gratitude for Maxwell's insight, "and later passed it on unhesitatingly to others, in letters of condolence, but now I'm not so sure. Most memories of my mother are affectionate and cheerful, but still center on the bottomless worries and overthoughts that descended on her late in her life."

Angell is private, though he is not shy. "He's not a hidden person," *New Yorker* editor David Remnick insists. "He's an emotional person. If you're his friend, he'll tell you a lot about how he's feeling, good, bad, and indifferent. And I value that. He's one of the least aloof people I've ever encountered." Yet Angell has spent the better part of his career writing personally rather than autobiographically, offering a carefully crafted persona that avoids intimate confession, though, in the long view, his themes of the urges to belong, the need to care, the whims of luck, and the binds of family are clear. And, of course, deeply personal.

He grew up with models of compositional reserve. "I was strongly influenced by the *New Yorker* conventions and the *New Yorker* writers, and by other writers, like Red Smith," Angell acknowledges, adding, "One of my big models was E. B. White— Andy White, my step father."

> If you read him, he can be intensely personal, but if you think about it—since I knew him—he's not showing much of himself at all. He's giving personal impressions of what he sees or thinks, but he doesn't tell much about himself, he doesn't talk about his family. In *One Man's Meat* he talks about his growing son—his son Joel, my brother, a kid doing this or that—or "My wife said . . . ," but it's not revelatory, it's not personal at all. It's not private. No, never.

Elsewhere Angell wrote of his stepfather's "instinctive, lifelong sense of privacy—a dated, almost Victorian consideration in these confessional times." Angell "comes from a background where you were simultaneously expected to be monastically devoted to your writing but completely unaffected about it," *New Yorker* staff writer Adam Gopnik remarks. "That's E. B. White. So I think if Roger ever stopped to think about *What is my real subject here?* he would feel that he couldn't go on writing. He would lose his monastic concentration on the writing in goo and blather."

As many young fiction writers do, Angell often used autobiographical materials in his stories. One case is the memoiristic "Tennis." A lesser known story, Angell's second appearance in the *New Yorker*, is "One for All." It ran on October 7, 1944, and is set in a classifications office at an Overseas Replacement Training Center, where Sergeant Longcope, a clerk, has convinced his captain that he, Longcope, belongs in public relations, not in the battlefield. The autobiographical details in "One for All," however camouflaged, are striking. While Europe was torn irrevocably, Angel was at a remove in Honolulu, reporting and writing for *Brief.* "I've kept quiet about my trifling Army career all these years," he wrote decades later, "because I was ashamed of my safe, lowly status." He'd known college friends who'd become commanders, many who'd seen active combat, and many who'd perished in that combat—all while he was "playing house," in his phrase. "I'd not been in the war, exactly, but like others back then I'd got the idea of it."

In the late 1980s, taking the opportunity to glance back at his career and mull the occasions of his work, Angell offers a particular definition of his impulse to write: "Friends and critics have sometimes called me a historian of the game or a baseball essayist or even a baseball poet, but I decline the honors. It seems to me that what I have been putting down for a quarter century now is autobiography: the story of myself as a fan."

And yet that fan's complex interior life—web of family connections, griefs, and complications—remains distant to the reader. Angell remarked in a 1988 interview with the SABR *Review of Books* that he views himself as a reporter. In a revealing aside he adds, "In my case, which is probably different from other writers, because of the space I am given, baseball is also a way of writing about myself." Acknowledging his fan credentials in 1982, he said, "I'm a fan, and one of the things I've permitted myself is to let my feelings show," adding, "So there's a lot of agony, a lot of self-examination." "He's certainly not merely a reporter, by any stretch of the imagination," Remnick observes.

Angell's hesitance in seeing himself as an essayist stems in part from the tradition he was writing in at the *New Yorker*, a magazine that historically has resisted the term "essay," preferring the more casual "piece." Adam Gopnik sensed this "bit of *New Yorker* affectation" upon his arrival at the magazine in the mid-1980s. "James Baldwin wrote a 'piece' and A. J. Liebling wrote a 'piece.' Not an 'article,' I should add. 'Articles' have a message, and we didn't in those days publish pieces with messages in that way. An article is about a trend, whereas a piece is reporting on an event. You can either think of it as a faith or an affectation, depending." However, Gopnik feels ("because I'm more corrupt") that Angell is an essayist more than he is a sportswriter. "The crucial thing about an essay to me is that it has an ostensible object and some other subject, whereas an 'article' or sports writing is about baseball, and it's about baseball—it's the subject and the object. In Roger's work, as in any first-rate essayist's, the objects and subjects are different. In a broad sense he's writing about baseball, but his subject is really belonging and all the varieties of belonging." He adds, "I say this with a catch in my throat because I know that Roger hates the kind of 'Roger Kahn/American Pastoral/I'm not really writing about baseball I'm writing about America' thing—he despises that kind of stuff, that kind of talk, really hates it with a passion. So I shudder when I say that his subject is different from his object, but it's just that his subject is as interesting as his object. We wouldn't respond to it as readers do if that weren't the case."

"The word 'essay' was verboten at the magazine," Charles McGrath acknowledges. "Roger's essays were just called 'The Sporting Scene,' but they were sui generis. He kind of invented this thing as he went along. And of course they changed. The pieces in *A Summer Game* really are essays, but as he got deeper into it, the essayistic thing gets submerged, I think. It comes up in a paragraph here and a paragraph there, but then you get real reporting. I don't know that the essayistic thing could've gone on forever for Roger; had that been, he would've turned into Bart Giamatti, this kind of maudlin elegist." "I'm not some 'poet laureate,'" Angell insists. "I'm not writing poetry. That sounds as if I'm doing no reporting, and that's not the truth. If you do enough reporting, then you don't have to gush about the emerald field, the white streak of the ball, and that."

McGrath too remarks on the lasting effect of E. B. White on Angell, "a huge influence, an empowering one, and it so easily could've been crippling. Instead it became something else." Angell wrote in the American essay tradition, McGrath concedes, but "his fictional background comes into it also, because there's a lot of very good scene-setting, perhaps not a characteristic essay trait, and at times the wealth of detail and the amount of dialogue that goes into a classic Angell baseball piece." He adds, "Roger would never say it, but his work is running parallel to the so-called New Journalism. He's doing some of the same kinds of things." Angell as an essayist is a "late development," Remnick feels, "unless you count reported narrative nonfiction as essay writing. I don't, but I could easily accede to your saying it is. He's definitely working in that tradition."

Angell's attitude about exploring his past in his writing changed dramatically in the 1990s during Tina Brown's reign as editor of the *New Yorker*. When Brown arrived at the magazine in 1992—succeeding Robert Gottlieb, whose five-year stint contrasted with the long tenures of founding editor Harold Ross and of William Shawn—she found Angell to be a friendly presence in a sometimes vexing work environment. Angell supported Brown and the bulk of the major, often controversial, aesthetic and editorial changes she made to the magazine. "When I first met him, everybody said, 'Oh Roger Angell, you're gonna have a tough time with him,'" Brown recalls.

> I was warned that he'd be curmudgeonly, that he would be somebody who would resist my ideas and my presence, that he was difficult. But actually he was incredibly welcoming because he believed in the *New Yorker*, didn't he, to do work in our factory, and he had a lot of his own feelings that the magazine had become stale. He wanted to give me a chance, and he was very helpful to me. He really was somebody I could turn to and ask for advice in an unvarnished way. He never, ever gave me anything but the truth. He has tremendous integrity like that. If he didn't like a piece, he'd absolutely say it, or he'd send me some kind of sharp, grumpy note. And I always paid attention!

Brown swiftly learned that as a "born bread-and-butter *New Yorker* writer," Angell was wonderful to converse with, that as they talked she realized "what a wonderful, interesting life he had and what a marvelous observationalist he was and a witty eye, and I also found pretty much everything out of Roger's typewriter was worth publishing. He would write memos that were critiquing things, or just his way of expressing himself at all times was entertaining. There was nothing that Roger could write, as far as I was concerned, that wouldn't entertain." She adds,

> One of the things that I try to do as an editor is really learn who that writer is. And one of the things I learned is that when you talk to writers about their life, you get all kinds of ideas of

what they may be writing about but perhaps they're not writing about now. I also tend to feel that the way they keep fresh as writers and stretch themselves is by taking on other things. And I felt that Roger should be writing about his own life. It did seem to liberate a vein in him that he hadn't tapped before.

Adam Gopnik acknowledges that Brown "encouraged a lot of the veterans, like Bud Trillin and Lillian Ross, not to shy away from more direct personal revelation. It was certainly the case that it was seen as an ideal at the magazine, even when I arrived, that you would write a first-person piece in which there would be absolutely no self-revelation of any kind! That was the goal. Not because it was seen as wrong to be revelatory, but you did the revelation through description and invocation rather than through direct confession."

"Roger's writing about baseball was perfectly candid, although I think it allowed him a deliberately limited show of his personality," says Daniel Menaker, former *New Yorker* fiction editor. "He was candid in his baseball writing and sometimes direct and critical, but always genial. I don't think he was being a hypocrite. I think he was genuinely that way, but it didn't allow the other parts through. There was not deeply intimate or embarrassing material in his baseball writing." David Remnick adds, "The character of quote-unquote Roger Angell, is to some degree, as it is in all the best writing, a thrown character. He's ebullient; he's enthusiastic; he's a happy, an intelligently happy enthusiast persona. It's not all of who Roger is. So it's a thrown character, to some extent." Charles McGrath insists, "He's too private to be a real autobiographer."

Indeed initially Angell balked at the notion of writing autobiography. "He said, 'Oh, I don't do that,' in that wonderfully curmudgeonly way," Brown recalls. "But I kept pushing. I can't remember when the dam broke, but he decided to do it." Brown knew in advance of her arrival that *New Yorker* literary conventions were quite formal. "It was a generational thing at the magazine, of keeping yourself out of the work."

And baseball was Roger's subject, and some people can only write about their subject. It was a different philosophy than what I have of editing. People at the *New Yorker* tended to get their beats and stay in them, whereas my whole thing was breaking people out of them. I think Roger just gets better and better the more he's packed into who he is. He's an old part of a certain era and generation who felt perhaps talking about things personal was somehow not done. And once that vein was tapped, it turns out he had so much to say.

Angell acknowledges as much. "Tina Brown came along and changed everything for me," he says. He gathered his scattered autobiographical essays, many of which he'd written under Brown's prompting, in the memoir *Let Me Finish*, published in 2006 to great acclaim. Mark Singer, a *New Yorker* staff writer and a longtime friend of Angell's, feels that these essays were Angell's way of "averting a biography, though I don't know if he thought of it that way. Roger loves to tell stories, he loves to have command of a group of people he's talking to. He's a wonderful storyteller and all that, but he's also shy and not always eager for attention. It's a paradox." Angell himself notes that these late excursions into personal writing weren't all-out confessionals. "In writing about myself, I'm still quite reserved," he says. "I'm not trying to get even with anybody or push things aside or reveal secrets. It's personal but not confidential."

"Early Innings," one of Angell's first essays in this vein, ran in the February 24, 1992, *New Yorker* as a "Personal History" and stayed within familiar white lines. A ruminative stroll through Angell's formative baseball memories, which often revolve around his father, the essay was the first occasion when he fully explored his autobiographical roots in the game.

He writes about attending early games at the Polo Grounds and Yankee Stadium and listening on the family radio, about his boyhood love for playing baseball and his dawning awareness of his limits of skill and drive, and of his favorite players and the poetry of their quirky names, still vivid to Angell decades later. (In his notes to the essay he wrote, "For a 10–13-year-old, names like this are the first real suggestion of the size of the world, and its flavor—its oddities.") He recalls his indulgences of other sports, the excitable buzz in the earnest and urgent politics of the era. Ernest Angell is in many ways the heart of the essay, gliding along the pages with conviction and athletic ease. Angell recalls watching him wash rivers of dirt off of his hands after playing in a local pickup game and throwing the ball back and forth with him. "Yes, reader: we threw the old pill around," Angell writes with a smile, "and although it did not provide me with an instant ticket to the major leagues, it was endlessly pleasurable." At their Sneden's Landing cottage, Angell and his father would set up in front of an old shed for a backstop. "My father had several gloves of his own, including an antique catcher's mitt that resembled a hatbox or a round dictionary. Wearing this, he would squat down again and again, putting up a target, and then fire the ball back (or fetch it from the weeds somewhere), gravely snapping the ball from behind his ear like Mickey Cochrane." When the occasional pitch from young Roger would thump firmly in his father's mitt, "he would nod silently and then flip the pill back again."

When Angell was sixteen, he worked for a summer in Missouri on a ranch and farm owned by an uncle and aunt. His father drove out from New York to visit and "soon discovered that there would be a local ballgame the next Sunday, with some of the hands on the ranch representing our nearby town. Somehow, he cajoled his way onto the team (he was close to fifty but looked much younger); he played first base, and got a single in a losing cause." Angell was sent in to pinch-hit in the late innings of the game. "The pitcher, a large and unpleasant-looking young man, must have felt distaste at the sight of a scared sixteen-year-old dude standing in, because he dismissed me with two fiery fast-balls and then a curve that I waved at without hope, without a chance." His father remained silent, but later, "perhaps riding back to supper, he murmured, 'What'd he throw you—two hard ones and a hook?'" Angell nodded, his ears red. "There was a pause, and Father said, 'The curveball away can be very tough.' It was late afternoon, but the view from my side of the car sud-denly grew brighter."

Such memories, which Angell affectionately carried with him for decades but which rarely found their way into his baseball writing, comfort Angell, of course, but raise a customary, cau-tionary flag. "It is hard to hear stories like this now without an accompanying inner smirk," he acknowledges. "We are wary of sentiment and obsessively knowing, and we feel obliged to put a spin of psychology or economic determinism or bored contempt on all clear-color memories." He adds, "My father was knowing, too; he was a New York sophisticate who spurned cynicism. He had only limited financial success as a Wall Street lawyer, but that work allowed him to put in great amounts of time with the American Civil Liberties Union." In those days, "The news was always harsh, and fresh threats to freedom immediate, but every problem was capable of solution somewhere down the line. We don't hold such ideas anymore—about our freedoms or about anything else. My father looked on baseball the same way; he would never be a big-league player, or even a college player, but whenever he found a game he jumped at the chance to play and to win."

Angell ends "Early Innings" in melancholy resignation. "If this sounds like a romantic or foolish impulse to us today, it is because most of American life, including baseball, no longer feels fea-sible." After instant replay and the avalanche of statistical data, we know everything about the game now, he sighs, and "what we seem to have concluded is that almost none of us are good enough to play it. Thanks to television and sports journalism, we also know everything about the skills and financial worth and private lives of the enormous young men we have hired to play baseball for us, but we don't seem to know how to keep their salaries or their personalities within human proportions." He adds, somberly, "We don't like them as much as we once did, and we don't like ourselves as much, either. Baseball becomes feasible from time to time, not much more, and we fans must make prodigious efforts to rearrange our profoundly ironic contemporary psyches in order to allow its old pleasures to reach us."

Let Me Finish will likely be regarded as among Angell's finest books. "I'd not planned a memoir, if that's what this is," he writes frankly in the book's introduction, "and never owned a diary or made notes about the passage of the days." For an untutored autobiographer, Angell produced a sturdy collection that adds dimension and depth to his persona and that brims with the narrative details, wry skepticism, anti-nostalgia, humor, and wide-angle wisdom that characterize his greatest baseball writing. In "Getting There," which he had originally attempted as a short story many years earlier, he can't quite recall a woman's physical appearance, "but when I thought of her golf swing, she'd reappear." He might as well have been writing about a long-forgotten journeyman Giants pinch-hitter from the 1950s. The essays move among portraits of Angell's parents; early, baffling romances and schooling; his experience during World War II; and lighter fare, such as favorite drinks, the many branches of his family tree, memories of long-ago movies and old colleagues, and Maine sailing, a passion for Angell that nearly rivals baseball. In composing these essays, most of which were written in a creative burst over a three-year period in the early 2000s, Angell makes contact with the seductive and complex authority of memory. "Our stories about our own lives are a form of fiction, I began to see, and become more insistent as we grow older," he observes. "Even as we try to make them come out in some other way." He adds that he doesn't pine for the past and, smartly, doubts that he could've written these intensely personal essays if he had. In *Let Me Finish* Angell allows the past, with its wealth of major and minor joys and losses and its private griefs to come to him.

"They're beautiful, great pieces," says Janet Malcolm, a long-time *New Yorker* writer. "They're Roger at his best, but he's almost always at his best." Malcolm's late husband, Gardner Botsford, edited Angell's baseball writing for many years, and she recalls that Botsford often wished that Roger would explore something other than baseball. "Had Gardner lived, he would've been so delighted by seeing the latest genre that Roger's working in. These personal essays would've pleased him." She adds, "I think maybe that's what he was thinking of, that it was all there, and he wished Roger would do that. And then Roger did."

Nearing his one hundredth birthday, more or less retired from the *New Yorker*, Angell still visits the offices, drops in on friends and colleagues, an icon on the outside looking in. Such informal trips have been curtailed considerably since early 2015, after the magazine moved downtown to the Condé Nast headquarters at 1 World Trade Center, having earlier departed the longtime offices on Forty-Third Street for 4 Times Square. All told, the enterprise is no longer a neighborhood hangout for Angell.

He still pops up in the print magazine. "Over the Wall," Angell's moving tribute to his wife, Carol, who died in May 2012, appeared in the November 19 issue that year. "What the dead don't know piles up," he writes," though we don't notice it at first. They don't know how we're getting along without them, of course, dealing with the hours and days that now accrue so quickly, and, unless they divined this in advance, they don't know that we don't want this inexorable onslaught of breakfasts and phone calls and going to the bank, all this stepping along, because we don't want anything extraneous to get in the way of what we feel about them or the ways we want to hold them in mind." But, he adds, "they're in a hurry, too, or so it seems." Grieving, Angell describes the beauty of his wife's hands, writes affectionately of her mild phobias and her tenderness and sociability, and closes the essay with a visit to her grave in the Brooklin, Maine, cemetery, where she lies very near Angell's mother and E. B. White and where Angell will one day rest too.

On February 17, 2014, readers of the *New Yorker* opened the annual anniversary issue to find, on page 60, a rare sight: a photo of Angell himself, sitting comfortably on a bench in Central Park, wearing a cap and holding a dark walking cane, gazing agreeably into the camera, his terrier Andy at his side. The photo accompanied "This Old Man," a landmark essay arriving as it did in Angell's sixth decade as a contributor to the magazine. The piece "presented itself unexpectedly one morning," Angell remarked. He wrote it in a week. Perhaps the surprise of its arrival accounts for its remarkable vulnerability and frank honesty. Reflecting on aging, its difficulties, pleasures, and wonders, Angell takes stock of himself physically—the essay opens in close-up, with a litany of his various bodily ailments; at ninety-three, he's suffered arthritis, macular degeneration, arterial stents, a heart clamp, weak knees, a herniated disc, rapidly deteriorating vision in his right eye, and one or two other minor setbacks—but he's as interested in the emotional and psychological sturdiness of the old man.

Loss, of course, permeates the essay. He writes of the heartbreaking death of his and Carol's beloved terrier Harry, who'd innocently leapt out of the couple's half-open apartment window ("I knew him well and could summon up his feelings during the brief moments of that leap: the welcome coolness of rain on his muzzle and shoulders, the excitement of air and space around his outstretched body"); memories of his retrieved body, splayed on the bathroom floor, and of his and Carol's uncontrollable weeping spur the frank revelation of a greater, more confounding loss: the suicide of his daughter Callie two months prior. "The oceanic force and mystery of that event had not left full space for tears," Angell wrote. "Now we could cry without reserve, weep together for Harry and Callie and ourselves. Harry cut us loose."

Why am I not endlessly grieving? Angell wonders. Friends and family help, as do surprising casseroles at the front door; memorizing light verse to keep the brain active; blogging; an evening scotch (Dewar's) with the Yankees on television; and daily walks, when possible, with Andy, the new terrier. Memories, stray or overwhelming, come unbidden and are usually fleeting. "Carol is around still, but less reliably," he writes. "For almost a year, I would wake up from another late-afternoon mini-nap in the same living-room chair, and, in the instants before clarity, would sense her sitting in her own chair, just opposite. Not a ghost but a presence, alive as before and in the same instant gone again. This happened often, and I almost came to count on it, knowing that it wouldn't last." He adds, "Then it stopped."

Angell squarely takes on mortality, "this hovering knowledge, that two-ton safe swaying on a frayed rope just over my head, that makes everyone so glad to see me again." Death is Angell's private, approaching visitor, but it is, he notes, on the news every moment, for all of us, no matter how old we are, or aren't: "We have become tireless voyeurs of death," he sighs, adding, "There's never anything new about death, to be sure, except its improved publicity. At second hand, we have become death's expert witnesses; we know more about death than morticians, feel as much at home with it as those poor bygone schlunks trying to survive a continent-ravaging, low-digit-century epidemic. Death sucks but, enh—click the channel." Such availability of the dead and dying may have inured us to its sobering finality, he muses, and at what cost?

Angell's at his most vulnerable when he complains of his "invisibility" in social situations (that old man going on again, to whom we politely listen before we resume the urgency of our, more youthful, matters) and when he turns his attention to physical desire, the "unceasing need for deep attachment and intimate love." Clear-eyed forthrightness in tension with Angell's still-palpable grief over losing Carol—she was seventeen years younger than he; "we had a different plan about dying," he'd written dryly in "Over the Wall"—these passages reveal a level of intimacy and wounded dignity scarcely present in Angell's baseball writing or even in his recent autobiographical essays. "No personal confession or revelation impends here," he writes near the finish, "but these feelings"—sensual longing—"in old folks are widely treated like a raunchy secret. The invisibility factor—you've had your turn—is back at it again. But I believe that everyone in the world wants to be with someone else tonight, together in the dark, with the sweet warmth of a hip or a foot or a bare expanse of shoulder within reach. Those of us who have lost that, whatever our age, never lose the longing: just look at our faces. If it returns, we seize upon it avidly, stunned and altered again."

"This Old Man" was widely applauded, remarked upon, and enthusiastically pinged around the Internet, Angell's first viral piece (and at age ninety-three!). Angell selected it as the title essay for a collection of miscellany—blog posts, reviews, profiles, obits, personal and professional correspondence, verse, "Talk of the Town" and "Comment" pieces, and of course some baseball things—published in 2015. "'This Old Man' is a really great piece," Tina Brown enthuses. "When I read it, I was really happy to see Roger doing this because it's a great voice now applied to the great subject of his own aging. It was just brilliant to read." "This Old Man" was awarded the 2015 Essays and Criticism prize from the American Society of Magazine Editors, remarkably Angell's first National Magazine Award. He acknowledged the essay's "amazing response," and was startled that "often children of old people have written me. . . . I think maybe because it's sad and because it's funny." "It's reassuring about their parents," he said on another occasion. "It's also reassuring about them. It's reassuring [to hear] that being old is—well, not easy, and not terrible, but better in some ways than we used to think." Elsewhere he remarked that the essay "brought a rush of personal and posted mail" and "more kindness than anything else I've written," adding, "That was a good day."

Always the long baseball seasons beckon, March to October, stuffed with trifling wins and heartbreaking losses and the steady accumulation of numbers and pleasures. Angell still watches and listens, blogging at the *New Yorker* occasionally during the season and serially during the postseason.

Angell's first blog post, about the actor Tommy Lee Jones, went live on October 5, 2008; his first baseball post, on Red Sox manager Terry Francona, appeared twelve days later. "We all shifted over," he says about blogging. "It was what to do. You can do something quick or something a little bit longer. It's over with in a moment. I enjoy it. It's short, and you don't have to take a million notes." In their imposed brevity his posts call to mind the writing of Red Smith, Angell's early writing mentor. "I think that blogging was a gift to him," Ann Goldstein, who edits Angell's posts, remarks. "He didn't like writing long pieces any more. It had to do with memory, as he's written about. Holding a whole piece in his mind was not something he felt he could do the way he used to, and he adapted to the form immediately, and he still writes these great sentences, with amazing metaphors and liveliness. Roger's a very good self-editor. Usually I just point things out to him, a long sentence, or a repetition, or something that the fact-checker caught." She adds, laughing, "*Very* occasionally the grammar!"

Angell continues to keep abreast of changes and developments in the game. During the vexing steroids era he remained skeptically philosophical where other commentators were reactively indignant, dryly citing the long history of deception in the game, from players gobbling energy-boosting "bennies" midcentury to the tradition of sign-stealing to doctored balls and corked bats to the radically differing, home-team-favoring dimensions and

grounds crew ministrations at ball parks. He was an early sup-
porter of Bill James and the Sabermetric revolution. As early as
1970 Angell observed that on the new AstroTurf playing fields, "a
thrown or batted ball jumps off the ungrass with such alacrity that
anything hit up the left- or right-field power alley almost invariably
streaks through for extra bases, but outfielders who remember to
keep their pegs down low"—to take advantage of the AstroTurf
bounce—"suddenly discover that they all have developed shot-
gun arms." He adds, skeptically, that this has altered the game in
"ways that have yet to be measured—if anyone should ever care
to conduct such useless, *ex post facto* researches."

Four years later Angell began to characteristically evolve on
the page, alert to the usefulness of valuing statistics as they form
"the critical dimension of the game. Invisible but ineluctable,
they swarm and hover above the head of every pitcher, every
fielder, every batter, every team, recording every play with an
accompanying silent shift of digits." Observing what future Saber-
metricians will ponder, he acknowledges that there are aspects
of the game—say fielding—that "are not perfectly measurable,
and good or bad managerial thinking is similarly obscure." He
adds, "None of this is secret; none of it is hard to understand.
The averages are there for us all to read and to ponder, and
they admit us to the innermost company of baseball." The true
fan, "comfortably at home with his newspapers and *The Sporting
News* and his 'Official Baseball Guide's and his various record
books and histories, notes the day's and the week's new figures
and draws his conclusions, and then plunges onward, deeper
into the puzzles and pleasures of his game."

One way Angell went deeper was to pay more attention and
respect to unconventional and refined ways of measuring suc-
cesses and failures on the field. "The great lesson that Roger has
for us all as people is to try and never become a Grumpy Old Man
in one's ideas of the world," Ben McGrath says. "He makes a point
of befriending the youngest people in the office every few years

because it keeps him fresh and gives him a reason to go to work. He's constitutionally receptive to new waves and phenomena because he believes that that's a virtue, essentially, as opposed to holding on to dogmas." Because Angell's way at looking at baseball is as a removed observer, as a fan, "anything that happens is good copy to him. This new group of people coming in with stats and computers, that's fun and something else to think about. He doesn't pick sides because he's not inside the game; he's outside the game. So it becomes yet another way in which this game obsesses and fascinates people and 'Isn't that interesting?'"

Yet as a fan who came of age in a less data-driven era, Angell remains comfortable with conventional, so-called back-of-the-card stats and will refer to this pitcher's win totals or that hitter's RBI numbers. In 2010 he couldn't resist poking some fun at the *Baseball Prospectus/Baseball Reference* crowd and its acronymic ways. "I treasure Bill James and can now readily employ the nifty sabermetrical OPS (On Base Plus Slugging) device to rate hitters," he blogged, "but I doubt that I will ever be entirely at home with the LI (Leverage Index) or the EXPWS (Expected Win Shares) or the EHL (Established Hit Level) in mulling over news of the pastime. I believe that I still know some stuff, however, and sometimes need only to slip in some formulaic representations of my own thinking to remind myself. I mean, I can see that Cliff Lee's UPUBB (Unexpectedly Passing Up Big Bucks) decision puts vastly more emphasis now on the Yankees' old WAPEAR (Will Andy Pettitte Ever Actually Retire?) dilemma." And so on.

Angell's most recent print postseason recap, "Daddies Win," appeared in the November 30, 2009, *New Yorker*. (The Yankees defeated the Philadelphia Phillies in the Series, four games to two.) Given his age and deteriorating eyesight, Angell no longer gets to the ball park. ("Nobody knows him there anymore," Charles McGrath remarks. "Which I think is sad and depressing.") He enjoys games on television with his wife, Peggy Moorman (whom he married in 2014), at home in Manhattan and at his beloved cottage in Maine, sitting close to the screen, aided by a magnifying glass and light apparatus and, here and again, by visiting friends. He still keeps score, posting his account of the heart-stopping sixth game of the 2011 World Series online at the *New Yorker*. Crammed with scrawled action, the scorecard looks like a storyboard for a Michael Mann thriller.

A grander celebration awaited. In 2013 Angell was awarded the J. G. Taylor Spink Award for meritorious contributions to baseball writing, voted by members of the Baseball Writers' Association of America (BBWAA). Named for the publisher and second editor of the *Sporting News*, the award was inaugurated in 1962 and had traditionally feted members of the BBWAA only. "Over the passage of the years there were a lot of writers who thought that I should be in Cooperstown," Angell acknowledged a few years before his election. "Some of the significant writer friends of mine, like Jerome Holtzman, who was the head of the Baseball Writers' Association at the time, launched a campaign to have me put in. And he got nowhere because of guys who felt I wasn't the real thing." He added, "And I, of course, never got a baseball writer's credential because you have to belong to a daily [newspaper]. And various people wrote or said, 'Well this is silly, let Roger in.'"

Susan Slusser of the *San Francisco Chronicle*, president of the BBWAA in 2012–13, had for some time been urging the New York chapter to nominate Angell but to no avail; she recommended Angell via the Bay Area chapter, and, at long last, he landed on the ballot. "I have been reading his work since I was 9," Slusser, a sportswriter herself, wrote, "but I never would have supposed that many mortals could write at that inspired, genius level. All Roger Angell ever has inspired me to do is to read more of his work." *New Yorker* editor David Remnick, opining on the occasion of Angell's election, wrote, "Not to be peevish, but the award is a teensy bit belated." The first non-BBWAA writer selected, Angell joined such lauded scribes as Holtzman, Ring Lardner, Grantland Rice, Fred Lieb, Damon Runyon, Shirley Povich, Dick Young, Murray Chass, Peter Gammons, Bill Madden, and his early mentor, Red Smith. "I'm really touched to see that [Smith] won this award earlier, so to be in the same room with him, so to speak, is very touching," Angell said.

The ceremony was held on July 27, 2014, at the Baseball Hall of Fame in Cooperstown, New York, during the annual inductions ceremonies. Twenty-five years earlier Angell had identified as a Hall of Fame skeptic. "I had resisted it, all these years," he wrote in "Up at the Hall" in the August 31, 1987, *New Yorker*. "I've been a baseball fan all my life—starting long before the Hall of Fame opened, in 1939—but lately when each summer came along I realized once again that I preferred to stay with the new season, close to the heat and fuss and noise and news of the games, rather than pay my respects to baseball's past. Cooperstown seemed too far away, in any case, and I secretly suspected that I wouldn't like it." He added, "I was afraid I'd be bored—a dumb idea for a baseball fan, if you think about it."

He warmed to the Hall over the course of his visit, and over the years, and though he remained doubtful of some of the overly earnest, Grand-Old-Game glories of the place, he was aware of affectionately embodied histories there too. In his notes to "Up at the Hall" he describes a visit to Doubleday Field, the local, charmingly rickety ball field built in 1920, no doubt put in mind of a few of his favorite old parks from the past, admiring the "church steeple nearby in left and just beyond the RF foul line a swaybacked green barn." "But this field is used. . . . It belongs to the town." By 2014 Angell was thrilled to be standing in the sweltering sun on the same dais as fellow inductees Greg Maddux, Tom Glavine, Frank Thomas, Bobby Cox, Tony La Russa, and his old friend Joe Torre. "I was surprised to find how much I secretly hoped this would happen because I was very moved and startled and extremely pleased," he said.

Wearing his trademark cap and an open-collar white shirt and dark blazer and not a little frail in his manner, Angell began his speech by indulging the familiar litany of old-time baseball names, the ones that gave—that give—so much pleasure to say aloud. "My gratitude always goes back to baseball itself, which turned out to be so familiar and so startling, so spacious and exacting, so easy-looking and so heart-breakingly difficult that it filled up my notebooks and seasons in a rush," he said. "A pastime indeed. Fans know about this too. Nowadays we have all sports available, every sport all day long, but we're hanging on to this game of ours, knowing how lucky we are." He sounded familiar themes. He recalled favorite players and their places of business. And he was, as always, careful to stress the difficulties of the game and the lessons we might learn, and forget and re-learn again, by observing the game's elegance and complexities. "Amazing men, extraordinary competitors, but there's too much winning here. Baseball is mostly about losing," Angel remarked, as many on the dais nodded along vigorously. "These all-time winners in the Hall of Fame are proud men—pride is what drives every player—but every one of them knows or knew the pain of loss, the days and weeks when you're beat up and worn down, and another season is about to slip away."

Angell thanked William Shawn, Robert Gottlieb, Tina Brown, and David Remnick for the decades of generosity, time, and space they gave and trusted him with. And he thanked baseball. His plaque now hangs in a quiet, sunny spot in the Hall near the library, just across from a corridor of windows that look out onto the statue courtyard, where, in the shade, Johnny Podres, pitching with his long follow-through, and Roy Campanella, squatting and receiving, are eternally playing.

First. In the sepia-tinged photograph, a small boy is pitching to his mother. It's 1931. The scene is pastoral, a vast field in apple-treed Bedford, New York. The boy is Angell, ten and half years old.

E. B. White is the photographer. Katharine White, in a "well-cut suit skirt and a silk blouse . . . in keeping with the Sunday-outing styles of that time," is exhibiting a superb batting stance at the plate, such as it is, her weight well-balanced, her front leg moving "boldly forward in preparation for the swing, which will initially take the bat up and back, then swiftly down into the reversing pivot and full-body turn that precede and accompany her Tris Speaker-esque, closed-stance cut at the ball." Down the decades Angell's pretty proud of his kid-heave to the plate too, "a combined heater and changeup that will parallel the lower profile of the apple tree and, descending, cross the plate hem-high: a pitch taken by my mom for a called—called by me—strike one."

Second. In the foreword to *The Summer Game*, his first baseball book, published in 1972, Angell reflects on his still-young career: "And this was the real luck, for how could I have guessed then that baseball, of all team sports anywhere, should turn out to be so complex, so rich and various in structure and aesthetics and emotion, as to convince me, after ten years as a writer and forty years as a fan, that I have not yet come close to its heart?"

Third. More than forty years after writing that sentence, in a blog post about the 2017 wild card game that propelled the New York Yankees into the Divisional Series to face the Cleveland Indians, Angell—wise, relaxed, grateful, ninety-seven years old now—wrote, "I will have an honorable fallback position if the Indians win, thanks to my father, who rooted for them throughout his life, without much reward. He was born in 1889, and his early home-town heroes were Nap Lajoie and Cy Young, at the dawn of the modern baseball era. Between us, we have this old game bracketed."

Home. "I'm not retired, which is good. So I'll keep at it. There will always be obituaries. At my age you write a lot of farewells."

Epilogue

Roger Angell died on May 20, 2022, at his home in Manhattan at the age of 101. He lives on, of course, in his many books, essays, casuals, and blog posts, in the extraordinary stories written by others who were graced by his editorial eye, and through his family.

He'd never really retired. He blogged at the *New Yorker* through 2020. Roger's final posts saw him weighing in on big events: memories of D-Day; imploring his readers to vote in the 2018 election; taking Donald Trump to task for his "grotesque display" at a presidential debate. The game he loved, of course, never deserted him. What turned out to be his final baseball post on May 2, 2018, was typically brief—blogging allowed Roger to weigh in on a moment or three in the games he chose to enjoy—and Angellian: an amused take on Houston Astros' pitcher Ken Giles's exit from an inessential May game after being shelled by the Yankees. Giles lost his temper on the way to the dugout. "What followed was transfixing, another Never Before," Roger wrote nearly half a century after his first *New Yorker* piece, "as the stalking-off Giles began punching himself, first in the chest and then in the jaw. The instant image was of a newborn flailing in his crib, and an adult baby." He added that the next night, "part of the fun will be watching Giles on the bench and looking for bruises."

A lifer fan, Roger indulged his native skepticism to the end. Speaking with Tyler Kepner at the *New York Times* in 2021, he complained about the new rule that placed a runner at second base at the start of each extra inning: "It violates everything in baseball. Every effort now is to shorten the game instead of letting it go on. The man on second is the first in baseball history to never earn what he got." He added, "There's an accounting for every space.

It balances, as we know. That's one of the fascinating, great things about the game. It balances so evenly and has so many astounding events in the middle of it." To the end, Roger was awestruck at the blend of surprise and routine so unique to baseball, and often doubtful of knee-jerk responses to dilute that mixture.

On August 8, 2020, a sunny Saturday, the town of Brooklin, Maine, threw a one hundredth birthday celebration for Roger on the lawn of the Friend Memorial Library. In front of an intimate, masked (it was the early days of the pandemic), and lively crowd, Maine governor Janet Mills proclaimed Roger Angell Day, thanking Roger and his parents for their long association with the library and praising him as a writer. "Roger Angell is someone who has used words to elevate us, to inspire us, to get at the truth," Mills observed. "He tells it straight. He writes about winning, and he writes about the pain of loss and regaining life again."

Roger sat comfortably on a tall stool on the library's banner-festooned porch, accompanied by his wife, Peggy, who'd occasionally whisper in his ear or adjust his microphone. He spoke for about nine minutes. He acknowledged that the governor was a new friend to him, noting wryly, "To make a new friend at this age is quite rare." He emphasized that though he was a born and bred New Yorker—someone *from away*, in the local parlance—he always felt deeply at home in Maine. He offered affectionate anecdotes about Peggy, thanked friends and family, and remarked that his mother exposed him to her children's book reviews in the *New Yorker* when he was a young boy, helping to set him along his literary path, "so thank you, mother." Roger's humor was sharp as he urged his guests to maintain social distancing, adding, to laughter all around, "If there's any impulse to rush the podium here and pick me up on your shoulders and carry me around, resist that, okay? Be careful."

He ended with a small story: a hundred years in the future "Zeke" and "Danny," two gents in their mid-sixties, find themselves in the Brooklin cemetery where they come across Roger's gravesite. "Wasn't he some kind of writer or something?" Zeke asks. "Yeah, yeah," Danny replies, "but, you know, he was *from away*." The crowd laughed warmly at the irony, the intimacies of this bright day ensuring that few city visitors would ever be as beloved in Brooklin as Roger was. The celebration ended with the crowd singing rousing versions of "Happy Birthday" and "Take Me Out to the Ballgame."

If I was startled to hear of Roger's death, it was because he'd been living his life so fully that the prospect of its ending had seemed remote, even as he lived beyond his hundredth year. Shortly after I heard the news I watched the Chicago White Sox host the Boston Red Sox. Boston's starter, the veteran Rich Hill, pitched well but ran into some difficulties in the middle innings. The Chicago announcer commented that Hill looked unhappy on the mound, and I instantly wondered—as I have countless times—what Roger would've made of the now-aggrieved Hill's countenance as he stared down potential trouble. It just as swiftly occurred to me, with a pang, that we'll never again enjoy a new observation—a new *sentence*—from Roger. His immense observational and writing gifts aside, there doesn't seem to be much room for long, languid, patient takes on baseball, where knowledge, amusement, curiosity, and skepticism blend, where the writing seems as boundless as the game itself. The great themes in Roger's baseball writing— the desire for community and attachment, the capacity and value of caring, the vagaries of luck—are eternal, and transcended the game. Simply put, Roger elevated the game of baseball; no one before or since has written about it as attentively and as thoughtfully, and with such droll literary panache. He loved baseball. He was endlessly enthused by its joys and disappointed by its disappointments, finding a cherished place there. The long seasons will go on, but something irreplaceable is now gone.

Notes

PREFACE

xiv   "We're all so impatient": Author interview with Angell, July 5, 2016.

xv   "stuffed with waiting": R. Angell, "That Yankee Win, Well Awaited."

TRYING OUT

1   On the afternoon of September 19, 1920: *New York Times*, September 20, 1920, 18; baseball-reference.com.

2   Born in 1889 in Cleveland, Ohio: "Ernest Angell, Lawyer, Dead"; R. Angell, "The King of the Forest," in *Let Me Finish*, 32; "Katharine White," A19.

3   "modern residence": "Tenement Deals," 36.

3   "like thousands of other young and youngish people": Franklin, "Lady with a Pencil," 429.

3   "I can hardly remember a time": K. Angell, "Home and Office," 318.

4   "My mother, for her part": R. Angell, "The King of the Forest," in *Let Me Finish*, 40.

5   Thus began young Roger's dual-home adolescence: Franklin, "Lady with a Pencil," 434.

5   "a big mistake for everybody": Mishkin, "One on 1 Profile."

6   "No Lincoln parent": R. Angell, "Early Innings," in *Let Me Finish*, 58.

6   "Tex saved my life": R. Angell, "The King of the Forest," in *Let Me Finish*, 44.

6   "The *lowly* Dodgers": R. Angell, "Early Innings," in *Let Me Finish*, 68.

7   "I liked it best": R. Angell, "Early Innings," in *Let Me Finish*, 61.

7   "If the Polo Grounds felt": R. Angell, "Early Innings," in *Let Me Finish*, 61.

8   "I listened either to Ted Husing": R. Angell, "Early Innings," in *Let Me Finish*, 71.

9   "There were occasional weekends": R. Angel, McGrath, and Miller, "Roger Angell Interview," June 4, 2010.

10   "I was entranced by Andy White": R. Angel, McGrath, and Miller, "Roger Angell Interview," June 4, 2010.

10   "When I got older, I realized": Haynes, "An Interview with Roger Angell," 134.

10   "I never had a choice": R. Angel, McGrath, and Miller, "Roger Angell Interview," June 4, 2010.

11   He asked for some help: "Angell, Roger, Editorial Correspondence, 1939," *New Yorker* records (hereafter NYR).

12   "*Brief* had already started": Author interview with Angell, July 5, 2016.

12   A twenty-page weekly: wartimepress.com; R. Angell, "To Herbert Mitgang," in *This Old Man*, 148

12   "My column was about anything": R. Angel, McGrath, and Miller, "Roger Angell Interview," June 14, 2010.

13   "I'd just had a story published": R. Angell, "Permanent Party," in *Let Me Finish*, 187.

14   "I'm going to *stop* this": R. Angell, "Three Ladies in the Morning," 55.

14   Angell was twenty-three: R. Angel, McGrath, and Miller, "Roger Angell Interview," June 14, 2010.

15   "practically a suburb of Buffalo": R. Angell, letter to Gus Lobrano, September 22, 1947, "Editorial Correspondence, Fiction, 1947," NYR.

15   *X* was a glossy photo magazine: Popp, *The Holiday Makers*, 49–50; Heller, "Frank Zachary, Catalyst-in-Chief."

15   "flashily upholstered but unexciting": "The Press: Holiday Troubles," 48.

16   "In America, the years after World War II": Callahan, "A *Holiday* for the Jet Set."

16   "I don't want stories about how": "The Press: Holiday Troubles," 48.

16   "*Holiday* is not an organ": Fadiman, *Ten Years of Holiday*, viii.

17   "We all tried to assign ourselves": Author interview with Angell, July 5, 2016.

17   "I think [White] did it for me": Quoted in Callahan, "A *Holiday* for the Jet Set."

18   While stationed in Honolulu: R. Angell, "Editorial Correspondence, Fiction, 1945," NYR.

18   "We felt that it was nicely written": Lobrano to Evelyn Angell, in "Editorial Correspondence, Fiction, 1945," NYR.

18   "grieved to report": Katharine White to Evelyn Angell, in "Editorial Correspondence, Fiction, 1946," NYR.

18   "it was somewhat forced": Lobrano to Roger Angell, in "Editorial Correspondence, Fiction, 1946," NYR.

19   "I'm awfully sorry, but the vote": Lobrano to Roger Angell, in "Editorial Correspondence, Fiction, 1947," NYR.

19 "the prevailing feeling": Lobrano to Roger Angell, in "Editorial Correspondence, Fiction, 1947," NYR.

19 [Ross] had various other suggestions: Lobrano to Roger Angell, in "Editorial Correspondence, Fiction, 1947," NYR.

20 "To put it quite bluntly": Lobrano to Roger Angell, in "Editorial Correspondence, Fiction, 1948," NYR.

20 "soul of the magazine": Ross, preface to *The Fun of It*, i.

20 "You're doing fine": Shawn to Roger Angell, in "Editorial Correspondence, 1950," NYR.

21 In 2016, Angell received an award: Author interview with Angell, July 5, 2016.

21 "a fine collection of *New Yorker* stories": Poore, "Books of the Times."

21 "The quality of these stories": Talbot, "Disasters That Skim the Surface."

21 "offbeat items, while convincing": *Kirkus Reviews*, February 21, 1960.

22 "what might happen if": Macauley, "The Love of Two Oranges," 20.

22 "When I look back on it": Author interview with Angell, July 5, 2016.

22 "I really didn't decide to stop": Quoted in Haynes, "An Interview with Roger Angell," 136.

22 "Mr. Angell's best and most frequent subject": Macauley, "The Love of Two Oranges," 19.

23 "Watching him take off his spikes": R. Angell, "The Arms Talks," in *Season Ticket*, 374.

24 "But for God's sake, Gloria!": R. Angell, "The Pastime," in *The Stone Arbor and Other Stories*, 137.

25 "Spring is sure here": R. Angell, "Opening Day," 80.

25 Einstein jokingly urged readers: Einstein, *The Fireside Book of Baseball*, 11.

26 "Here's another one with those two": Roger Angell to Lobrano, "Editorial Correspondence, Fiction, 1950," NYR.

26 More than a half century later: Author interview with Angell, July 5, 2016.

26 "some history-minded fans": R. Angell, "Farewell, My Giants!," 165.

26 "absolutely heartbreaking": Quoted in "Inning Four—A National Heirloom," in Burns, *Baseball*; originally broadcast on PBS on September 21, 1994.

27 "a solidly hit triple": R. Angell, "Baseball—The Perfect Game," 397.

27 "Unknowing people, new to the game": R. Angell, "Baseball—The Perfect Game," 400.

28 "writes so well about baseball": Fadiman, *Ten Years Of Holiday*, viii.

29 In fact, Angell and Katharine White: Franklin, "Lady with a Pencil," 429–30.

29 "When I came to work": Quoted in Dellinger, "The Veteran."

29 "surrounded me on every side": R. Angell, "Congratulations! It's a Baby," in *This Old Man*, 53.

30 "'Ross,' they called him": R. Angel, McGrath, and Miller, "Roger Angell Interview," June 4, 2010.

30 "was important. It mattered": Haynes, "An Interview with Roger Angell," 134.

30 "It's hard to think about": Quoted in Pappu, "Roger Angell."

31 "If we are going to continue": R. Angell, "Comment," *New Yorker*, May 20, 1950.

31 "The more you analyze": R. Angell, "Baseball—The Perfect Game," 401.

31 One afternoon in the winter of 1962: Author interview with Angell, July 5, 2016; Plimpton, "Talk With Roger Angell," 33; R. Angell, *Once More Around the Park*, xi; Kettmann, "Roger Angell"; Yagoda, *About Town*, 269; Haynes, "An Interview with Roger Angell," 136; "Sep. 19, 2016: Birthday: Roger Angell"; C. Smith, "Influences."

31 But tell me, again, what exactly: "I told him about spring training; he didn't know there was such a thing" (quoted in C. Smith, "Influences"). (David Remnick: "I don't know how you live in American life and don't know what spring training is, but there are a lot of things I don't know, either!" Author interview with David Remnick, September 14, 2016.)

GOOD NEWS FOREVER

33 Following the New York Giants': Shapiro, *Bottom of the Ninth*; Creamer, *Stengel*; Breslin, *Can't Anybody Here Play This Game?*; Meehan and Gill, "Deserving."

33 "We've already got five cities": Meehan and Gill, "Deserving," 33–34.

34 Before he headed south: Author interview with Angell, July 5, 2016; Yagoda, *About Town*, 269. It's unclear whether Shawn offered the instruction to Angell directly or via an office memo. In 2014 Angell related the anecdote this way: "The only advice he gave me was, 'There are two dangers in sportswriting: Toughness and sentimentality. Don't be tough, and don't be sentimental.' And I said okay" (quoted in Green, "Annotation Tuesday!").

34 "That was just like [Shawn]": Quoted in Kettmann, "Roger Angell."

35 "It was just natural for me": Author interview with Angell, July 5, 2016.

35 "By going down at age forty-one": Author interview with Ben McGrath, October 6, 2016.

35 "It occurred to me fairly early": Quoted in Kettmann, "Roger Angell."

35 "Kind of team this is": R. Angell, "S Is for So Lovable" (May 25, 1963), Roger Angell Papers (hereafter RAP), Box 1, Folder 9.

35 "press-box peer": Remnick, *The Only Game in Town*, xii–xiii. On Libeling detesting baseball: R. Angell, note in "A Tale of Three Cities," in *The Summer Game*, 82.

36 "[a] great model for me": Quoted in Haynes, "An Interview with Roger Angell," 146.

37 "joyful participation": Quoted in Green, "Annotation Tuesday!"

37 "Red wrote about sports": R. Angel, McGrath, and Miller, "Roger Angell Interview," November 19, 2010.

37 When [Robinson] was involved: R. Smith, "Negro Outspoken," in *Red Smith on Baseball*, 273.

38 "Shakespeare of the Press Box": Ira Berkow, in R. Smith, *Red Smith on Baseball*, vii, x.

38 "a bleachers guy": Ray Robinson, foreword to Hano, *A Day in the Bleachers*, n.p.

39 "in curiously sharp focus": Updike, "Hub Fans Bid Kid Adieu."

39 "When [Updike] and I talked about the article": R. Angell, "Past Masters: John Updike," in *This Old Man*, 253.

40 "though it took me a while": R. Angell, "The Fadeaway," 39.

40 "He put himself and his grownup sensibility": Quoted in Green, "Annotation Tuesday!"

40 Cruising into its fourth decade: Yagoda, *About Town*, 309.

40 "By the midfifties": Yagoda, *About Town*, 309.

41 "part-time, nonprofessional baseball watcher": R. Angell, *The Summer Game*, ix.

41 "It was clear to me": R. Angell, *The Summer Game*, ix.

41 "in the stands watching": Quoted in Green, "Annotation Tuesday!"

41 "not just on the events": R. Angell, *The Summer Game*, x.

42 "Every piece contained boundless possibilities": R. Angell, *Once More Around the Park*, xi.

42 "People who write about spring training": Quoted in Platt, *Speaking Baseball*, 31.

43 He used the official fifteen-cent scorebooks: R. Angell, "The Old Folks behind Home" (April 7, 1962), RAP, Box 1, Folder 2.

44 "Watching the White Sox work out this morning": R. Angell, "The Old Folks behind Home," in *The Summer Game*, 9–10, 17.

45 "gulf between the players": R. Angell, "A Terrific Strain," in *The Summer Game*, 147.

45 He'll eventually acknowledge: Angell played baseball as a kid. In 1992 he revealed that a few years before his inaugural 1962 spring training visit, he'd had a dream wherein he stumbled across a grave-

stone in his backyard with his birth and death dates ominously written upon it. He brought the vision to his psychiatrist who, when informed by the dreamer that the gravestone was reminiscent of "those monuments out by the flagpole in deep center field at [Yankee] Stadium," helped Angell in realizing the symbolism: his "dreams of becoming a major-league ballplayer had died at last" (see R. Angell, "Early Innings," in *Let Me Finish*, 78).

45 "have a curious sight": R. Angell, "The Old Folks behind Home" (April 7, 1962), RAP, Box 1, Folder 2.

45 Suddenly I saw: R. Angell, "The Old Folks behind Home," in *The Summer Game*, 9–10, 17.

46 "The ultimate shape, essence, and reputation": R. Angell, "S Is for So Lovable," in *The Summer Game*, 54–55.

46 In his notes: R. Angell, "S Is for So Lovable" (May 25, 1963), RAP, Box 1, Folder 9.

47 Off to the side of the page: R. Angell: "Starting to Belong," "Mets Redux," and "Agincourt and After," in *Five Seasons*, 39, 35, 144, 303; *A Pitcher's Story*, 296, 217; "Onward"; and "Pluck and Luck," in *Late Innings*, 320.

47 "rich, deplorable, and heartwarming": R. Angell, "S Is for So Lovable," in *The Summer Game*, 54–55.

48 In a "Talk of the Town" piece: Retitled "Farewell" for inclusion in Angell's first baseball book, *The Summer Game*.

49 "Carl Hubbell's five strikeouts": R. Angell, "Farewell," in *The Summer Game*, 57–58.

50 "struck by something odd": R. Angell, "So Long at the Fair," in *Late Innings*, 14.

51 The notion of baseball: R. Angell: "The Leaping Corpse, the Shallow Cellar, the French Pastime, the Walking Radio, and Other Summer Mysteries," in *The Sumer Game*, 208; "Voices of Spring," in *Late Innings*, 84; and "Warming Up," 40.

51 "a row of shirts": R. Angell, "The Old Folks behind Home" (April 7, 1962), RAP, Box 1, Folder 2.

51 "The game went on": R. Angell, "La Vida," in *Season Ticket*, 12.

52 "cramped but delightful": R. Angell, "Warming Up," 40.

52 "That country flavor": "Roger Angell: Mr. Baseball."

52 "My [spring training] trip was ending": R. Angell, "Sunny Side of the Street," in *Five Seasons*, 220–21.

53 "I am a baseball fan in good standing": R. Angell, "In the Counting House," in *Five Seasons*, 311–12.

56 "that's too bad": R. Angell, "In the Counting House" (May 10, 1976), RAP, Box 10, Folder 3.

56 "may be in the thick of things": R. Angell, "In the Counting House," in *Five Seasons*, 340.

58 "All this seemed to be happening with unusual clarity": R. Angell, "Walking into the Picture," in *Late Innings*, 177–78.

59 "The sun would be slanting": R. Angell, McGrath, and Miller, "Roger Angell Interview," November 19, 2010.

60 "A Learning Spring": Retitled "Sunshine Semester" for inclusion in Angell's third baseball book, *Late Innings*.

60 "Baseball is simple but never easy": R. Angell, "Sunshine Semester," in *Late Innings*, 228.

61 "You can write long, but be clear": Quoted in Verducci, "The Passion of Roger Angell."

61 "perfect writer's sport": Quoted in Charkes, "The Great Roger Angell Interview," 5.

61 "Every thought in my writing": Quoted in Green, "Annotation Tuesday!"

61 "the foul-ground territory around home": R. Angell, "One Hard Way to Make a Living," in *Late Innings*, 348.

62 "reporters reëncountering the game": R. Angell, "A Heart for the Game," 63.

64 "Baseball is changing at warp speed": R. Angell, "Are We Having Fun Yet?," 44.

64 "how great Spring Training was": R. Angel, McGrath, and Miller, "Roger Angell Interview," November 19, 2010.

65 "With Opening Day gone by": R. Angell, "Here Comes the Sun," in *This Old Man*, 226–29.

67 "seining of the notes and scorecards": R. Angell, "Summery," in *Season Ticket*, 176.

67 "Alfresco" in the August 5, 1985, *New Yorker*: Retitled "Summery" for inclusion in Angell's fourth baseball book, *Season Ticket*.

67 "Midseason baseball is a picnic": R. Angell, "Summery," in *Season Ticket*, 174.

68 As I studied the box score: R. Angell, "Fortuity," in *Season Ticket*, 309.

70 "one baseball sentimentality": R. Angell, *A Pitcher's Story*, x.

71 Baseball is not life itself: R. Angell, "La Vida," in *Season Ticket*, 3.

71 "This is kind of extraordinary": Author interview with Charles McGrath, October 20, 2016.

72 "People have said to me": Quoted in Charkes, "The Great Roger Angell Interview."

DELAY ON THE FIELD

75 "The long, almost insupportable strain": R. Angell, "Comment," *New Yorker*, May 13, 1967, 37.

76 "I think that a man should grasp": R. Angell, "The Dignity of Man."

77 "We couldn't help observing": Navasky, "A Perfect Palindrome of a Book," 298.

77 *Publishers Weekly* called the book "delightful": *Publishers Weekly*, August 1970, 276.

77 "scintillating commentary": *Booklist*, February 1971, 434.

77 "absolutely first rate": Lasson, "The Foe Is Folly," 6.

77 "actually makes one laugh": *Library Journal*, October 1970, 3283.

78 "I worked out for an hour": R. Angell, "Over My Head," in *A Day in the Life of Roger Angell*, 33.

79 "Angell was, and remains": Remnick, introduction to *The Only Game in Town*, xii.

79 "one must conclude": R. Angell, "A Terrific Strain," in *The Summer Game*, 156.

79 "For fifty some years": Author interview with Ben McGrath, October 6, 2016.

80 "He's got a freshness in his view": Author interview with Tina Brown, October 26, 2016.

80 "first breakdown": R. Angell, "In the Fire," in *Season Ticket*, 29.

80 "People have no idea": Author interview with Angell, July 5, 2016.

80 "It's not just baseball": Author interview with Remnick, September 14, 2016.

81 "Baseball has changed more": R. Angell, introduction to Bernard Malamud, *The Natural*, xviii–xix.

81 "a decade ago when we all knew": R. Angell, "The Leaping Corpse," in *The Summer Game*, 202.

82 "I persist in a belief": R. Angell, *A Pitcher's Story*, 10.

82 "opening a family album": R. Angell, "So Long at the Fair," in *Late Innings*, 10.

82 "Baseball is like joining an enormous family": Quoted in "Inning Four—A National Heirloom," in Burns, *Baseball*.

82 "biggest altering force": R. Angell, introduction to E. B. White, *Here Is New York*, 12.

83 "commanded an extensive view": McGowen, "Games Are Televised," 121.

83 Alas, if Angell was settling: "Angell, Roger, Editorial Correspondence, 1939," NYR.

83 "could baseball fade so quickly": R. Angell, "Baseball's Strike Zone," 29.

84 "emotions and suggestions": R. Angell, "On the Ball," in *Five Seasons*, 22.

85 "Baseball is a game where the mind": Author interview with Mark Singer, November 2, 2016.

86 "true Yankee fan in his October retreat": R. Angell, "Taverns in the Town," in *The Summer Game*, 84.

86 Angell scribbled: R. Angell, "Four Taverns in the Town" (October 26, 1963), RAP, Box 1, Folder 11.

87 "most shameful and destructive year": R. Angell, "Two Strikes on the Image," in *The Summer Game*, 96.

88 "excited, rapid-fire delivery": R. Angell, "Cast a Cold Eye," in *Five Seasons*, 396.

89 "Typical, I think": R. Angell, "Several Stories with Sudden Endings" (November 14, 1977), RAP, Box 13, Folder 1.

89 "The baseball planners have increased": R. Angell, "The Game's the Thing," 74.

90 "radio and television have been responsible": R. Angell, "Baseball— The Perfect Game," 397.

91 "almost up to the baseball": R. Angell, "Ninety Feet," in *Game Time*, 330–31.

91 "I turn it off or go out of the room": Quoted in R. Angell, "Homeric Tales," 78.

91 "ESPN keeps us up to the moment": R. Angell, *Game Time*, xvi.

91 "I watch quite a lot of televised baseball": Quoted in Welch, "Roger Angell."

92 "dull, showery game": R. Angell, "Several Stories with Sudden Endings" (November 14, 1977), RAP, Box 13, Folder 1.

92 "You should enter a ballpark": Quoted in Pahigian, *Baseball's Most Essential and Inane Debates*, 217.

93 "More and more these stadia remind one": R. Angell, "The Baltimore Vermeers," in *The Summer Game*, 243.

93 "I don't much admire the much admired": R. Angell, "Pluck and Luck," in *Late Innings*, x.

94 "Not since the ancient seven wonders": *Astrodome: Eighth Wonder of the World!*, in "The Cool Bubble" (May 14, 1966), RAP, Box 3, Folder 2.

94 "It will mark the first time that baseball": Daley, "Ballpark, Texas Style," 24.

95 The Astros' first season under the dome: Shannon and Kalinsky, *The Ballparks*, 96; R. Angell, "The Cool Bubble," in *The Summer Game*, 126.

95 "During my stay, I found": R. Angell, "The Cool Bubble," in *The Summer Game*, 130.

96 "This park keeps 'em interested enough": Quoted in R. Angell, "The Cool Bubble," in *The Summer Game*, 134.

97 "Perhaps 'traditional' should now be reserved": R. Angell, *A Pitcher's Story*, x.

97 "The expensive Houston experiment": R. Angell, "The Cool Bubble," in *The Summer Game*, 137.

97 "I do not wish them luck": R. Angell, "The Cool Bubble," in *The Summer Game*, 138. Dodger Stadium, which opened in 1962, presaged the era of baseball-as-spectacle, as it shared values with another southern California amusement destination, Disneyland. It was "everything the contemporary major league baseball park was not and all that [Dodgers owner Walter] O'Malley envisioned for Dodger Stadium," historian Jerald Podair observes. (See Podair, *City of Dreams*, 94.)

98 The observations he made while visiting: R. Angell, "The Cool Bubble" (May 14, 1966), RAP, Box 3, Folder 2.

98 "the first All-Carpet Championship": R. Angell, "Pluck and Luck," in *Late Innings*, 305.

99 "More domes are coming": Quoted in R. Angell, "Celebration," in *Once More Around the Park*, 316.

99 "This is a *fans'* park": R. Angell, "The Pit and the Pendulum," 79.

100 "The whole nature of what we think": Author interview with Angell, July 5, 2016.

101 "On the far side of the site": R. Angell, "The Pit and the Pendulum," 83.

101 "a lot of cheap home runs": Quoted in Welch, "Roger Angell."

101 "massive and relentless add-ons": R. Angell, "The Silence of the Fans," in *This Old Man*, 297–98.

102 "Now, you know, we have less space": Quoted in Green, "Annotation Tuesday!"

102 "There's a great freedom and blessing": Author interview with Ben McGrath, October 6, 2016.

103 "This was a new thing": Quoted in Green, "Annotation Tuesday!"

104 "pink and freshly shaved": R. Angell, "Front Running," 34.

105 "No one—well, no one since Casey Stengel": R. Angell, "One for the Good Guys," in *Game Time*, 34.

105 "instinctive fairness": R. Angell, "Trust," 71.

105 On another occasion he observed: R. Angell, *A Pitcher's Story*, 133.

105 "prairie mortician's gait": R. Angell, "One for the Good Guys," in *Game Time*, 340.

106 "the marvel of the third game": R. Angell, "Some Pirates and Lesser Men," in *The Summer Game*, 281.

106 "Blass was not a great talker": Quoted in Green, "Annotation Tuesday!"

107 "I noticed that it seems difficult": R. Angell, "Gone for Good," in *Five Seasons*, 232.

108 the death of teammate Roberto Clemente: A twelve-time All-Star and the 1966 National League MVP, Clemente died in a plane crash on December 31, 1972, while traveling to deliver aid to earthquake victims in Nicaragua. He was thirty-eight.

108 "the reader has gone through a lot": Quoted in Green, "Annotation Tuesday!"

108 "It had occurred to me": R. Angell, "Gone for Good," in *Five Seasons*, 257.

110 "Gibson, hardly taking a deep breath": R. Angell, "The Flowering and Deflowering of New England," in *The Summer Game*, 175.

110 "the shock of this went out": R. Angell, "Distance," in *Late Innings*, 266.

112 SAY THAT: I too understand: R. Angell, "Distance" (September 22, 1980), RAP, Box 19, Folder 4.

113 "No, I'm not sad": Quoted in R. Angell, "Distance," in *Late Innings*, 292.

113 "Say that he was sounding like the man": R. Angell, "Distance" (September 22, 1980), RAP, Box 19, Folder 4.

114 "overattachments and repeated buffetings": R. Angell, "The Arms Talks," in *Season Ticket*, 352.

114 "rewards in trying": R. Angell, "Taking Infield," in *Season Ticket*, 153.

114 "I learned more about baseball": R. Angell, *Once More Around the Park*, xii.

114 "pleasing roundhouse curve": R. Angell, "Early Innings," in *Let Me Finish*, 73.

115 "Everybody was interested": "Roger Angell: Mr. Baseball."

116 "Everything else in the game": "Roger Angell: Mr. Baseball."

116 "watching and talking with someone": R. Angell, *A Pitcher's Story*, 11.

117 "The pain and sadness we feel": R. Angell, "The Arms Talks," in *Season Ticket*, 351–52.

118 "Sports renew us": R. Angell, *A Pitcher's Story*, 276.

119 "We were friends": Author interview with Angell, July 5, 2016.

120 "My book was nothing": R. Angell, *A Pitcher's Story*, 254.

120 "confidently through a succession": R. Angell, *A Pitcher's Story*, 257–58.

121 "A typical modern ball team": R. Angell, "The Companions of the Game," in *Five Seasons*, 261.

121 "prove day after day that they consider": Greenberg, "Baseball's Con Game."

122   The owners rarely opened their franchises' books: In October 1969
       the St. Louis Cardinals traded center fielder Curt Flood to the Phil-
       adelphia Phillies. Flood refused to report, believing, as did many
       players, that baseball's decades-old reserve clause was unfair in that
       it kept a player beholden for the length of his career to the team
       with which he had first signed. "After twelve years in the major
       leagues, I do not feel I am a piece of property to be bought and
       sold irrespective of my wishes," Flood wrote famously in a letter
       to baseball commissioner Bowie Kuhn. "I believe that any system
       which produces that result violates my basic rights as a citizen and
       is inconsistent with the laws of the United States and of the several
       States" (Record Group 21: Records of District Courts of the United
       States, 1685–2009; Series: Civil Case Files, 1930–1968; File Unit:
       Curtis C. Flood vs. Bowie K. Kuhn, et al.; Item: Letter to Bowie K.
       Kuhn, Commissioner of Baseball from Curtis C. Flood stating that
       he had the right to consider offers from other baseball clubs before
       signing a contract, 12/24/1969, National Archives Catalog, catalog
       .archives.gov). Flood demanded that the commissioner declare
       him a free agent rather than a component of the trade to the Phil-
       lies, a transaction over which he had no say; Kuhn denied Flood's
       request, citing the sanctity of the reserve clause, explicitly stated in
       Flood's 1969 contract. In January 1970 Flood filed a $1 million law-
       suit against Kuhn and Major League Baseball, alleging violation of
       federal antitrust laws. In June 1972 the Supreme Court ruled 5–3 in
       favor of Major League Baseball, but the waves caused by Flood's law-
       suit built and crested. In December 1975 arbitrator Peter Seitz ruled
       that since pitchers Andy Messersmith and Dave McNally had each
       played a season without a contract, each was entitled to become a
       free agent. This influential ruling effectively invalidated the reserve
       clause and allowed for widespread free agency, which has funda-
       mentally altered the business of the game.

122   "There's a big misconception": Author interview with Angell, July 5, 2016.

123   "friend of ours here in the city": R. Angell, "Comment," New Yorker,
       July 6, 1981, 30. The piece was later retitled "The Silence" for inclu-
       sion in Late Innings.

125   "Fans looking back on the strike": R. Angell, "Asterisks." In an
       edited version and sans title, "Asterisks" was included as the second
       part of "The Silence" in Late Innings.

126   "interconnections and possibilities and opportunities": R. Angell,
       "One for the Good Guys," in Game Time, 345.

126 "turned up again at Yankee Stadium": R. Angell, "Bob Feller," in *This Old Man*, 108.

126 "sixteen different but familiar faces": R. Angell, "Early Innings," in *Let Me Finish*, 68.

126 "fell over the big crowd": R. Angell, "Yan-kee Ac-cent," 69.

126 "as familiar to us as our dad's light cough": R. Angell, "Mo Town," in *This Old Man*, 260.

127 "kept coming back as a shock": R. Angell, "Wilver's Way," in *Late Innings*, 199.

127 "Sometimes I wish I had private portraits": R. Angell, *Once More Around the Park*, x.

128 "Like a lot of other fans": R. Angell, "Asterisks," 56.

129 "Without realizing it, the clueless owners": R. Angell, "Bad Call," 4.

129 "The owners (and the players, too)": R. Angell, "Hardball," 76.

YOU WANT TO LAUGH

131 On March 31, 1995: The chapter title comes from R. Angell, "Fish Story," 88.

131 "I came home from Arizona and unpacked": R. Angell, "Called Strike," 50–51.

132 "For once, the right answer": R. Angell, *Game Time*, xviii.

132 "slovenly and excessive": R. Angell, "Hardball," 66–67.

132 "a powerful, and complicated, and beautiful sport": Author interview with Angell, July 5, 2016.

133 "Much is expected of the World Series": R. Angell, "Agincourt and After," in *Five Seasons*, 282.

133 Listening, he imagined the throng: Drebinger, "Giants Win World's Series," 8s.

133 "odd conviction that this championship": R. Angell, "A Tale of Three Cities," in *The Summer Game*, 81.

134 "After the game: Carl Hubbell": R. Angell, "A Tale of Three Cities" (October 20, 1962), RAP, Box 1, Folder 7.

135 "Frame 1: Chris Chambliss has just swung": R. Angell, "Cast a Cold Eye," in *Five Seasons*, 401–2.

137 "Given a choice of watching": Remnick, "The Literature of Baseball."

137 "the greatest night of my life": Author interview with Remnick, September 14, 2016.

138 "passionate boyhood attachments": R. Angell, "The Companions of the Game," in *Five Seasons*, 261.

138   "the transistor [radio] goes everywhere": Letter from Katharine
      White to Angell, in "The Flowering and Subsequent Deflowering of
      New England" (October 28, 1967), RAP, Box 3, Folder 5.

139   "Maybe my last look at this beautiful landscape": R. Angell, "Agin-
      court and After" (November 17, 1975), RAP, Box 10, Folder 2.

139   "the cheerless, circular, Monsantoed close": R. Angell, "Agincourt
      and After," in *Five Seasons*, 297.

139   "Stands on hill like sunstruck archeologist": R. Angell, "Starting to
      Belong," in *Five Seasons*, 40; retitled from "In Search of a Season."

140   "The venerable stopper": R. Angell, "Agincourt and After," in *Five
      Seasons*, 296.

140   "Game Six, Game Six . . .": R. Angell, "Agincourt and After," in *Five
      Seasons*, 302.

140   "WHAT AN INNING!": R. Angell, "Agincourt and After" (November
      17, 1975), RAP, Box 10, Folder 2.

141   "I was watching the ball, of course": R. Angell, "Agincourt and
      After," in *Five Seasons*, 305.

141   "Sudden thoughts of my friends in Maine": R. Angell, "Agincourt
      and After" (November 17, 1975), RAP, Box 10, Folder 2.

141   For the second time that evening: R. Angell, "Agincourt and After,"
      in *Five Seasons*, 305.

143   "It's still extremely quiet here": R. Angell, "City Lights: Heartthrobs,
      Prodigies, Winners, Lost Children" (November 20, 1978), RAP, Box
      14, Folder 1.

143   "dark, ancient grandstand": R. Angell, "City Lights: Heartthrobs,
      Prodigies, Winners, Lost Children," in *Late Innings*, 112.

143   "I'm in crowd with weak knees": R. Angell, "City Lights: Heart-
      throbs, Prodigies, Winners, Lost Children" (November 20, 1978),
      RAP, Box 14, Folder 1.

144   "A whole season, thousands of innings": R. Angell, "City Lights: Heart-
      throbs, Prodigies, Winners, Lost Children," in *Late Innings*, 112–13.

144   "YAZ: it had to come to this—": R. Angell, "City Lights: Heartthrobs,
      Prodigies, Winners, Lost Children" (November 20, 1978), RAP, Box
      14, Folder 1.

144   "In the biggest ballgame of his life": R. Angell, "City Lights: Heart-
      throbs, Prodigies, Winners, Lost Children," in *Late Innings*, 113.

145   "Disbelief persists, then": R. Angell, "Days and Nights with the
      Unbored," in *The Summer Game*, 216, 223.

146   "As readers of these reports may know": R. Angell, "Not So, Bos-
      ton," in *Season Ticket*, 312–13.

147   "Shea goes dead": R. Angell, "Not So, Boston" (December 8, 1986), RAP, Box 34, Folder 5.

147   "happened slowly but all at once": R. Angell, "Not So, Boston," in *Season Ticket*, 341.

147   "Horribly sad for Buckner.—Jesus": R. Angell, "Not So, Boston" (December 8, 1986), RAP, Box 34, Folder 5.

148   "ready for a dash to the clubhouses": R. Angell, "Not So, Boston," in *Season Ticket*, 341.

148   "Throngs of sportswriters were climbing": Dawidoff, "The Power and Glory of Sportswriting."

148   Three hastily written observations: R. Angell, "Not So, Boston" (December 8, 1986), RAP, Box 34, Folder 5.

149   "There was a surprise for me": R. Angell, "Not So, Boston," in *Season Ticket*, 347.

149   "New England paranoias": R. Angell, "Papiness," in *This Old Man*, 266.

149   "*Use a lot of myself": R. Angell, "Distance" (September 22, 1980), RAP, Box 19, Folder 4.

150   Carol had attended Bucknell University: "Paid Notice."

150   "'Parenting' in its contemporary sense": R. Angell, "The King of the Forest," in *Let Me Finish*, 41.

150   "Unlike his colleagues, [Angell] is intensely competitive": Gill, *Here at The New Yorker*, 294.

150   "The plain truth about him": R. Angell, *Ernest Angell*, n.p.; remarks delivered at memorial for Ernest Angell at the Century Association, New York City, February 23, 1973.

151   "never played well against him": R. Angell, "Tennis," in *The Stone Arbor*, 57.

151   "I think that [the narrator] would hate to admit": R. Angell to Lobrano, "Editorial Correspondence, Fiction, 1950," NYR.

151   "I'd never wanted to beat him": R. Angell, "Tennis," in *The Stone Arbor*, 64.

151   "drew heavily on the struggles": R. Angel, "The King of the Forest," in *Let Me Finish*, 48.

152   Joy. Dash. Verve. Panache: R. Angell, *Ernest Angell*, n.p.

152   "To me, the Whites' later concern": R. Angell, "Andy," in *Let Me Finish*, 127–28.

153   "I suspect that his enshrinement": R. Angell, "Walking into the Picture," in *Late Innings*, 171.

153   "one of the great mercies": R. Angell, "Here Below," in *Let Me Finish*, 267–28.

154   "He's not a hidden person": Author interview with Remnick, September 14, 2016.

154   "I was strongly influenced by the *New Yorker* conventions": Author interview with Angell, July 5, 2016.

155   "instinctive, lifelong sense of privacy": R. Angell, "Foreword to *One Man's Meat*," in *This Old Man*, 16.

155   "comes from a background": Author interview with Adam Gopnik, October 4, 2016.

155   "I've kept quiet": R. Angell, "Permanent Party," in *Let Me Finish*, 187.

155   "I'd not been in the war, exactly": R. Angell, "Permanent Party," in *Let Me Finish*, 193.

155   "Friends and critics": R. Angell, *Season Ticket*, ix.

156   "In my case, which is probably different": Quoted in Johnson, "A Conversation with Roger Angell," 45.

156   "I'm a fan": Quoted in Langdon, "Is Winning the Only Thing?," 82.

156   "He's certainly not merely a reporter": Author interview with Remnick, September 14, 2016.

156   "bit of *New Yorker* affectation": Author interview with Gopnik, October 4, 2016.

157   "The word 'essay' was verboten": Author interview with Charles McGrath, October 20, 2016.

157   "I'm not some 'poet laureate'": Quoted in Pappu, "Roger Angell."

157   "a huge influence, an empowering one": Author interview with Charles McGrath, October 20, 2016.

157   "late development": Author interview with Remnick, September 14, 2016.

158   "When I first met him, everybody said": Author interview with Brown, October 26, 2016.

159   "encouraged a lot of the veterans": Author interview with Gopnik, October 4, 2016.

159   "Roger's writing about baseball": Author interview with Daniel Menaker, October 22, 2016.

159   "The character of quote-unquote Roger Angell": Author interview with Remnick, September 14, 2016.

159   "He's too private to be a real autobiographer": Author interview with Charles McGrath, October 20, 2016.

159   "He said, 'Oh, I don't do that'": Author interview with Brown, October 26, 2016.

160   "Tina Brown came along": Author interview with Angell, July 5, 2016.

160   "averting a biography": Author interview with Singer, November 2, 2016.

160   "In writing about myself": Author interview with Angell, July 5, 2016.

161 "For a 10–13-year-old": R. Angell, "Early Innings" (February 1992), RAP, Box 47, Folder 6.

161 "Yes, reader: we threw the old pill around": R. Angell, "Early Innings," in *Let Me Finish*, 72.

163 "I'd not planned a memoir": R. Angell, "Introduction," in *Let Me Finish*, 1.

163 "but when I thought of her golf swing": R. Angell, "Getting There," in *Let Me Finish*, 154.

163 "Our stories about our own lives": R. Angell, "Introduction," in *Let Me Finish*, 1.

164 "They're beautiful, great pieces": Author interview with Janet Malcolm, October 24, 2016.

164 "What the dead don't know": R. Angell, "Over the Wall," in *This Old Man*, 229.

165 "presented itself unexpectedly one morning": R. Angell, "Introduction," in *This Old Man*, 2.

165 "I knew him well and could summon up": R. Angell, "This Old Man," in *This Old Man*, 270.

167 "we had a different plan about dying": R. Angell, "Over the Wall," in *This Old Man*, 231.

167 "No personal confession or revelation impends here": R. Angell, "This Old Man," in *This Old Man*, 281.

167 "When I read it, I was really happy": Author interview with Brown, October 26, 2016.

167 "amazing response": Osborn, "Love Lives Don't Have an Expiration Date."

167 "It's reassuring about their parents": Quoted in Schube, "Roger Angell's Not Going Anywhere."

168 "We all shifted over": Author interview with Angell, July 5, 2016.

168 "I think that blogging was a gift": Author interview with Ann Goldstein, September 19, 2016.

169 "a thrown or batted ball jumps": R. Angell, "The Baltimore Vermeers," in *The Summer Game*, 245.

169 "the critical dimension of the game": R. Angell, "Landscape, with Figures," in *Five Seasons*, 149–50.

169 "The great lesson that Roger has": Author interview with Ben McGrath, October 6, 2016.

170 "I treasure Bill James": R. Angell, "Stats."

170 "Nobody knows him there anymore": Author interview with Charles McGrath, October 20, 2016.

171 In 2013 Angell was awarded: Francis, "2014 J. G. Taylor Spink Award Winner Roger Angell."

171 "Over the passage of the years": R. Angell, McGrath, and Miller, "Roger Angell Interview," November 19, 2010.

171 "I have been reading his work": Slusser, "*New Yorker*'s Roger Angell Receives Spink Award."

171 "Not to be peevish": Remnick, "Roger Angell Heads to Cooperstown."

172 "I'm really touched to see": Quoted in Francis, "2014 J. G. Taylor Spink Award Winner Roger Angell."

172 "I had resisted it, all these years": R. Angell, "Up at the Hall," 36.

172 "church steeple nearby in left": R. Angell, "Up at the Hall" (August 31, 1987), RAP, Box 36, Folder 1.

172 "I was surprised to find how much": Quoted in Francis, "2014 J. G. Taylor Spink Award Winner Roger Angell."

173 "My gratitude always goes back to baseball": R. Angell, "Spinked," in *This Old Man*, 283.

174 "well-cut suit skirt and a silk blouse": R. Angell, "Lineup," in *This Old Man*, 5–6. A reproduction of the photograph is included in the book.

174 "And this was the real luck": R. Angell, "Foreword," in *The Summer Game*, x.

174 "I will have an honorable fallback position": R. Angell, "Wild, and Then Wilder."

174 "I'm not retired, which is good": Author interview with Angell, July 5, 2016.

Bibliography

ARCHIVAL AND UNPUBLISHED SOURCES

Angell, Roger, Chip McGrath, and Allan Miller. "Roger Angell Interview." Oral history, New York City, June 4 and 14 and November 19, 2010. Unpublished.

New Yorker records. Manuscripts and Archives Division. New York Public Library. Astor, Lenox, and Tilden Foundations. Courtesy of the *New Yorker*. All rights reserved. Cited as NYR.

Roger Angell Papers. BA MSS 41. National Baseball Hall of Fame Library, National Baseball Hall of Fame and Museum. Used by permission. Cited as RAP.

PUBLISHED SOURCES

Angell, Katharine S. "Home and Office." *The Survey*, December 1, 1926.

Angell, Roger. "Are We Having Fun Yet?" *New Yorker*, May 17, 1999.

———. "Asterisks." *New Yorker*, November 20, 1981.

———. "Bad Call." *New Yorker*, August 15, 1994.

———. "Baseball's Strike Zone." *New York Times*, April 8, 1972.

———. "Baseball—The Perfect Game." In Fadiman, ed., *Ten Years of Holiday*.

———. "Called Strike." *New Yorker*, May 22, 1995.

———. "Comment." *New Yorker*, May 20, 1950.

———. "Comment." *New Yorker*, May 13, 1967.

———. "Comment." *New Yorker*, July 6, 1981.

———. "Conversation: Roger Angell and Mark Singer." New York Society Library. New York, June 22, 2015.

———. *A Day in the Life of Roger Angell*. New York: Viking, 1970.

———. "The Dignity of Man." Radio broadcast, 1952, thisibelieve.org.

———. *Ernest Angell*. Lunenburg VT: Stinehour Press, 1973.

———. "The Fadeaway." *New Yorker*, February 9, 2009.

———. "Farewell, My Giants!" *Holiday*, May 1958.

———. "Fish Story." *New Yorker*, November 24, 1997.

———. *Five Seasons*. New York: Simon and Schuster, 1977.

———. "Front Running." *New Yorker*, August 17, 1998.

———. "The Game's the Thing." *New Yorker*, November 27, 1995.

———. *Game Time: A Baseball Companion.* San Diego: Harcourt, 2003.

———. "Hardball." *New Yorker*, October 17, 1994.

———. "A Heart for the Game." *New Yorker*, May 2, 1988.

———. "Homeric Tales." *New Yorker*, May 27, 1991.

———. "Introduction." In Bernard Malamud, *The Natural.* New York: Time Life, 1966.

———. "Introduction." In E. B. White, *Here Is New York.* Melbourne: Little Bookroom, 1999.

———. *Late Innings.* New York: Simon and Schuster, 1982.

———. *Let Me Finish.* San Diego: Harcourt, 2006.

———. *Once More Around the Park: A Baseball Reader.* New York: Ballantine, 1991.

———. "One for All." *New Yorker*, October 7, 1944.

———. "Onward." *New Yorker*, October 16, 2015, newyorker.com.

———. "Opening Day." *New Yorker*, April 22, 1950.

———. "The Pit and the Pendulum." *New Yorker*, May 21, 1990.

———. *A Pitcher's Story: Innings with David Cone.* New York: Warner Books, 2001.

———. *Season Ticket: A Baseball Companion.* Boston: Houghton Mifflin, 1988.

———. "Stats." *New Yorker*, December 15, 2010, newyorker.com.

———. *The Stone Arbor and Other Stories.* Boston: Little, Brown, 1960.

———. *The Summer Game.* New York: Viking, 1972.

———. "That Yankee Win, Well Awaited." *New Yorker*, October 12, 2017, newyorker.com.

———. *This Old Man: All In Pieces.* New York: Doubleday, 2015.

———. "Three Ladies in the Morning." *New Yorker*, March 18, 1944.

———. "Trust: Joe Torre's 'The Yankee Years.'" *New Yorker*, March 9, 2009.

———. "Up at the Hall." *New Yorker*, August 31, 1987.

———. "Warming Up." *New Yorker*, April 7, 1997.

———. "Wild, and Then Wilder: The Young Yankees Rebound." *New Yorker*, October 4, 2017, newyorker.com.

———. "Yan-kee Ac-cent." *New Yorker*, October 4, 1993.

Astrodome: Eighth Wonder of the World! Houston Sports Association, 1965.

Breslin, Jimmy. *Can't Anybody Here Play This Game?* New York: Viking, 1963.

Burns, Ken. *Baseball: A Film by Ken Burns.* 1994.

Callahan, Michael. "A *Holiday* for the Jet Set." *Vanity Fair*, April 11, 2013, vanityfair.com.

Charkes, Evan. "The Great Roger Angell Interview." *Columbia Spectator*, October 6, 1980.

Creamer, Robert W. *Stengel: His Life and Times.* New York: Simon and Schuster, 1984.

Daley, Arthur. "Ballpark, Texas Style." *New York Times*, April 9, 1965.

Dawidoff, Nicholas. "The Power and Glory of Sportswriting." *New York Times*, July 28, 2012, nytimes.com.

Dellinger, Matt. "The Veteran: Roger Angell Talks to Matt Dellinger about His Recent Memoir, Fifty Years of Editing Fiction, and the Major-League Playoffs." In "Q. & A.," *New Yorker*, October 9, 2006, newyorker.com.

Drebinger, John. "Giants Win World's Series, Beating Senators in Tenth Inning of Fifth Game." *New York Times*, October 8, 1933.

Einstein, Charles, ed. *The Fireside Book of Baseball.* New York: Simon and Schuster, 1956.

"Ernest Angell, Lawyer, Dead; Former Chairman of ACLU." *New York Times*, January 12, 1973.

Fadiman, Clifton, ed. *Ten Years of Holiday.* New York: Simon and Schuster, 1956.

Francis, Bill. "2014 J. G. Taylor Spink Award Winner Roger Angell." National Baseball Hall of Fame, baseballhall.org.

Franklin, Nancy. "Lady with a Pencil." In *Life Stories: Profiles from The New Yorker*, ed. David Remnick. New York: Random House, 2000.

Gill, Brendan. *Here at The New Yorker.* New York: Random House, 1975.

Green, Elon. "Annotation Tuesday! Roger Angell and the Pitcher with a Major-League Case of the Yips." *Nieman Storyboard*, March 11, 2014.

Greenberg, David. "Baseball's Con Game." *Slate*, July 19, 2002, slate.com.

Hano, Arnold. *A Day in the Bleachers.* Cambridge MA: Da Capo, 1995.

Haynes, Jared. "An Interview with Roger Angell: 'They Look Easy, but They're Hard.'" *Writing on the Edge*, Fall 1992.

Heller, Steven. "Frank Zachary, Catalyst-in-Chief." *Print*, June 16, 2015, printmag.com.

Johnson, Dick. "A Conversation with Roger Angell." *SABR Review of Books*, vol. 3, 1988.

"Katharine White, Ex-Fiction Editor of *The New Yorker*, Is Dead at 84." *New York Times*, July 22, 1977.

Kettmann, Steve. "Roger Angell: Long before He Started Writing about Baseball for the *New Yorker* He Was a Fan of the Game, and He Has Never Been Afraid to Show It." *Salon*, August 29, 2000, salon.com.

Langdon, Dolly. "Is Winning the Only Thing? Not in His Book, Says the Keeper of Baseball's Flame, Roger Angell." *People Magazine*, July 26, 1982.

Lasson, Robert. "The Foe Is Folly, the Weapon Wit." *Book World*, November 1970.

Macauley, Robbie. "The Love of Two Oranges." *New Republic*, May 1, 1961.

McGowen, Roscoe. "Games Are Televised: Major League Baseball Makes Its Radio Camera Debut." *New York Times*, August 27, 1939.

Meehan, Thomas, and Brendan Gill. "Deserving." *New Yorker*, October 3, 1959.

Mishkin, Budd. "One on 1 Profile: At 95, Baseball Writer Roger Angell Still Has His Fastball." Spectrum News NY1, January 26, 2016, ny1.com.

Navasky, Victor S. "A Perfect Palindrome of a Book." *New York Times*, November 8, 1970.

Osborn, Jennifer. "Love Lives Don't Have an Expiration Date, According to Author." *Ellsworth American*, August 16, 2016.

Pahigian, Josh. *Baseball's Most Essential and Inane Debates*. Guilford CT: Lyons Press, 2010.

"Paid Notice: Deaths. Carol Rogge." *New York Times*, April 13, 2012.

Pappu, Sridhar. "Roger Angell, A Hall-of-Famer at 93." *Women's Wear Daily*, June 2, 2014, WWD.com.

Platt, David, ed. *Speaking Baseball*. Philadelphia: Running Press, 1993.

Plimpton, George. "Talk with Roger Angell." *New York Times*, May 15, 1977.

Podair, Jerald. *City of Dreams: Dodger Stadium and the Birth of Modern Los Angeles*. Princeton NJ: Princeton University Press, 2017.

Poore, Charles. "Books of the Times." *New York Times*, March 9, 1961.

Popp, Richard K. *The Holiday Makers: Magazines, Advertising, and Mass Tourism in Postwar America*. Baton Rouge: Louisiana State University Press, 2012.

"The Press: Holiday Troubles." *Time*, July 8, 1946.

Remnick, David. "The Literature of Baseball—The Joy Is in the Reading." *Los Angeles Times*, April 13, 1986.

———, ed. *The Only Game in Town: Sportswriting from The New Yorker*. New York: Random House, 2010.

———. "Roger Angell Heads to Cooperstown." *New Yorker*, December 10, 2013, newyorker.com.

"Roger Angell: Mr. Baseball." *A.V. Club*, June 20, 2001.

Ross, Lillian, ed. *The Fun of It: Stories from The Talk of the Town*. New York: Modern Library, 2001.

Schube, Sam. "Roger Angell's Not Going Anywhere." *GQ*, November 21, 2015, GQ.com.

"Sep. 19, 2016: Birthday: Roger Angell." *Writer's Almanac*, September 19, 2016.

Shannon, Bill, and George Kalinsky. *The Ballparks*. New York: Hawthorn Books, 1975.

Shapiro, Michael. *Bottom of the Ninth: Branch Rickey, Casey Stengel, and the Daring Scheme to Save Baseball from Itself*. New York: Holt, 2009.

Slusser, Susan. "*New Yorker*'s Roger Angell Receives Spink Award—Nominated by Bay Area Chapter." SFGate, December 10, 2013, sfgate.com.

Smith, Chris. "Influences: Roger Angell." *New York*, n.d., nymag.com.

Smith, Red. *Red Smith on Baseball*. Chicago: Ivan R. Dee, 2000.

Talbot, Daniel. "Disasters That Skim the Surface." *New York Times,*
     March 26, 1961.

"Tenement Deals." *New York Times,* April 9, 1924.

Updike, John. "Hub Fans Bid Kid Adieu." *New Yorker,* October 20, 1960.

Verducci, Tom. "The Passion of Roger Angell: The Best Baseball Writer in
     America Is Also a Fan." *Sports Illustrated,* July 22, 2014, si.com.

Welch, Dave. "Roger Angell: Still Throwing Strikes." Powell's Books, April
     16, 2003, powells.com.

Yagoda, Ben. *About Town: The New Yorker and the World It Made.* New York:
     Scribner, 2000.

Index

RA refers to Roger Angell. Page numbers in italics refer to illustrations.

acronyms, 170
Alderson, Sandy, 68
Al Lang Park, 42, 61
Allen, Mel, 31, 86, 91
Alou, Matty, 134
Angell, Abigail, 150
Angell, Alice, 15, 18
Angell, Callie, 15, 18, 20, 26, 50, 165–66
Angell, Carol Rogge, 59, 92, 123, 150, 164–67
Angell, Christopher, 150
Angell, Elizabeth Brosius Higgins, 150
Angell, Ernest, 2–8, 150–52, 161–62
Angell, Evelyn Baker, 11–12, 15, 17–18, 150
Angell, John Henry, 92, 150
Angell, Katharine Sergeant. *See* White, Katharine Angell
Angell, Nancy, 2–3, 5
Angell, Peggy Moorman, 170–71
Angell, Roger, personal life: as baseball fan, xiii–xiv, 53, 68–70, 138, 145, 148–49, 155–56, 170, 172; birth of, 2; children of, 15, 18, 20, 26, 50, 165–66; divorce of, from Evelyn, 150; education of, 6, 9–11; family of, 2–10, 71–72, 150–52, 162–64, 173–74; father of, 2–8, 150–52, 161; life

summary of, 173–74; loneliness of, 71–72; on loss and grieving, 164–67; marriage of, to Carol Rogge, 59, 92, 123, 150, 164–67; marriage of, to Evelyn Baker, 11–12, 15, 17–18, 150; marriage of, to Peggy Moorman, 170–71; military service of, 11–13, 155, 163; mother of, 9–11, 18, 29, 152, 165, 174; nearsightedness of, 11; professional background of, xii–xv; social invisibility of, 166–67; youthful interest of, in baseball, 6–8, 133, 161, 179n; as youthful pitcher, 114–15
Angell, Roger, as writer: on acronyms, 170; on annoying announcers, 86–88; autobiographical material in writing of, 149–52, 155–68; on ballpark evolution, 92–102; on baseball movies, 104; baseball parks described by, 47–51; best idea of, as reporter, 109; blogging by, 92, 166–70, 174; on catchers, 103, 126–27; central theme in baseball essays by, 27–28; on changes in baseball, 80–91; on changes in sports news delivery, xiv–xv; on cheating players, 168–69; compassion of, for players, 106–9; as cultural archaeologist, 46; disenchantment of, with baseball,

Angell, Roger (*continued*)
53–61, 64, 85–88; earliest baseball essays of, 30, *32*; empathy
of, 76; on envy of players' fame
and fortune, 112; favorite teams
of, xii, 69; fictional parodies of,
76–77; film reviews by, 75; on
hitters, 103; at *Holiday*, 15–18,
20, 26–29; on home runs, 103–
4; humor of, 26–28, 44, 76–79,
103, 140, 163, 167; on impulse
to write, 155; on infielders, 103;
influence of other writers on,
35–40; and luck, 40–41, 67–70;
at *Magazine X*, 15; memory of,
8; on Minor League baseball,
104; on mortality, 166; and nepotism suspicions, 29; *New Yorker*
baseball essay debut of, 43; *New
Yorker* essay debut of, 18; as *New
Yorker* fiction editor, 29–31, 75–
76; *New Yorker* short story debut
of, 14–15; non-baseball sports
writing by, 75–76; note taking by,
42–43, *74*, *130*, 134, 148–49; obituary writing by, 75; on players'
salaries, 122; poetry by, 75; radio
essay by, 75–76; and rejection
letters, 18–20; on relationship
between baseball stars and press,
111; satire by, 76–79; scorekeeping by, xiii, 42–43, 133; sense of
privacy of, 154–55; short story
television adaptations of, 21; as
short story writer, 18–22; skepticism of, 53, 76, 91, 163; on televised baseball, 82–92, 101–2, 110,
122, 124, 132, 141, 163, 170; on
Vietnam War, 75; writing philosophy of, 61; writing style of, 35,

38, 41–51, 54–55, 61–64, 70–72,
76–80, 98, 151–52, 155–68
Angell, Roger, essays by (baseball):
"Agincourt and After," 143–45;
"Alfresco," 67; "Are We Hav-
ing Fun Yet?," 64; "The Arms
Talk," 114–15; "Bad Call," 129;
"The Bard in the Booth," 104;
"Baseball's Strike Zone," 83–84;
"Baseball—The Perfect Game,"
27–28, 31, 90; "Being Green,"
103; "Call the Osteopath," 140;
"Cast a Cold Eye," 57, 88, 135;
"City Lights," 144–45; "The
Companions of the Game,"
103; "Conic Projection," 115–21;
"The Cool Bubble," 97, 184n;
"Daddies Win," 170; "Days and
Nights with the Unbored," 145;
"Dinosaur," 104; "Distance,"
109–14, 149; "Down for Good,"
76; "Down the Drain," 106–9;
"Early Innings," 160–63; "Fall
Classic," 31, 77; "Falling off
the Fence," 140; "Farewell, My
Giants," 26; "Fortuity," 67–70;
"Four Taverns in the Town,"
85–87; "Front Running," 104;
"The Game's the Thing," 89;
"A Heart for the Game," 62–64;
"Here Comes the Sun," 65–
67; "Homeric Tales," 104; "In
Search of a Season," 139–40; "In
the Counting House," 53–57; "In
the Country," 103; "In the Fire,"
103; "It Got by Buckner!," 70;
"La Vida," 70–72; "A Learning
Spring," 60; "No, But I Saw the
Game," 104; "Not So, Boston,"
145; "The Old Folks behind

Home," 43–46, 51, 75, 79; "One
Hard Way to Make a Living,"
103; "On the Ball," 57, 84–85,
103; "Over My Head," 77–78;
"Personal History," 160–63; "The
Pit and the Pendulum," 99–101;
"Quis," 103–4; "The Series: Two
Strikes on the Image," 87; "Sev-
eral Stories with Sudden End-
ings," 89; "Sharing the Beat,"
103; "S Is for So Lovable," 46;
"The Slipper-Kick," 140; "Sport-
ing Scene" columns, 32, 43, 157;
"Taking Infield," 103; "Three
for the Tigers," 103; "Up at the
Hall," 104, 172; "Walking in the
Picture," 58; "The Web of the
Game," 103; "Wilver's Way," 127;
"Wings of Fire," 104
Angell, Roger, essays by (non-
baseball): "Just a Matter of Time,"
20; "Over the Wall," 165–66;
"Talk of the Town," 10, 36, 48, 65,
75, 167; "This Old Man," 165–67
Angell, Roger, short stories by:
"Côte d'Azur," 21; "Flight
through the Dark," 21; "In an
Early Winter," 21; "A Killing,"
20–21, 23, 25; "My Own Master,"
21; "The Old Moxie," 23–25;
"One for All," 155; "Opening
Day," 23–26; *The Stone Arbor and
Other Stories*, 21–22, 25, 29, 77, 151;
"Tennis," 151–52, 155; "Three
Ladies in the Morning," 14–15
announcers, television, 86–88
antitrust laws, 34, 121–22, 186n
Arizona Diamondbacks, 135
artificial turf, xiii, 93–94, 98, 169
Astrodome, 47, 94–98

AstroTurf, xiii, 94, 98, 169
Atlanta Braves, 91, 101, 105, 131
Aurilia, Rich, 66
Autry, Gene, 71

Backman, Wally, 145
Baerga, Carlos, 90
Bailey, Ed, 134
ballparks: domed, 93–98; evolution
of, 92–102; field dimensions of,
80; as neighborhoods, 100; retro,
64, 98. *See also specific ballparks*
Barber, Red, 83
Barnes, Jesse, 1
Barrett, Marty, 147
baseball: and antitrust laws, 34,
121–22, 186n; as business, 121–29;
capriciousness of, 69; changes
in, 64, 80–91; and changes in
news delivery, xiv–xv; cheating
players in, 168–69; as city sport,
100; clichés of, 58–59; and collective bargaining, 128; as country game, 51; and disillusionment
of fans, 81; evolution of, 52–53,
55, 64–67; as family, 82, 126–27;
female fans of, 90; and football,
83–84; and free agency, xiii, 81,
122–23, 125, 186n; and league
expansion, xiii, 34, 53, 81–82,
89–90; luck in, 67–70; as metaphor for life, 70–72; midseason,
67; Minor League, 104; owner-
player strife in, 121–29, 131–32;
as personality-driven entertainment, 88–89; players' salaries in,
122; players' size in, 80; players'
speed in, 80; and players' strike
of 1995, 89, 121; postseason, 82–
83, 132–49; RA as fan of, 92;

baseball (*continued*)
radio coverage of, 8; RA's disenchantment with, 53–61, 64; rural charm of, 51–52; and strikes and work stoppages, 121–29, 131–32; surprises in, 79–81; televised, 82–92, 101–2, 110, 122, 124, 132, 141, 163, 170; as thinking fan's game, 85; wild card teams in, 82
Baseball (Burns), 26, 82
baseball movies, 104
Baseball Prospectus/Baseball Reference, 170
Baseball Writers Association of America (BBWAA), 171
Baylor, Don, 69
Beatles, 50
Blass, Steve, 76, 106–9, 119–20
blogging, 92, 166–70, 174
Boggs, Wade, 69, 147
Bonds, Barry, xiii, 66
Boston Red Sox: and American League East Division playoffs (1978), 143–44; David Cone's return to, 118; as family, 82; and luck, 67–70; RA as fan of, 2, 69, 138, 146; and spring training, 51; and World Series, 70, 91, 110, 114, 128, 133, 138–42, 146–49
Brock, Lou, 80
Brooklyn Dodgers: cartoon about, 36; E. J. Kahn Jr. on, 36; in first televised Major League baseball game, 83; move of, to California, 26, 33; in National League Divisional Series, 47; RA's scorn for, xii, 6, 23, 25; and spring training, 42, 45; and World Series, 23, 86, 137
Brown, Tina, 80, 157–60, 167, 173

Buck, Jack, 91
Buckner, Bill, 70, 147–48
Buffalo Stadium, 94
Bunzel, Peter, 36
Burleson, Rick, 143–44
Burns, Ken, 26, 82
Busch Memorial Stadium, 93, 111

Callahan, Michael, 16–17
Camden Yards, 99–102
Campanella, Roy, 173
Candlestick Park, 134
Cano, Robinson, 123
Carbo, Bernie, 141
Carraway, Nick, 75
Carter, Gary, 147
Central Park, 165
Chambliss, Chris, 88, 135–37
Championship Series, 82, 87–88, 135, 149
cheating players, 168–69
Cheever, John, 18, 126
Chicago White Sox, xi, 39, 42, 44, 47, 101
Cincinnati Reds: and Dave Parker, 63; on day of RA's birth, 1; in first televised Major League baseball game, 83; and offer to relocate to New York, 33; and playoffs (1967), 57; and spring training, 42, 45; and World Series, 31, 133, 138–42
Clemente, Roberto, 108
Cochrane, Mickey, 161
Coffee Club, 9
collective bargaining, 128
Colt Stadium, 95
Comiskey Park, 47, 99–100, 139
"Comment" pieces, *New Yorker*, 10, 31, 75, 123–25, 129, 167

Cone, David, 47, 104, 115–21
Conger, Hank, xi
Conley, Renee, 65–66
Continental League, 33–34, 36
Cosell, Howard, 88–89
Costas, Bob, 148
Coumbe, Fritz, 1
Cowens, Al, 136
Cox, Bobby, 172
Craig, Roger, 69
Curse of the Bambino, 149

Daley, Arthur, 94–95
Darcy, Pat, 141
Darling, Ron, 103
Dawidoff, Nicholas, 148
A Day in the Bleachers (Hano), 38
A Day in the Life of Roger Angell (RA), 76–79
Dekinger, Don, 135
Dent, Bucky, 143
Dickey, Bill, 7
DiMaggio, Joe, xiii, 27, 56
Divisional Series, 47, 131, 174
Dodger Stadium, 184n
domed ballparks, 93–98
Doubleday Field, 172
Doyle, Brian, 140
Doyle, Larry, 1
Duncan, Pat, 1

Ebbets Field, xii, xv, 36, 83, 100, 137
Eisenhardt, Roy, 69, 103
essay, definition of, 156–57
Evans, Dwight, 140
exhibition games, 35, 51–52, 66, 78
exhibition season. *See* spring training

Fadiman, Clifton, 16–17, 28
Fehr, Donald, 128

Feller, Bob, 37
female sportswriters in the locker room, 103
Fenway Park, 38–39, 47, 99–100, 139–43
film reviews, 75
Fisk, Carlton, 91, 139–42
Flood, Curt, 122, 186n
football, 83–84
Forbes Field, 100
Ford, Whitey, 45–46, 79
Foster, George, 140
Francona, Terry, 168
Franklin, Nancy, 3
free agency, xiii, 81, 122–23, 125, 186n
Freese, David, 135
Frick, Ford, 28
Fuller, Walter D., 15–16

Game Time (RA), 91
Gammons, Peter, 148, 172
Gehrig, Lou, xii, 7, 92
Giamatti, A. Bartlett, 98–99, 157
Gibson, Bob, 109–13, 120–21, 149
Gibson, Kirk, 135
Gill, Brendan, 36, 150
Glaus, Troy, 47
Glavine, Tom, 172
Goldschmidt, Tex, 6
Goldstein, Ann, 168
Gomez, Lefty, 7
Gooden, Dwight, 117
Gopnik, Adam, 155–56, 159
Gossage, Goose, 143–44
Gottlieb, Robert, 158, 173
Gowdy, Curt, 39
Gray, Freddie, 101
Greenburg, David, 121
"Greetings, Friends!" (RA), 75
Griffey, Ken, 140

Griffith Stadium, 133
Gutteridge, Don, 44

Haller, Tom, 58
Hamilton, Josh, xi
Hano, Arnold, 38
Harris, Brendan, xi
Harvard University, 9–10
Henderson, Dave, 147
Henderson, Rickey, 80
Hernandez, Keith, 69, 147
Hershiser, Orel, 90
Higgins, Elizabeth Brosius, 150
Hiller Muggins Field, 42
Hodges, Gil, 145
Hofheinz, Roy, 94, 96–97
HoHoKam Park, 52
Holiday magazine: celebrated writers
    of, 17; and E. B. White, 17; RA's
    baseball essays in, 26–29, 90; RA's
    travel stories in, 15–18, 20
Holtzman, Jerome, 171–72
"Home and Office" (White), 3–4
Houston Colt .45s, 94
Hubbell, Carl, 7, 49, 115, 134
Hubert H. Humphrey Metrodome, 93
humor: of Red Smith, 37; of Roger
    Angell, 26–28, 44, 76–79, 103,
    140, 163, 167
Humphries, Rolfe, 36
Hurth, Charlie, 34
Husing, Ted, 8

instant replay, xv, 8, 84, 91, 162

Jackson, Keith, 88
Jackson, Reggie, 58, 60, 88, 135
James, Bill, 169–70
Jarry Park, 51
Jeter, Derek, 138

J. G. Taylor Spink Award, 36, 79,
    171–73
Johnson, Randy, 90
Jones, Nate, xi
Jones, Tommy Lee, 168

Kael, Pauline, 75
Kahn, E. J., Jr., 36
Kansas City Royals, 35, 88, 98, 104, 116
Kaufman Stadium, 117
Kendricks, Howie, xi
Kiley, John, 141
Kingdome, 93
Kittell, Linda, 103
Knight, Ray, 147
Koufax, Sandy, 42
Kuhel, Joe, 133
Kuhn, Bowie, 121, 186n

Lansford, Carney, 69
Larsen, Don, 135
La Russa, Tony, 68, 172
Lasson, Robert, 77
Lavelle, Gary, 58
league expansion, xiii, 34, 53, 81–
    82, 89–90
Lee, Bill, 92–93
Lee, Cliff, 170
Lee County Sports Complex, 52
Leonard, Jeffrey, 104
Let Me Finish (RA), 160–64
Liebling, A. J., 14–15, 35, 156
Lindstrom, Matt, xi
Littell, Mark, 135
Lobrano, Gus, 15, 18–20, 26, 29, 151
locker room, female reporters in, 103
Loretta Young Show, 21
Los Angeles Angels, xi, 71, 74, 149
Louis, Joe, 56
Lowry Field, 11

luck, 40–41, 67–70
Luque, Adolfo (Dolf), 1, 7, 133
Lynn, Fred, 140

Macauley, Robbie, 22
MacPhail, Larry, 35
Maddux, Greg, 172
Magazine X, 15
Major League Baseball: and anti-
  trust laws, 34, 121–22, 186n;
  and collective bargaining, 128;
  and expansion announcement
  (1960), 34; video archive of, 91.
  See also baseball
Malamud, Bernard, 81
Mantle, Mickey, 56, 67, 78
Marberry, Firpo, 104
Martin, Charles Elmer, 50
Matsui, Hideki, 65, 67
May, Carlos, 88
Mays, Willie, 38, 49, 60, 78, 134–
  35, 153
Mazeroski, Bill, 135
Mazzilli, Lee, 145
McCallister, Richard, 36
McCarver, Tim, 91, 104
McCovey, Willie, 134
McEnaney, Will, 140
McGrath, Ben, 35, 79–80, 102,
  169–70
McGrath, Charles, 71–72, 157, 159,
  170–71
McGwire, Mark, 64
McNally, Dave, 186n
McNamara, John, 147
McNamee, Graham, 8
McNulty, John, 35–36
McRae, Hal, 136
Meehan, Thomas, 31, 36
Menaker, Daniel, 159

Messersmith, Andy, 186n
Metropolitan Baseball Club. *See*
  New York Mets
Miller, Marvin, 122
Milwaukee Braves, 42–43, 45, 51
Minnesota Twins, 52, 56, 68, 91, 93
Minor League baseball, 104
Mitchell, Kevin, 147
Moorman, Peggy, 170–71
Morgan, Joe, 108–9, 140
Morris, Jack, 135
Municipal Field, 51
Munson, Thurman, 126–27
Murphy, Daniel, xiii

National Baseball Hall of Fame and
  Museum, 79, 104, 109, 153, 172–73
The Natural (Malamud), 81
Navasky, Victor, 77
Nettles, Graig, 144
New Yorker: "Comment" pieces in,
  10, 31, 75, 123–24, 129, 167; and
  E. B. White, 5, 10; and Katharine
  Angell White, 3, 5, 9–10; and
  nepotism suspicions, 29; peak
  of, 40–41; RA as fiction editor
  of, 29–31; RA's essay debut in,
  18; RA's short story debut in,
  14–15; rejection by, of RA's early
  submissions, 18–20; "Talk of
  the Town" essays in, 10, 36, 48,
  65, 75, 167; typical issue of, 12–
  15. *See also* Angell, Roger, essays
  by (baseball); Angell, Roger,
  essays by (non-baseball); Angell,
  Roger, short stories by
New York Giants: Callie Angell's
  comment on, 50; on day of RA's
  birth, 1–2; move of, to California,
  26, 33, 138; RA as fan of, 6–8, 92,

New York Giants (*continued*) 138, 149; RA's nostalgia for, xii; in short stories, 23–25; and spring training, 35–36; and World Series, 8, 23–25, 128, 133–34

New York Mets: and David Cone, 115–16, 118; exuberance of fans of, 46–47; inaugural season of, 33–36, 138; last year of, at Polo Grounds, 46; at National League Divisional Series (2015), 47; RA as fan of, 2, 69, 92, 138, 145–49; RA's nostalgia for, xii–xiii; and spring training, xii–xiii, 33–36, 42; and Willie Mays, 153; and World Series, 70, 114

New York State Writers Hall of Fame, 21, 36–38

New York Yankees: in American League Championship Series, 88; in American League East Division Championship Series, 143, 174; and baseball as country game, 51; and David Cone, 116–18; RA as fan of, 2, 6, 138; and reopening of Yankee Stadium, 55–56; in short story "Opening Day," 25; and spring training, 45, 62, 65; and unexpected moments in games, 45; and WAPEAR dilemma, 170; and World Series, 23, 31, 57, 86–87, 104, 118, 133–37

Niekro, Phil, 23–24

note taking, *ii*, 42–43, *74*, *130*, 134, 148–49

Oakland A's, 63, 68, 69

Olympic Stadium, 93

O'Malley, Walter, 184n

Oneonta Yankees, 104

Oriole Park, 98

orthopedic surgery, 104

Ott, Mel, xiii, 7, 133

Owen, Mickey, 137

owner-player strife, 121–29, 131–32

palindromes, 77

Parker, Dave, 63

Patek, Freddie, 88

Patrick, Ted, 15

Payne Park, 44, 51

Perez, Tony, 108–9

Piniella, Lou, 143

A Pitcher's Story (RA), 115–21

pitching, 23–24, 45–46, 52, 57–59, 78, 83–86, 103–21, 139–40, 173–74

Pittsburgh Pirates, 26, 33, 93, 101, 106–7, 118

Plimpton, George, 77–78

Podair, Jerald, 184n

Podres, Johnny, 173

Polo Grounds: Arnold Hano on, 38; last year of baseball at, 46–47; New York Giants' final game at, 50–51; RA's nostalgia for, 1–2, 6–7, 22–23, 26, 31, 49–50, 92, 100, 161; razing of, xii, 48–50; remodeling of, 36; Rolfe Humphries on, 36

Polo Grounds Towers complex, 48

Pomfret School, 9

Poore, Charles, 21

Pujols, Albert, xi

Pulitzer Prize, 36

Quisenberry, Dan, 104

racism, 37–38

Remnick, David, 30, 79–80, 137, 154, 156–57, 159, 171, 173, 178n

Remy, Jerry, 143
Rendezvous, 21
retro ballparks, 64, 98
RFK Memorial Stadium, 93
Rice, Jim, 89, 143
Rice, Robert, 35
Richards, Paul, 95
Richardson, Bobby, 134
Rickey, Branch, 33–35
Rivera, Mariano, 126, 138
Riverfront Stadium, 93, 139
Robinson, Floyd, 44
Robinson, Frank, 52
Robinson, Jackie, 37–38
Rose, Pete, 58, 108–9, 124
Ross, Harold, 3, 13, 19–20, 29–30, 158
Ross, Lilian, 159
Royals Stadium, 93
Ruth, Babe, xii, 7, 92, 134, 137, 149

Sabermetrics, 168–70
Sadecki, Ray, 52
San Diego Padres, 54
San Diego Stadium, 93
Sanford, Donald S., 21
San Francisco Giants, 65, 68–69,
    81–82, 92, 101, 121, 133–34, 138
satire, 76–79, 103
Schiraldi, Calvin, 147
Schulte, Fred, 133
Schumacher, Hal, 23
scorecards, 42
scorekeeping, xiii, 42–43, 133
Scottsdale Stadium, 65
Season Ticket (RA), 70
Seaver, Tom, 69
Shanahan, Tim, 69
Shawn, William: and beginning of
    RA's baseball writing career, xii;
    encouraging RA at *New Yorker*,

20, 31, 34, 42, 178n; and nepo-
    tism suspicions, 29; at RA's Base-
    ball Hall of Fame induction, 173;
    and women sports reporters, 103
Shea, William, 33–34
Shea Stadium, xiii, 46–47, 50, 55,
    92–93, 145–47
Shepard, Larry, 58
Sheppard, Bob, 116, 126
Shibe Park, 100
Shuck, J. B., xi
Singer, Mark, 85, 160
skyboxes, 96
Slusser, Susan, 171
Smith, Red, 36–38, 61, 154, 168, 172
Snyder, Frank, 1
Sondheim, Stephen, 21
Sorensen, Lary, 60–61
Sosa, Sammy, 64
Sotomayor, Sonia, 131
Spahn, Warren, 45–46, 79
"Sporting Scene" columns, 32, 43, 157
spring training: David Cone's med-
    ical problems at, 117; David
    Remnick on, 178n; evolution of,
    52–53, 55, 64–67; and exhibition
    games, 35, 51–52, 66, 78; familiar-
    ity of, 62–64; and pitching, 114;
    RA's disenchantment with, 57;
    RA's effect on, 64–65; RA's first
    season at, xii, 34–36, 41–48; RA's
    nostalgia for, 52–58; RA's proba-
    ble last on-site report on, 65–67;
    at rural baseball fields, 51–52;
    Sandy Koufax on, 42; usefulness
    of, 52–55; William Shawn on, 31
Stanley, Bob, 147
statistics, 168–70
Steinbrenner, George, 104, 138
Stengel, Casey, 31, 34, 49, 105

steroids, 168
Stewart, Donald, 36
St. Louis Cardinals, 33, 54–55, 61, 93–94, 105, 110, 138, 186n
The Stone Arbor and Other Stories (RA), 21–22, 25, 29, 77, 151
Stoneham, Horace, 103, 121
Strawberry, Darryl, 69
strikes and work stoppages, 121–29
Sullivan, Frank, 75
The Summer Game (RA), 67, 83, 87, 134, 174, 184n

Talbot, Daniel, 21
"Talk of the Town" essays, 10, 20, 30–31, 36, 48, 65, 75, 167
Taylor, Robert Lewis, 35
television, 82–92, 101–2, 110, 122, 124, 132, 141, 163, 170
Ten Years of Holiday (Fadiman), 16, 28
Terry, Bill, 7, 134
"This Is New York" (White), 17
This Week In Baseball, 91
Thomas, Frank, 172
Thomson, Bobby, 49
Three Rivers Stadium, 93
Tiant, Luis, 139–40
Tiger Stadium, xv, 47, 64, 99
Torre, Joe, 104–5, 117, 137–38, 172
Trillin, Bud, 159
Trout, Mike, xi
Trumbo, Mark, xi

Updike, John, 38–41

Vaughn, Mo, 65
Verducci, Tom, 61
Vermeule, Emily, 144
Veterans Stadium, 93, 98

Vietnam War, 75
Viola, Frank, 103

Wagner, Robert, 33
Waitkus, Eddie, 25
WAPEAR (Will Andy Pettitte Ever Retire?) dilemma, 170
Washington Senators, xv, 8, 24, 93, 133
Weaver, Earl, 71, 104
Weiss, George, 34
White, E. B. "Andy": burial place of, 165; death of, 152–55; influence of, on RA, 10, 19–20, 29–30, 154, 157; and Katharine Angell White, 5, 174; and radio broadcasts of baseball, 138; relocating of, to Maine, 9–10; and "This Is New York," 17
White, Joel, 9, 154
White, Katharine Angell: burial place of, 165; death of, 152–54; divorce of, from Earnest Angell, 5; education of, 9; favorite team of, 138; influence of, on RA's writing, 30; marriage of, to Earnest Angell, 3–5; and nepotism suspicions, 29; as *New Yorker* editor, 9–11, 18–19, 29; pitching of, to youthful RA, 173–74; RA's fond memories of, 152–54; and rejection of RA's submission, 18–19; relocating of, to Maine, 9–10; retirement of, 29; as working mother, 4
wild card teams, 82
Williams, Ted, xvi, 24, 38–40
Wilson, Mookie, 147
Wolcott, Bob, 90
women: as fans, 90; in the locker room, 103

Wood, Smokey Joe, 103

Woodward, Stanley, 37

work stoppages and strikes, 121–29

World Series: and Boston Red Sox, 70, 91, 110, 114, 128, 133, 138–42, 146–49; and Brooklyn Dodgers, 23, 86, 137; cancellation of, 121, 128; and Cincinnati Reds, 31, 133, 138–42; and New York Giants, 8, 23–25, 128, 133–34; and New York Mets, 70, 114; and New York Yankees, 23, 31, 57, 86–87, 104, 118, 133–37; and Oakland A's, 63, 68; theatrical moments in, 134–35

World Series 1933, 8, 23–24, 133

World Series 1941, 137

World Series 1954, 38

World Series 1955, 23

World Series 1961, 31, 77

World Series 1962, 133–34

World Series 1963, 86

World Series 1964, 87

World Series 1967, 57, 110, 137–38

World Series 1968, 110, 137

World Series 1971, 106, 137

World Series 1974, 87

World Series 1975, 47, 91, 133, 138–42

World Series 1976, 57

World Series 1977, 137

World Series 1980, 98

World Series 1986, 114, 146–49

World Series 1988, 68

World Series 1989, 68

World Series 1990, 68

World Series 1991, 91, 137

World Series 1995, 131–32

World Series 1998, 104

World Series 2000, 118–19, 137

World Series 2004, 70, 149

World Series 2007, 70, 143

World Series 2009, 170

World Series 2011, 171

World Series 2013, 70, 149

Wrigley, William, Jr., 121

Wrigley Field, 99–100

Yankee Stadium: David Cone's perfect game at, 118; RA's dream about, 179–80; RA's nostalgia for, xii–xiii, 6–7, 23, 92, 126, 131–34, 161; reopening of, xii–xiii, 55–57

Yastrzemski, Carl, 60, 124, 138, 140, 144

Zimmer, Don, 104–5, 137

BOOKS BY ROGER ANGELL

The Stone Arbor and Other Stories (1960)

A Day in the Life of Roger Angell (1970)

The Summer Game (1972)

Five Seasons (1977)

Late Innings (1982)

Season Ticket (1988)

Once More Around the Park: A Baseball Reader (1991)

A Pitcher's Story: Innings with David Cone (2001)

Game Time: A Baseball Companion
(edited by Steve Kettmann) (2003)

Let Me Finish (2006)

This Old Man: All in Pieces (2015)

Ingram Content Group UK Ltd.
Milton Keynes UK
UKHW012130160323
418699UK00005B/204

9 781496 234780